PRAISE FOR *PROCESSED MEATS*

"Candidly personal . . . Walker frames contrasting concepts of stability versus risk, abundance versus dearth, self-sufficiency versus reliance within the context of the larger global imperatives of climate change, pollution, and sustainability. The result is the kind of deeply thoughtful and relatable discussion one might have with one's best friends around a dinner table, back in the day when one could safely do that kind of thing."

—*BOOKLIST*

"This is some brilliant, snappy, poetic, serious, hilarious stuff."

—CRAIG CHILDS, author of *Virga and Bone*

"Walker plays her way linguistically deep into the grotesque and marvelous realities of what it means to live in a female body and to depend on other bodies—chicken, raven, pig, veal, cougar, husband and child—for one's sustenance. I woke from this book as from a sweet and slightly dirty dream, sex and cooking swirling in my mind, saying yes and yes to the bizzare beauty of a fleshly existence."

—ALISON HAWTHORNE DEMING, author of
Zoologies: On Animals and the Human Spirit

"Walker gathers seemingly disparate scraps of earthly experience and sniffs out their secret connections, before stitching them together into the sort of tapestry that is as colorful as it is interrogative, as disarming as it is bursting with light."

—MATTHEW GAVIN FRANK, author of
The Mad Feast and *Preparing the Ghost*

"To think about food is to think about life, and Walker does so with brilliant complexity and insight."

—BICH MINH NGUYEN, author of
Stealing Buddha's Dinner

"This book is more than funny, more than tough. It's about appetite—food as, life as, place as, memory as, hope as—and about how, through the act of articulation itself, we can make a meal of life's pain and peace."

—CHRISTOPHER COKINOS, author of
Bodies, of the Holocene

PROCESSED MEATS

PROCESSED MEATS

Essays on Food, Flesh, and Navigating Disaster

Nicole Walker

TORREY HOUSE PRESS

Salt Lake City • Torrey

First Torrey House Press Edition, March 2021

Published by Torrey House Press
Salt Lake City, Utah
www.torreyhouse.org

International Standard Book Number: 978-1-948814-34-8
E-book ISBN: 978-1-948814-35-5
Library of Congress Control Number: 2019955068

Cover illustration by Deborah Griscom Passmore
Cover design by Kathleen Metcalf
Interior design by Rachel Leigh Buck-Cockayne
Distributed to the trade by Consortium Book Sales and Distribution

Torrey House Press offices in Salt Lake City sit on the homelands of Ute, Goshute, Shoshone, and Paiute nations. Offices in Torrey are in homelands of Paiute, Ute, and Navajo nations.

Acknowledgments

"Tongue," Witness (Spring 2015)
Notable Essay, Best American Essays 2016

"Out of Place," River Teeth (Spring 2014)

"On Anger," Passages North (Spring 2014)
Notable Essay, Best American Essays 2015

"The Unkindness of Ravens," Triquarterly Summer/Fall (2013)
Notable Essay, Best American Essays 2014

"Antibodies" in Fifth Wednesday (Fall 2013).

"Veal" Animal Magazine (August 1, 2013).

"Move Out" Precipitate: A Journal of the
Environmental Imagination.

"A Permanent Home." New Ohio Review (2009): 22-30.

"Dissociation." Agni Online (Fall 2007).

"Making It Palatable." Hotel Amerika 7.1 (2008): 6-10.

"Amalgamated Products Are Us." Slice 1.3 (2008): 105-109.

CONTENTS

PREFACE

FIVE PINT-SIZED MASON JARS sit on the windowsill of my kitchen. Two with butts of romaine hearts. One with the butt of a celery. One with a garlic clove and another with the roots of a scallion swimming in ounces of water encouraging new roots to swirl in their depths. There was a time when the only butts I worried about were the butts of cigarettes I smoked. Now, I wonder how much lettuce can I grow to feed my family. Or at least make a reasonably sized salad.

It is day fifty-three of the COVID-19 lockdown. I've planted peas. Their thin-as-spiderweb tendrils have begun to unfurl and reach for something even stronger than the sun to defy gravity. My son, Max, and I strung twine fifteen different ways up and around some old tomato cages because the truth is, trying to grow anything in Flagstaff, at a seven-thousand-foot elevation, is a bit of a crapshoot. Still, every day, we check the dirt in the garden bed Erik built. We open the wood frame gate to crawl up and over the edges of the box. Erik raised the beds two feet high and wrapped the upper levels with plastic fencing. The fencing is to keep out the deer. The two-foot-high box is meant, I guess, to accommodate six hundred square feet of perfect dirt. So far, we've filled it only halfway. Still. The dirt is perfect. Max sticks his finger an inch deep.

"Is it still wet?"

"I just watered it this morning, Mom. Of course it is."

All babies are born teenagers these days but his smart-ass comment is truly unhelpful. The weather has become unpredictable. Sometimes, it is actually humid in this semi-arid desert climate now that the jet stream has shifted. Now that it rains more than it snows.

With the pandemic, everything has changed. What does one do with a book about fear of apocalypse and desperate cooking when the whole world is now contending with these issues without hyperbole? In *Processed Meats*, the narrator (me) is batted around by life challenges, but nothing compares to this news. How does one publish a narrative about disaster without recasting those challenges in light of a global pandemic? The past still exists, and still matters, but the perspective must change. It's going to take a lot of work to make this work not only artistic and meaningful, but culturally relevant.

My friend, the climate scientist Bruce Hungate, directs the Center for Ecosystem Science and Society. He serves the Department of Energy as part of the climate change task force. We usually meet once a month for Cobb salads to discuss his writing and my freaking out about climate change. He studies microorganisms in soil. I bug him about an essay I want to write about these pictures showing the Himalayas in Nepal and downtown LA. Is there really that much less pollution? Does a lack of visible particulates suggest fewer carbon emissions?

He answers that there are dangers in seeking silver linings. I am embarrassed to tell him that I live for silver linings. I prefer a slight bit of ignorance if I can, pea-tendril-like, fling my hopes on the warming edge of a little bit of cloud. I don't want to be a fool but I do want to believe that the tiny changes I've made lately have been more than just a privileged time to grow some peas and to cook for my family six days a week instead of the usual five.

In a pandemic, cooking at home is its own kind of silver lining—at least we can eat dinner together every night. At least I'm challenged to make dinner interesting.

My family disagrees about which meal I've cooked is the best. Erik says it was the wedge salad, filet mignon, and baked potato. Max says the spicy curry. Zoë says the Cobb salad even though she eats it without the bacon or the blue cheese, making the Cobb salad really just a chicken and egg salad. "With avocado and tomatoes," she corrects.

My favorite meal was lentils and soufflé. If and when I truly manage to become vegetarian, I will eat that every day. I make the lentils like I make risotto. I make soufflé like everyone makes soufflé—with more egg whites than egg yolks. But then Zora and Bear, the dogs, get the extra yolks and I get to watch the soufflé defy gravity like pea tendrils. One day, I'm going to figure this sun and heat mixture out perfectly. One day, I'm going to buy a solar stove. One day, I'm going to figure out how to make a meal that is everyone's favorite, and everyone will include not only Erik and Max and Zoë but the students who didn't get to finish their semester, the instructors who lost their jobs, the surviving members of the Navajo Nation, which suffered the greatest per capita deaths next to New York and New Jersey because of the pandemic. It will be a big feast. If these peas work out, a pod for everyone. It's a big if, but uncertainty is what we're learning to live with. Maybe these little changes will lead to big changes.

In this essay collection, I try to control a series of disasters by cooking complicated meals. I displace a feeling of ineffectiveness and loss of stability with the illusion of control. The book traces the Y2K scare, countenances the H1N1 virus threat, and worries air pollution effects on premature babies with the larger threat of climate change beckoning in the background. Disasters of different levels threaten to make what was stable, like computers or husbands or fertility, feel precarious.

However, since March of 2020, COVID-19 has redefined disaster. The stakes are different now, and the stories I tell in this collection can be deepened and intensified with a new perspective on what disaster, stability, precarity, and control signify. To revise and restructure this book with an actual disaster infusing my understanding of stability, scarcity, abundance, and control I hope will make the book more widely relevant.

Even the act of cooking has changed with the onset of quarantines and stay-at-home directives. I've never cooked so much in my life. With the advent of the new coronavirus, our relationship to food is brought into specific relief: emotional eating, emotional cooking, food waste, sourdough starters, cooking with what you have in your cupboard, growing plants from scraps, talking to the pea starts every morning, telling them to produce their pods before it gets too hot. It's one of the few things we can control and yet, access to food is now more precarious. The safety of our food suspect. Now, to some degree, middle-class people are experiencing what a large percentage of people in the world experience: food is not available at your fingertips. In fact, there may be trouble getting food at all.

During the 1990s and early 2000s, the part-time do-it-yourself culture became a full-time occupation for some people. Words from the counter-culture, like *sustainability*, *self-sufficiency*, and *off-the-grid* became everyday words. Informed by environmental concerns like sourcing sustainable timber or bamboo for building, to slow-food movements like conscientious and cruelty-free animal husbandry, the movement began as one concerned with the health of the planet. But, as capital markets feared diminishing profits, DIY became quickly commodified. Big business co-opted the DIY industry. Home Depot and HGTV assigned a price to the products; Food Network made cooking a contest that you could never win without the proper, expensive, tools.

Processed Meats wonders how to make a real self-sufficiency that is neither self-indulgent nor selfish. Real DIY requires the collaboration of many people bringing many gifts, none of them necessarily commodified. The challenge now is to refine this collaborative effort through the lens of the coronavirus.

The virus has laid bare the fundamental flaws inherent to capitalism: the inequity in an economy built upon the backs of Black people who now suffer at disproportionate rates from COVID-19 and the police system that serves to keep them unequal, the lack of protection for essential workers, the neglected infrastructure necessary to ramp up production of health care to quickly meet demand, the fragility of the industrial meat complex, the environmental damage caused by an economy built on resource extraction and excessive consumption. With the advent of the virus and the subsequent lockdown, we've developed new relationships with food and control. Some of those may be more severe—some of them may be desperate. Some of them may lead to a kind of self-sufficiency that threatens the capital economy. Excessive consumption has been clipped—we can make do with less now. The emotional power of precarity may be diffused.

If this new perspective is to gain any currency, it's going to need to be culturally reinforced. By the end of this book, I hope I've shown that real self-reliance threatens capitalism by recasting what we understand to be unstable and precarious. The coronavirus is a big disruption that may presage the big disruption the climate crisis presages and social justice requires. Perhaps this changed relationship between food and precarity will lead to a thoughtfulness about individual versus collective impact. Perhaps a new vision of self-sufficiency that loses the "self"—a vision less invested in control and more invested in repair and connection— will restore the collaborative nature of growing and cooking food.

INTRODUCTION

B ABIES' CHEEKS ARE DELICIOUS. WE nibble and kiss. We say, "I'm going to eat you up," in a growly, hungry voice. Think of all the food that went into making that baby. How much butter the pregnant woman ate. How many leafy greens with that folic acid. Would the baby taste like Swiss chard?

It's a daunting choice—deciding to have kids. When I was growing up, my mom was an establishing member of the Zero Population Growth society. In the doctor's office, at the mall, in the grocery store, whenever we saw a family of eight kids, the eldest daughter managing the little kids, she would loud-whisper, "The planet cannot take so many humans." In a state where women marry youngest and have babies right soon after, having kids isn't a decision. It's an expectation. To be in Utah is to be pregnant, so I left for Oregon to attend college ASAP.

After leaving Salt Lake for even-more-progressive-than-my-mom city of Portland, I was not having kids anytime soon. In Portland, it was well established that there were already too many people on the earth. Every house had a *Diet for a Small Planet* cookbook on the countertop next to the homegrown bean sprouts. In Portland, it was a given that food choices were political. Even in the late nineties, liberal Portlanders knew that eating red meat harmed the environment. I stuck a sticker to the bumper of my not-so-ecofriendly Isuzu Rodeo that read "Cows Kill Salmon" because of the way grazing cows trotted through small creeks, turning spawning grounds into muddy, grazeable land even though I, occasionally, ate burgers at McMenamins.

Growing up in Salt Lake City, I was a picky eater, but after Portland's mind-opening ways, now I eat, and make, almost anything. I love to cook. Soufflés and beef roulade, cassoulet and lengua tacos. I love sauces: gravy, béarnaise, beurre blanc, béchamel, raspberry jam compote, and beef broth reduction. I blow through a pound of butter on a regular dinner party night and three pounds for Thanksgiving. Fish! I love branzino, sea bass, trout, salmon, chicken thighs without skin, chicken thighs with. I love turkey and I love filet mignon.

It's not very ladylike to eat an eight-ounce filet mignon covered in béarnaise. It's really not ladylike to eat a twenty-two-ounce prime rib. My sisters and I all have a capacity to eat an enormous amount of red meat. My parents fostered a kind of feminism: choose what you want for dinner. Choose whether or not you want to have kids. As much as my father may have wanted a son, he didn't complain about how many daughters he had. All three of us were told we could be anything we wanted to be. My mother, who eventually divorced my dad, not so much for his infernal drinking as for his clumsy cheating, reminded my sisters and me never to rely on the money of men. So, like boys we ate huge steaks. Like men, each of us got big jobs. We are not the tiniest people you've ever met. "At least," my mom said, "you stopped at one or two." Kids, I thought she meant. Or maybe she meant steaks.

When I returned to Salt Lake from Portland for grad school, even my grad school friends were having kids. Maybe there is something in the water but the part of me that wanted to have kids that had lain dormant in the back of my brain erupted. Now, when I saw families of eight, instead of thinking "planet," I thought, "can I borrow one?" I've always liked kids. I've always thought I'd be a good mom. How could I have known that deciding to have kids is one thing, having them and raising them is quite another? But, if being a good mom meant wringing your hands over every decision and wondering how the planet could survive your individual desire to procreate, then I was already the best mom in the world.

Processed Meats is a book about wanting everything and knowing that there is a price to pay for getting it. *Processed* because hand-wringing and overthinking and mechanized worry. *Meats* because these babies and these steaks are so delicious and there is only one life to live and we should dig in and enjoy it. Well, maybe we should forego the red meat but keep the béarnaise. The sauce is the best part.

SALMON OF THE APOCALYPSE

W HAT OF THE FUTURE CAN you divine from a single detail? It's like trying to discern a recipe from only one ingredient. Although that one ingredient gives you a bit of a clue of what it is you're trying to make.

I could see the horse's ribs. The brown fur stretched across the stomach like bark on a tree. Like it was already practicing to be leather. There was nothing green on the ground for him to eat. Nothing even straw-colored. Barren dirt. Gray fences. A hawk stood on a post. Even its feathers looked thin. Thirsty. I hadn't seen a patch of water since we'd passed Utah Lake in Provo where not even a drawn-out horse would drink that mercury-filled pretender. I reached for my Nalgene, took a sip. I thought for a minute about asking Erik to stop the car. Erik, whom I had been dating for a year, didn't like to stop on road trips. He liked to make good time. He liked to keep the radio going. But I thought maybe I could help the horses. I could pour the rest of my water in the trough. Then I thought better of it. He and his fellow horses would fight over the droplets. It would just prolong his thirst. What would I drink for the rest of the car trip? Maybe it would rain soon. Maybe the owners would come out. The horse needed real water, not just drops. We kept driving.

It was as we had predicted. We had left the metropolis of Salt Lake City for the safety of a middle-of-the-desert small town to avoid the crushing traffic jam predicted at the end of this world. But, like most versions of movies about the ends of the worlds, the narrator of this version survives. I'd lived through it. I was the star of my own apocalypse. Erik and I had advance warning. We had preparations. We had a trunk full of beer. An entire salmon. Twenty-four unshucked oysters. A six-pack of chicken broth. An end-of-the-world emergency kit of sorts— if your emergency is New Year's Eve in the desert trying to be New Year's Eve in Portland, Oregon. Although, if our gas tank ran out, we would be trapped in central Utah. Why had we driven south and east instead of north and west to the real Portland? At least then, we'd be nearer places where we could harvest oysters instead of transporting them first by boat, then by plane, then by car to the middle of the desert where, without supplies, the world would feel like it had reached its end.

Unlike the pandemic that would upend global health and the global economy two decades later, Y2K wasn't supposed to bring about complete planetary collapse. It wasn't avian flu or a monkey virus mutated or a cure for cancer gone rogue. It wasn't nuclear. But drought plus technological disaster plus the middle-of-nowhere brought us to this full-stop. I'd been prepared for this happening—for me being the last one standing. I may have always been what would one day be called "a prepper." When I was eleven, after I had mown the lawn, I stored handfuls of grass for my horse, in this case, my bike, in a shoebox in the garage. I stored cough syrup for my dolls. I kept under my bed a pound of white chocolate. I would eat only a fingernail-scraping full at night. I had to make it last. Who knew when the next chocolate would appear? Who knew when my mom would realize the cough syrup I hid under my bed to administer to my dolls had gone missing and start keeping it under lock and key? I stole tiny jars of jam from fancy hotel restaurants. At the age of three, I had already realized the toilet provided plenty of water in a tea-party-for-Grandma crisis.

I blame my grandmother for this hoarding problem. Grandma Mayhew kept a ball of foil growing in her pantry.

She put up pickles, peaches, pears, cherries, apricots, and jam. She reused paper towels, drying out wet ones on the loop of the kitchen sink faucet. At Christmas she collected the bows from everyone's ripped-away wrapping. She was a good Mormon. Grandma kept a two year supply of food stuffs as encouraged by her church to sustain her family while they awaited the second coming of Jesus Christ—or a husband prone to losing his job. She staved off end-of-the-world questions like why did my husband run off to leave me to raise four daughters on my own by shoving her anger into something strong and permanent, like a Mason jar.

Erik and I are storer-uppers but we stored all the unwise, according to the church, substances. Neither beer nor cigarettes nor wine would have been on my grandma's list. Erik and I, although not baptized into the church ourselves, absorbed the admonition to prepare but our three-month supply would not be bishop-approved.

We believed we could hold out, in Torrey, Utah, Erik and I. Between us, maybe we could repopulate the world. Here, we would live. We could pillage the gas station for its cans of beans, its cans of sardines, its boxes of peanut butter crackers, its rows of candies: spice drops, red hots, gummy worms—all the preserves in the world ready to preserve us into the future. Rows of Reese's Peanut Butter Cups. Our children could be grateful to such parents who raised them on Reese's and Kit Kats, on Doritos and beef jerky. We could take some of the food back to those horses we drove past. Horses will eat Reese's too. Everybody likes peanut butter cups. It didn't seem fair, now that I had found someone who wanted to go into the future with me, that the future itself looked bleak. At least he was a carpenter. He could rebuild.

I'm from Mormon stock, even though I don't practice. I did practice canning with my mother and grandmother.

Transforming summer fruit to winter sustenance is an all-day event. Canning takes bodies under siege, although not mine, at least not at first. The room, filled with the sweating skins of my mom, my grandma and great-grandmother, and those of a hundred or so peaches, pulsed. It was August and 105 degrees outside. The air conditioner ran nonstop and yet my mom still had to wipe the sweat from her forehead with a washcloth. She stood over a pot of boiling water that was about the size of one of my nine-year-old twin sisters. The twins were three years younger. I would not fit in the pot anymore, but just barely.

My mom had hands made of Kevlar. She could dunk one into the pot, retrieve a Mason jar, and pass it to my grandmother, whose hands were made from whatever preceded Kevlar—iron or maybe uranium. My grandmother filled the jar with halved peaches. She gave the jar to my great-grandmother, who covered the peaches in sugar water, tapped on the sealing lid, and popped the jar into the rack that would be plunged into another kettle of boiling water.

My mom and grandma still can plum jam but they don't jar all the fruit of summer. They, like the rest of us, realized it's easier to buy peaches in light syrup from the grocery store. Still, I wish I'd paid more attention. I wish I'd taken to heart the idea that sometimes, there are no peaches at the store. Sometimes, there are no stores. If I don't learn to put up peaches, when the apocalypse comes, what use will I be? My ex-brother-in-law could jerry-rig any electrical device. With enough batteries we could probably still run a few necessary appliances like the Cuisinart and the air-conditioning. Perhaps he could have at least have taught me how to rewire a lamp before he left. My husband could build a two-room house with the remnants of a picnic table and an old mailbox, although he likes a perfect joint and mailboxes and picnic tables don't make ideal corners. My friend Misty could grow beans under the parching desert sun of Tucson or in the over-soaked soil of Portland. She has taught me to like beans. My sister Paige could catch brine shrimp, amassing them in a Mason jar, in her own kind of canning-chic, and then use those shrimp as bait for bigger fish like trout. My sister Val could sell ice in the Arctic and with the ever-decreasing ice shelf, the value of ice increasing dramatically, we'd be some of the few with cash. Even if money's no good, she could barter our fine sets of matching pine needles for a bag of flour or two, a gallon of milk, or, more probably, an entire cow. My main skill is speed—I can read books fast, chop onions quickly. I can clean a bathroom in five minutes or less. But after the apocalypse, I don't think quickly cleaned bathrooms will come in that handy. My Mormon family should have taught me better. It wasn't until it was too late that I received the following list of what my doomsday pantry should consist of:

Table 1: From my mother-in-law's Mormon brother.

Two Year supply cycle	**Two Year supply optional substitutions**
Week 1 - Grain: wheat, oats, rice, corn (25 lbs/person/month)	Macaroni and cheese mixes
	Soups (cans or packets)
	Peanut butter
Week 2 - Water	**Canned goods and preserves**
Week 3 - Sugar	
Week 4 - Baking soda, salt	
Week 5 - Grain: wheat, oats, rice, corn	
Week 6 - Water	
Week 7 - Nonfat dry milk	
Week 8 - Cooking oil	
Week 9 - Grain: wheat, oats, rice, corn	
Week 10 - Water or juice	

Week 11 - Beans, peas, and
other legumes (5 lbs/person/
month)
Week 12 - Dried fruit, pudding,
vitamins

Of course, my mother and grandmother would severely object to the idea that canned goods and preserves were anything like optional.

Like any time-consuming project, putting up fruit requires a lot of equipment. To can peaches you need at least a few essentials. From The Canning Pantry, you can get the Water Bath Canner Package which includes:

- Our enameled steel, 21.5-quart liquid capacity water bath canner.
- The canner rack that holds seven (7) quart jars.
- Our Home Canning Kit with lid lifter, canning funnel, jar lifter, jar wrench, and kitchen tongs.
- Canning Lid Sterilizer—an essential canning tool that provides a quick and easy way to sterilize your canning lids.

Our price: $49.99. Fifty dollars, plus the cost of peaches, plus the cost of jars isn't a lot of an investment to protect the future of your peaches. Of course, it's the time commitment that's the expensive part. Weeks upon weeks of fruits marching through your kitchen. Summer is seen through a fog steaming out of an enameled pot.

We hadn't completed our pantry diligently, but everyone knows that you should gas up before the apocalypse. But how do you know exactly when "before" is? We did need gas and the road was a lonely one. No other cars drove by as we pulled into the station. I couldn't see anyone through the windows of the store. I got out of the car because the tank was on my side. But the lever on the pump wouldn't pull. Through the car window, I told Erik I couldn't get the pump to turn on. He got out and came over to my side.

"OE," Erik presumed but then he tried to release the hose. No operator error here. The pump's gauge wouldn't zero out. We were trapped at empty.

We were more paranoid than your average people about Y2K. Erik's mom and stepdad worked in IT for the phone company. They were in lockdown for the weekend, awaiting whatever crisis would unveil when the computer clocks allowed for only two digits of date data. When the clock flipped to zero, the fear was we'd be transported back to the 1900s, possibly figuratively, meaning several computers would break down and possibly literally, like we would have no computers and therefore no infrastructure at all. Transmitters down, electrical grid down, pumps from the water treatment plant could go down. This would make people panic. There would be a run on gas, guns, and salmon AND oysters.

I wonder if we were flung back to 1900 and knew where our fossil fuels would take us, would we still pull them from the earth and transform them into electricity, plastics, and tailpipe exhaust? Knowledge about how fossil fuels damage the planet didn't stop us before. Some scientists predicted climate change in 1900. And by 1999, everyone who was paying attention knew. Al Gore was running for president. His inconvenient truth turned out to be the beginning of the end for democracy and for babies being named Chad. No new parent wants to name their kid after something so unable to commit.

We knew about ocean acidification, about losing the polar bears, the general potential extinction, the rising seas, the eroding coastlines, the shifting, disappearing habitats. Y2K was about the loss of technology—but that was also kind of a dreamy apocalypse. The "get-back-to-the-land" kind of apocalypse where we could learn from our Indigenous neighbors. Without tech, we could undo the deforestation, the overfishing, the mining, the driving, the plastic, the shipping. Y2K made us feel like we had a chance to go back. Repair. Hit the reset button. But, like the car we were driving, like the computers that managed to handle the two-digit to four-digit date change, like the clocks themselves, we hurtled into the future.

There's a giddiness to imagining you're the only person left on the planet. You could ban fossil fuel use. You could spearhead an all-solar economy, just for you. All that open forest (assuming it hasn't burned). All that prime real estate on the oceans (assuming they haven't turned totally acidic). All that free food (assuming it hasn't all been irradiated by nuclear bombs). Just you and the animals (assuming the animals bore some resistance to the virus/bomb/flood/drought that knocked everyone else out) roaming the countryside, eating berries, picking flowers. You don't have to wait in line, assuming, of course, there's anything left to wait in line for.

But after the giddiness, the freedom turns to fear. You realize that there are no lines to wait in to see the movie because movies aren't being made and there's no electricity to project the film. Animals think you're a tasty treat. Fresh food has rotted. The ocean is a dead, salmon-less sea. You become a little desperate. You start to look around at the ground. You wonder how the Indigenous people who lived here centuries ago made pots. You're going to need to learn how to make one to gather water. If you can find any water.

I followed Erik toward the station.

Erik pressed on the door. It opened. The lights were off. The place was silent. Not even the freezers buzzed.

I asked Erik, "Don't these Kit Kats look dusty?" It had only been two hours since we left Salt Lake. If the world had ended, perhaps it ended in a sandstorm. I looked around the store for what would need to be eaten now and what could be saved for later. String cheese and orange juice from the refrigerated section first. Packs of nuts and Cheetos could be saved, presumably, for eternity. Beer. We would need all the beer for now and for eternity even if it was 3.2 percent beer by volume, ala Utah law.

And then the lights flickered on.

A vision appeared. The vision of an angel wearing Carhartts and a button-down shirt. Praise be. Hallelujah. The second coming. Etc.

"We're closed, you know."

"The door was open." Erik, who doesn't really believe in the end of the world, answered more practically.

"It's New Year's Eve," the vision spoke. As if this was an explanation. It certainly didn't explain the dust.

"We just needed some gas."

"Chevron. Half a mile down the road. Their pumps are on."

When we got to the Chevron, I understood why the other place was so dusty. This place, well-lit, freezer-buzzing, was open all year round. This was the real gas station. The other one was just a placeholder, a sign of disaster and the end of the small town. This travel plaza was the sign of people on the move, one of those places recognizable wherever you were, like you hadn't even left home: Chevron, Shell, Texaco.

Torrey, Utah, in the middle of the state, just outside of Capitol Reef National Park, where the rocks are red and the permanent population is under three hundred, is a good place to hide from disasters of the urban kind where swarms of people will be storming the grocery stores for bottled water and canned tomatoes, crowding the freeways trying to get out of town, and loading their shotguns. But, in terms of places to stay forever, it lacks a couple of things: a sustainable source of water—the Fremont River is allocated for hay and alfalfa to feed cattle; and a sustainable amount of food—unless you know how to kill and butcher your own cow, or have taught your single stomach to digest alfalfa in the manner of the cow's four stomachs.

As we drove, the wind blew hard across Highway 24, shaking the car. Winter in the desert means freeze but still also dry. Almost no one visits Capitol Reef National Park in the winter. In Torrey, no store was open. Not the Chuckwagon, the general store, not the Robber's Roost bookstore and coffeehouse, not Café Diablo, which serves rattlesnake cakes, empanadas, a tower of pork ribs surrounding a haystack of French fries, mixed grill with trout, tenderloin, and rabbit sausage.

At the cabin, we met my old friend from middle school, Rebecca, her husband, Todd, Erik's cousin, Emily, and her boyfriend. We turned up the thermostat. The heat, fed by the propane tank outside, kicked on. Erik turned on the water and flushed the toilets to restore their waste-conveying abilities. We carried the cooler full of beer, the meat, cheeses and vegetables, a bag of potatoes and the bottles of wine, and the chicken broth up the long staircase to the main floor. The perishables we put in the refrigerator and hoped that the electrical grid would make it through the night. Admittedly, this amount of food would not sustain us through the end of the world. It probably wouldn't sustain us through the whole weekend if we ate like I expected us to. I bought a fish poacher just for this occasion. Should the world end, one should be able to poach a fish whole.

When I chopped the head off the fish and tossed it in the garbage, Rebecca, chopping garlic next to me, asked, "Shouldn't we save that?" Rebecca is from Utah too and her mother would not waste a fish head, were she to cook fish.

"For what?"

"Fish stock or something. Fumet?"

"I didn't bring any carrots or celery. It'd make kind of a lame stock. Maybe the dogs could eat it."

"Remember that time we gave the dogs all that salmon? They threw up all over the car."

"What would we do with the fish stock? I don't think we'll be making bouillabaisse down here."

"Maybe if we could freeze the heads." I saw where she was coming from. Channel our mothers. Practice self-sufficiency. Do not let things go to waste. Both Rebecca's mom and my mom were the first to start recycling in our neighborhoods—each of them packing up the back of their cars with separated glass and paper. It was my dream to be frugal. I should have at least been practicing for the future pandemic, if not the immediate catastrophe. But if the freezer lost electricity that night, the fish heads would go to waste. If the electrical grid did fail and we couldn't keep them frozen, we'd have to throw out the fish heads, which would bring ravens. Ravens and vultures. Then we'd be eating by the campfire, trying to see by campfire light, trying to keep the coals hot until morning to warn the ravens away, waving away vultures and ravens. Here's the thing about playing disaster. It's like playing dolls. One day, you might find yourself with real babies. What do you do then?

I tried to think of ways to preserve the fish heads if the electricity went out. I dug the fish head out of the garbage and put it in the pot with the skins of an onion to make a stock, if only to keep me from thinking about an influx of hungry ravens.

The directions said to place the poacher directly in the oven. Rebecca and Kurt, Emily's boyfriend, wanted to stick with a more familiar method of cooking—sautéing the salmon. Apocalypse threatened: they thought I would overcook the salmon. Everyone agrees that overcooked salmon is the worst kind of salmon. But even temperature equals even cooking, I argued. The salmon would saturate with liquid heat, cooking the inside simultaneously with the outside rather than shocking the outside and leaving the inside to absorb heat like a contagion.

Eventually, I convinced them of the logic of the oven. Two hundred and fifty degrees should prevent the leeching out of all fat and the absorption of wine and lemon and herb liquid. This could be the last salmon of our lives. Or, at least, the last good salmon of the year.

Emily's boyfriend Kurt thought I should add thyme.

"I think thyme always tastes moldy," Rebecca said.

As we each chewed on a sprig, trying to decide if we should add it, Rebecca asked, "What would our sixteen-year-old selves think of us waiting for the apocalypse? It's so Mormon." Rebecca and I had been friends since junior high. But she had been baptized Mormon. The edict to procreate soaked through her skin as much as it swirled through the thick air of Salt Lake City.

"If you were still Mormon, you'd have four kids by now," I said.

"My mom had six by the time she was twenty-eight," Rebecca said. "We are so old."

"We always have been."

Emily, who was a vegetarian, came in to see if I was going to use chicken stock in the soup. "Sometimes, people put in chicken stock when they say they're going to use veggie stock. I can taste the difference."

"You can't get the same mouthfeel from vegetable stock. Plus, chicken stock uses the throwaway parts of the chicken," Kurt argued for me.

"It's just gross though," she pointed out.

I picked up my car keys. "I'll go into Loa for some."

"It'll take an hour," Erik noted.

"It's just fifteen miles. I'll be fast." In the future carbon crisis, I would weigh the carbon output against the necessity of broth making. I could have just made veggie stock if I'd remembered to bring any vegetables.

"I thought that was the point. To make do."

"But if we can still go to the store, shouldn't we?" Privilege is being able to imagine a happy ending to an apocalypse, being able to take off into the desert and eat salmon. Privilege is also being able to take off the hat of imaginary crisis and put on the run-to-the-store-hat, even if the run is a twenty-minute drive.

Going to the store was, of course, before. Before the time when every trip to the store required some mathematical estimation of the carbon each item emitted in production, how much carbon each item cost to be transported to the store, how to add the cost of one more bit of plastic to wrap the head of lettuce and then subtract the speed of decay when you denied yourself the pleasure of plastic-wrapped lettuce. Before the pandemic, when we could, at the drop of a hat, not put anyone's health at risk by popping by a different store every five minutes to pick up the most esoteric ingredient. I once traveled all of Salt Lake Valley to look for the herb rue to follow one of Thomas Keller's recipes. I ended up at the garden store.

It is a long, arduous process, going to the grocery these days. The year 1999 might not have been the end of the world, but it may have been antediluvian. The flood of information coupled with the flood of carbon filling the skies was about to deluge us, with the admonition to only expose yourself and others once a week at most.

In 1999, you could still pretend a little ignorance about carbon. You could still pretend that the math at the end of the millennium was going to be worse than the math of carbon particulates amassing in the atmosphere. You could pretend there was a place to hide from the world as if you yourself were not the world incarnate.

On New Year's Eve, in 1999, going to the store wasn't contributing to disaster; it was an attempt to avert it. The list of what you could buy at the Loa Food Town in 1999, the grocery store fifteen miles from the cabin in Torrey, included: Tillamook cheese, tomatillos, red cluster tomatoes for $1.49/lb, Fresh Express spring mix, portobellos, shitakes, a package, though dusty, of dried wild mushroom mix (oyster mushrooms, enoki, shitake), bone-in, skin-on chicken thighs, bamboo skewers, and live baby chicks.

Things you couldn't get at the Food Town in Loa: truffles, fresh porcini, fresh chanterelles, boneless, skinless chicken thighs, organically grown spring mix, Vidalia onions, poblano peppers, kosher salt, organically grown anything, panko breadcrumbs, truffle oil, vegetable broth.

I bought the package of dried shitakes. I would rehydrate those and toss them in with the button mushrooms to bring out the underlying woodsy-ness in the soup. If I were really worthy of middle-of-nowhere living, I would have hunted mushrooms on my own.

As I served the salmon, I could already tell the attempt to avert disaster had failed. It was awful. So overcooked it fell apart on the spatula. By poaching it too long, I had washed all the color out of it, turning the flesh white. Tasting more of wet clay than red fish, the meat caught on the roof of my mouth. I had to push it off with my tongue. Only the citrus sauce I made with the juice of blood oranges and butter alleviated the tackiness of the flesh, but even that didn't disguise the pastiness of the salmon. We ate the bites we could and stuck the rest, along with the fish head, in the refrigerator, forgetting about the threat of electronic oblivion and turning instead to chips, salsa, and the cooler of beer.

There is food to be found in the desert but it takes someone who has studied deserts or had knowledge passed down to them to figure out which are the good foods to eat. You don't just get it by wandering into the red rock and hoping a fruit from a cholla cactus seduces you.

The *Phoenix New Times* advises this delicious and nutritious dish:

> You've seen prickly pear jam at the supermarket, but did you know many varieties of cholla cactus are edible straight from the ground? According to the James Beard Foundation's Foods of the Southwest Indian Nations, the Tohono O'odham Indians regularly consumed cholla buds—a smart move considering a palm-size dollop contains as much calcium as a glass of milk. All you need to prepare your cholla in the wild is a lighter and a pocket comb.
>
> Grasp the comb and rake in a downward motion along the shaft of the plant. The fruit should pop right off and be trapped in the teeth of the comb. Skewer your cholla onto a small branch and use the lighter to spark a pile of brush. Cook until the spines char and break off. Once the fruit is clear of spikes, simply peel the skin and roast until warm. Voilà! Cactus appetizers. For a Martha Stewart touch, pluck additional needles and use them as cocktail toothpicks.

But in the apocalypse, there will be very little Internet to guide you to this recipe and the Tohono O'odham are probably not too jazzed to give a lot of free how-to-live-without-electricity advice. Desert plants cling to survival. They make tight, skinny roots. They want to poke you away for good reason. Still, if you know what you're looking for, you might not starve. Miner's lettuce, nettles, prickly pear and pine nuts. Some Mormons knew their wild plants. John Hyrum Barton (1868-1944) wrote in his diary, "We considered pigweed greens a dessert." You need to find someone named Hyrum to help you figure out which weed is a dessert-worthy pig.

⋏⋏⋎

I should have served pigweed. At least that would have been vegetarian and Emily wouldn't be eating only reconstituted shitake soup.

"It's okay, Nik. It's not the end of the world," Rebecca said.

But it was. At least for that minute. All that work, all that preparation, that whole production—a waste. I was sad that whole salmon had died just to be turned to thyme and roof-of-the-mouth stick.

I should have made something more Torrey-like. Something with pine nuts and river trout, not ocean salmon. Food that they eat down here, that you can get fresh in Loa. Steak and cheese—ranch food. The reason they keep the horses. When you drive north and west, think pink. When you drive south and east into the red and orange and desolate desert, don't plan your menu to match the ripples of red rock. Look at the dirt. Match your food to ground.

The clocks turned midnight and the lights stayed on. At least our part of the grid stayed safe. We opened a requisite bottle of champagne.

"I guess we won't have to repopulate the planet," Todd said as he flicked the lights on and off. "Though we could try."

"We're probably all infertile, all this booze," Rebecca said.

Sitting against the fireplace in the living room, Erik's hand on my knee, Rebecca put her head on my shoulder. Emily poked my ribs. We're one big gelatinous goo of warm bodies. I could give up the idea of having kids, if I could keep these bodies connected to me all the time.

"All these years of not getting pregnant. A toast to birth control pills." I raised my glass.

Nobody cheered.

"How about 'to condoms'?"

That got a half a lift of their glasses.

Emily said that she intended not to get pregnant. "If I decide to have kids, I'll communicate with my ovaries."

Neither she nor Rebecca had ever been pregnant. Not one pregnancy scare for either of them. A prophylactic the equivalent of scare quotes kept sperm away from egg. I stared at each of their stomachs, envious of bodies that will do the brain's bidding. Emily just thought "control" and had it. She was thin with mental discipline and vegetarianism. She had self-control. As for me, I cooked. I made spaghetti sauce for pregnancy tests, mashed avocados for cysts, packed up the car for Y2K, cut carrots into French brunoise, strained soup through a chinois, took a pill with the word "control" written into it. Those were the kinds of methods I understood.

"Do you think you'll have kids?" I asked them.

"Not any time soon," Kurt said.

"We're going to be thirty."

"One day."

"One day pretty soon," I said. I could feel the wrinkle in my forehead fat as a crack.

I didn't expect the guys to worry about it. But my friends. They weren't even thinking kids. They were making me feel like the Mormon in the room. Like I'd lost whatever population consciousness my mother had conferred upon me. Maybe they just weren't planners like me. Or maybe they didn't believe that worry was its own kind of prophylactic. None of us knew then what we would have to give up for the children we would or wouldn't have.

As the climate crisis hurtles the fertile valleys of the planet into desertification, learning what plants can grow in sandy soil and arid climates would be more productive than learning how to poach salmon. Pigweed, nettles, prickly pear. These foods require more processing to eat than some of the foods we are used to. The desert is full of thorns to keep the foragers away. Perhaps we'll learn how to transform them from pokey vegetation into smooth, apple-like edibles—burn the needles of cholla berries like the *Phoenix New Times* suggests. We're good at making hybrids, teaching plants to adapt to us. It keeps us from having to adapt ourselves.

I have yet to try to grow pigweed, or even look for it, but, in another quixotic attempt to approximate some kind of preparation, I have figured out which pine cones produce pine nuts. It's not easy. Piñon trees fruit only once every few years. If you're lucky enough to find a fully-seeded cone, you have to dig out the nut with your fingernail or wait for the pine cone to dry in the hot sun. I'm not patient. I end up with bruised fingers and hangnails. When I do get a seed out, I eat it. I suppose one could save them, reserve them to make pesto. In the desert, Native peoples would have told the pioneers as part of their three-month stores to keep the pine nuts in their shells. Pine nuts are full of oil. They pack more protein than any other seed or nut. Outside of their shells, the rich white seeds go rancid quickly. They are best preserved in the freezer. In a total power failure situation, or in pioneer times, shelled seeds would rot. To survive in the desert, you have to shell on demand. No preservation. No prophylactic. And it's fine to have stored no pine nuts, to not know the ways of pigweed, to make fun of salmon fumet and your inability to hook a trout—until it's not.

AMALGAMATED PRODUCTS ARE US

ONE HUNDRED PERCENT CANADIAN BEEF in your hamburger is not the same thing as one hundred percent American beef. I had this problem in Germany and England, too. In Canada, at Niagara Falls, a day before the wedding, I ordered a hamburger. I should have known better by then than to order a hamburger outside of my home country. The hamburger lay flat on the bun as if it were a whole piece of meat rather than *of* a piece—like a fine knit rather than an open weave. Like it had been pressed and stitched. Or cut from the whole cloth of a bolt of hamburger fabric. American hamburgers retain the grind, keep the fibers stretched. In the American hamburger, the cow is reduced to its smallest quantity. It is pea-sized steak showcasing the fundamental level of meat, stitched together loosely—the seams made of dissolvable fat. American hamburgers—you can eat them with just your teeth; the meat falls apart right in your mouth.

To make American hamburger from a chuck roast: Whether you use a food processor or a KitchenAid-type grinder or a hand grinder, you should freeze all the parts. Keeping things cold makes sure the cut is precise. Freeze a chuck roast for half an hour to make it easier to slice into chunks. Press the chunks through the grinder. Be careful of the speed. Too fine and the whole burger will turn to mush. Too large and you won't be able to pack the meat into a self-contained unit. Pea-sized is what you need so the meat is big enough to take a stitch and exactly small enough to want to stitch others to itself. There is safety in numbers.

Restaurants in the US have perfected the hamburger. You know what to expect from state to state, town to town. Cross that international border though, even to attend a wedding, and you'll be ordering at your own risk.

But no matter the cut, the serving of meat is a thread that ties weddings together, even across borders, as if all weddings are united by one very large cow.

A new season of amalgamation has arrived in the form of Beyond Burgers and Impossible Burgers. These burgers are as full of secrets as wedding nights and certainly as processed as weddings themselves. What is the joy in perception? Why is the faintly metallic taste of the fake burger more disturbing than the metallic taste of blood? They talk about the uncanny valley when a robot is almost too human. The freakiness stems not from its similarity but from the vast, vast distance between the mirror and the self. Do I really look like that? Do you think I look like that? Thank God for wedding pictures that make us look exactly like what we are not. Veggie burgers are the most beautiful robot versions of ourselves. We should love them, and ourselves, more than we do.

My wedding was as processed as the next one. Erik and I made few attempts to distinguish ourselves from the march of brides wearing white, ordering prime rib, matching flower colors to tablecloths. I wore white. We served prime rib at the buffet, in keeping with my sisters' weddings, in keeping with the expectations of our meat-loving relatives. We did not serve a vegetarian option, not even for Emily. The bridesmaids' dresses were fuchsia—matched already to many a flower, although I didn't have many flowers. My desire to have fancy things runs counter to my desire to save money, unless the cost involves food. So instead of huge bouquets of flowers, we had bowls of figs and grapes. Erik and I, in one moment of nobody's-advice-but-our-own, shopped for the wedding at Deseret Industries, the local thrift store, and bought platters and bowls upon which to set this fruit.

We chose a reception hall that let us bring in our own liquor—magnum-sized bottles of Concha y Toro, hundreds of cans of Bud Light, handles of Smirnoff and Jack Daniel's. The way our would-be united families drank, this saved us three thousand dollars. On the expensive side, we also served hors d'oeuvres of goat cheese and sundried tomato bruschetta and shrimp ceviche. Otherwise, pretty standard wedding. We had carrot cake for cake. It might have tasted good. We didn't have a minute between shaking hands of friends of uncles whose names we wouldn't remember and cutting the cake just one more time—the flash didn't go off—to try a bite.

The meat: it might have been prime. It might have been medium rare. Who can be sure? We didn't have a moment to chew.

Prime Rib Facts:
- *Prime* is a distinction. *Rib* is a place on a body. Prime rib is designated by its agedness (the prime) and the part of the cow it comes from (the front ribs). Roast cut from the rib is what you're eating.
- A twelve-ounce slice of prime rib has 1,165 calories and offers 225 percent of the suggested saturated fat intake for the day.
- Rib roast from bison is available to order. The bison roast offers only 145 percent of the suggested saturated fat intake for the day.
- To cook a perfect rib roast: Rub all over with salt and other seasonings like pepper. Cook in the oven at 500 degrees for twenty minutes. Then cook for twelve minutes a pound at a low 300 degrees. Remove when the

meat thermometer reads 135-140 degrees. Let rest for half an hour. Even an hour.

- Cattle are the number one agricultural source of greenhouse gases worldwide. Each year, a single cow will belch about 220 pounds of methane, which is shorter lived than carbon dioxide but twenty-eight times more potent in warming the atmosphere.
- The Texas and Utah Beef Councils would prefer you forget about the calories, the carbon output, and the bison and recognize the cow-beefy deliciousness for what it is.

The first wedding I attended was in New York City. I was twelve or fourteen. I don't think I smoked cigarettes full time yet so I must have been twelve. The pictures of me from that time look sweet and innocent—a blond bob, bangs, big cheeks, smiley-smiley, so I'm pretty sure I wasn't smoking yet—but I always looked smiley-nice, even when I did smoke.

My parents weren't big on taking kids to weddings—for their wedding they'd specifically had the printer engrave "no children please" on the invitation. This was partially a budgetary consideration in Utah, where if every couple brought every kid, your catering budget would skyrocket. Unless you had a cake-and-punch wedding in the church gymnasium. But this New York wedding was of the fancy kind and my twin sisters and I were expressly invited. It was my dad's college mentor's son's wedding, held at the Hyatt Regency. Glass chandeliers and gold ice buckets—it was the eighties—and plates and plates of cocktail shrimp. Even though the Friedmans were Jewish, Robert's fiancé wasn't. Cold shrimp were 1980s de rigueur New York wedding food. This wedding may have informed my deep desire to have a raw bar at my wedding—although all Erik and I could afford was the shrimp ceviche. The New York wedding became the standard for my ideal wedding: the offering of fancy meats that work to transcend religious edicts, suturing the rifts between families from different cultures. So as we two wed, so shall the raw bar be served alongside the prime rib.

If prime rib is the heavy weave convincing you that this marriage is substantial, sustaining, and fulfilling, then shrimp is its gauzier cousin—the tat between weddings suggesting a more cautious hope, a more realistic eye, a bit of a cynical nod to the idea that weddings are an event but a marriage is a life and it's going to take more than chandeliers and gold ice buckets and slabs of meat to make it past the honeymoon.

Shrimp, sea-meat that it is, are farmed like cows. They're bred and fed in small ponds or confined in ocean-adjacent pens. The problems with shrimp farms are the same as with any farms—complications brought upon by a single organism growing against what was a natural ecosystem. In the case of shrimp, the complications include viruses, overproduction, market fluctuation, and environmental factors like flooding clean estuaries with shrimp waste. Over one hundred countries grow shrimp. More than grow corn or wheat. The shrimp—little water insect, tasty with butter or deep fried, or sautéed with garlic or best eaten simply with cocktail sauce extra horseradish—has become a fundamental protein for dozens of countries. If the shrimp were to disappear tomorrow, many tables would turn vegetarian overnight. And the weddings? All prime rib, no gauzy shrimp cousin.

The shrimp of the 1980s are different than the shrimp of today. Shrimp's ability to process the effects of ocean acidification brought about by global warming have changed their flavor. Sam Dupont, a researcher at the University of Gothenburg in Sweden, studies the effect of acidification on Northern shrimp. "Dupont's team exposed the shrimp to water chemistries that mimicked the levels of carbon dioxide forecast a few decades from now. Then, they asked chefs to prepare them side by side with shrimp grown in 2019 conditions. A panel of tasters sampled each plate. Surprisingly, most could taste a difference. And most preferred today's shrimp over the shrimp grown under acidified conditions—a taste of things to come. 'That was kind of the first step: You know, like you can actually taste acidification,' Dupont says."[1, 2]

The process of harvesting fish from the oceans doesn't help the climate crisis. As more people host more shrimp-infused weddings and as more people find Red Lobster a reasonable place to dine, more fishing boats trawl for shrimp. As those heavy nets draw fish from the ocean, they create more drag, forcing the boats to burn more gasoline. The more shrimp you eat, the more carbon in the atmosphere.[3]

There is a tiny bit of good news. Shrimp, albeit brine shrimp, super tiny shrimp that seahorses and other creatures eat, swim around the ocean. They have the capacity to swim upwards as well as downwards. If they could do a little more upward swimming, they could reach the carbon-saturated, warmer waters and, with the forces of their swimming parts, could drag those warmer waters into the colder waters, effectively stirring up the oceans, inviting the water to trap a little more heat and a little more carbon. The only bad news is that shrimp are as lazy as humans and don't like to expend the energy to swim up toward the top layers of water. To get the experiment to work, the research team, led by Dr. John Dabiri, had to "trick" the brine shrimp by attracting them upwards with seductive LED lighting. In the non-lab ocean, the upwards is where the boats with their nets live. Better to play it safe and tuck into the cold, dense waters of the bottom layers.[4]

When I lived in Portland, I worked at a place called Orlo—Raising Awareness about the Environment through the Creative Arts. We published a literary magazine, performed Word on the Street where we stood on the steps of Pioneer Square and the library and read volubly from *Cadillac Desert* and *Silent Spring*. We had an outfit for Vinnie the Fire Boy and one for a bear-looking creature so we could compete with Oregon's other mascots—the Beavers and the Ducks. Vinnie and Orlo the Bear walked along the Willamette River, handing out bumper stickers that read "YouENDanger" and "Cows Kill Salmon."

Cows do kill salmon. Their hooves skim across the small creeks from which the salmon were first spawned. When the salmon try to return to do their own spawning, chunks of dried mud stand, as forceful as a concrete dam, in their way. Salmon already had it rough to begin with, this upstream going just to lay eggs and die. Now, they have to dodge stomping cows, cow pies, cow paths intersecting spawning streams with no lifeguard to help the would-be parents cross.

There is little debate that eating less meat would have an effect on climate change. Emissions from cattle in the form of methane are a concern because methane molecules can hold three times the amount of heat as CO_2. Transporting cows, feeding cows, slaughtering cows—the climate toll, and possibly the moral toll, adds up. Humans exhale their guilt in batches of CO_2.

I look at the mournful eyes of the cow as I drive through the middle of Utah. They seem sad, already. How is it possible I look him in the eye and still manage, not even two hours later, to consider whether to broil or grill, baste or sauce?

To persist in eating meat is to privilege tradition over beliefs. Growing up, to celebrate birthdays, good report cards, anniversaries, we ate prime rib. My dad didn't cook much but he prided himself on the best burger. My parents hosted New Year's Eve for both sides of our extended family, serving rare roast beef and horseradish sauce. When the Friedman's visited us from New Jersey, mom made sure to serve the steaks without a butter sauce to keep it kosher. Beef stitched our family together. It still does. That's why a wedding ceremony requires beef—to knot the stitch. Even the vegetarians don't disapprove.

Our eyes are more connected to our stomachs than our hearts. Or perhaps, our hearts are preoccupied with human constructs like romance and celebrations and love. Not all hotel weddings are held on the upper floors of New York Regency Hyatt ballrooms. Most weddings I've attended have been held in the bottom layer of the hotel in the conference center where the chairs aren't wood draped with linen but aluminum-framed jobs with polyester upholstery. Usually pink. The ceremony is performed over the dramatic vista of the hotel lobby stairwell. As a bridesmaid, I walk as I've always been taught to in the procession, with that special step, toes together, step. I hold my flowers too high. My sister has to remind me to lower the bouquet to its pubic, not breast, decoration.

In Utah, the weddings come fast and often. With so many children in each family and so many of them getting married so young, you can, at the age of eighty, attend your great-grand-daughter's wedding. The old Utah joke that says you know it's a Mormon wedding if the bride's not pregnant but her mother is, is both a joke and also sometimes true. There are two kinds of Mormon weddings—the LDS temple kind, to which I'm never invited because I haven't been recommended by my bishop (because I have no bishop) and the other kind where some one-time, wanton friend of mine returns to the fold of the church—most likely because she got pregnant and the families pressed her to marry the guy who knocked her up for the sake of the child. The bishop also can't recommend pre-marriage pregnant people to the temple for the wedding, so these weddings take place in the wardhouse's gym where punch, cookies, and ice cream are served by the young women in Mutual (the Mormon answer to 4-H Club). There's a chance you might be served meat, but it will be the least prime of the meats: the bolognas, the hot dogs, the overcooked, freezer-burned game that someone's relative shot three years ago. So many wards, so many weddings. There's a processed feel to the reception line. The glazed-over look in the parents' eyes looks like so much glistening, slightly over-the-date deli slices. There are no chairs for the guests so everyone stands up to drink the bad punch and chew the bad meat into the rescuing tuck of a napkin. In the receiving line you notice the dress on the bride is one size too big because she borrowed it from her mother and it has stains on it from carrying her little brother and you think that in twenty years, she'll just shift one spot over to the left and receive the new relatives of her daughter with the same we're-all-one-big-family-now glance that suggests that there's no way she is able to remember all the names in this family in the first place. The knitting together is much less fancy a stitch when you're sewing together so vast a blanket.

What is the process behind the Impossible Burger? It's a secret—but Sophia Hampton, a farmer who raises cows and pigs in small numbers, humanely, and with the philosophy of the Slow Food Movement, says in an article in *Bon Appétit* that two of the ingredients are two kinds of soy, "textured soy protein, which looks like stale breadcrumbs, and barrels of soy leghemoglobin, aka heme, the genetically engineered red liquid that flavors an Impossible burger."

Another main ingredient is coconut oil. Coconuts must be the current mainstay of our economic system—coconut oil for popcorn, for face cleansing, for lotion. Coconut water for proper hydration. Coconut milk for proper tom kha kai. The coconut oil is what makes the Impossible Burger as saturated in fat as a regular burger and gives it as many calories. It's the soy protein concentrate and the product called heme that help make the Impossible Burger burger-like. The heme, or soy leghemoglobin, is what makes the Impossible Burger bloody-like. Laura Reiley, for the *Washington Post*, writes, "Impossible Burger is made by taking the DNA from the roots of soy plants, inserting it into genetically engineered yeast and then fermenting that yeast (much the way Belgian beer is made). Soy contains estrogen-like compounds called isoflavones that some findings say can promote the growth of some cancer cells, impair female fertility and mess with men's hormones."[5] But we've met the health warnings on beef before. We're all dying of heart disease. And, thanks to the beef industry, the whole planet is dying of cow-making. *Our World in Data* shows that eating beef contributes 60 kilograms of CO_2 per kilogram of food product. Poultry produces 6 kilograms. Apples, 0.4 kilograms.[6]

Think how many degrees cooler the temperature of the planet will be. There are enough kids on the planet (she says, hypocritically, now that she's had her own). Your female fertility isn't helping, anyway. Your men's hormones have been messed up from the get-go. Process that soy. Ferment those genetically engineered yeasts. Humans are amazing cooks. Let them make a burger that mimics the process of making Belgian beer.

Sophia Hampton worries about what will happen to the 1 percent of growers of sustainable meat products if all flesh-based meat is replaced by vegetarian meat. She argues that it's not really the animals themselves but the system of production, the big companies getting bigger and bigger, warehousing animals for meat, where the real greenhouse gases become a problem. The animals of small producers, she notes, can, like plants, help sink carbon into the soil if they are grazed properly. But she can't deny Impossible Burgers' large-screen advertisement as she walks out of the production plant: "The Impossible Burger takes 87 percent less water, 96 percent less land, and 89 percent fewer emissions than any conventional beef burger in America."

The beef and pork industries counter plant-based meat claims by calling them "highly processed." Like Hampton writes, it's two kinds of weirdly processed soy that go into the burgers. Soy isn't always healthful. Additives and preservatives combine to make the food taste more like meat and be more shelf stable. The plant-based meat industry counters that claim by noting no antibiotics go into plant-based meat as they do in almost all industry beef and pork. And, processed isn't always bad. The Academy of Nutrition and Dietetics, American Society for Nutrition, Institute of Food Technologists, and International Food Information Council all show that processed foods like bread and canned goods add valuable nutrients to diets.

Personally, I'm waiting for lab-grown meat. Although I don't know if I believe in progress—before industrialization, meat was a very rare treat—I do believe in science. If meat is what we have been culturally acclimated to eat and a low-carb diet keeps me from swelling up like a true balloon (instead of a partial balloon), then I'm excited by the idea of chicken thighs, hewn from a stem cell of a proper, long-lived chicken, grown in a vat of serum with a battery of lab assistants attending to its pain-free cultivation. Unless it really is cruelty that gives meat its flavor. But I'm sure there is enough cruelty in this world to incorporate into the test tube chicken babies.

In the US, hot dogs, bologna, hamburgers, and roast beef are all kinds of processed. And yet we recoil from the idea of processed fish. Canned tuna is one thing; churned and amalgamated fish products are another. Many Americans find the idea of shrimp paste repugnant even though many of the meats they usually eat have been, at one point, a paste. Fermented shrimp are pressed into blocks and then sliced into sauces and soup broths in Thailand and Laos, Myanmar and Vietnam, Indonesia and Southern China. Certain food wouldn't be that food without a slice of fermented shrimp. To make the paste: dry the shrimp to preserve its sea-salty characteristic and count on microbes to make their home inside the shrimp that will shortly be mashed into a paste and then buried in the ground in earthen jars. When the paste comes up, it's fermented. Scoop out a spoonful. Toss it with chili peppers, some shallot paste and garlic and sugar, fry it up and you are eating a traditional Malay dish. If you are Malaysian, you know you'd be in for a delicious snack just like I know I am when I drive up to the window at Arby's.

Prime rib is really just a beef roast—something from which you could make a sandwich the next day. At Arby's they allow you to skip the teeth work and turn beef into a perfect paste for you. Neither fork nor knife required.

Someone from Myanmar might be a bit taken aback when they looked at a slice of Arby's beef. Why is it see-through? Where did all the sinew go? Arby's knows you don't want to trouble with that resistance. Like many processed meats, the meat is cooked like a regular roast beef that is then chopped and mashed and reformed. By adding salt and sodium phosphate and then massaging the pureed and infused beef into a malleable mixture, myosin rises to the surface. The myosin helps glom the pieces together. Formed into a football-sized mound, the beef mixture is cooked, then sliced, then piled high on a buttery bun. In both the cases of the shrimp and the Arby's roast beef, the chunking apart of meat and then the stitching it back together reminds me of the way we pull apart from our original family units and knit ourselves into a new one. Maybe, if we're lucky, we weave some of those origins together. A different kind of lab experiment.

The sinews that try to tie together this marriage blanket, in an attempt to cross cultural, religious, and just plain family-specific predilections, are the rites of ceremony. The ceremonial rote words, when they begin, are always the same. This should provide me a feeling of continuity and ritual, but where I once imagined marriage stitching together the past with the future, this family extending onward, I wonder, what kind of blanket are we making? Who's going to need a blanket? The planet is getting warmer and warmer. This family quilt has become redundant. Traditional, patriarchal, wedding vows read "Christ told us that the wife must submit herself unto her own husband as unto the Lord. For as Christ is Head of His Church so is the husband head of his wife. [Name], I submit myself to you." Perhaps instead the bride and the groom submit to an unpredictable future. We'll move to higher ground. We'll prepare for a more acidic ocean. We'll hurry this union along, eat all the Arby's. We'll have the prime rib and the shrimp.

The last wedding ended in the usual way. After seventeen minutes of congratulations-you're-one-big-family-now, the officiator of ceremonies interrupts the back-slapping to remind you that the balcony is reserved for club room guests. A wedding staffer ushers you into the conference center room where the ceiling is seven feet tall and the lighting is either full-on or full-off. You dance to CD compilations over crackly speakers. The dinner is sit-down. The prime rib is medium rare. All as perfect as the last wedding you attended when you sat down and ate delicious prime rib. You are thankful the dinner is not the ubiquitous conference chicken. You raise your glass to all the toasts that suggest this wedding is different—that he's the trunk and she's the leaves, that he's the car to her road, that he's the knife to her fork and maybe they'll have spoon babies. The metaphors are unique, slightly off and sometimes revelatory.

Years later, after their divorce, you remember the toast by groomsman number two and wonder if his suggestion that she is the knife and the groom is the fork was prescient; at dinner one night after the groom said something perfect like "the roast beef is a little rare," the fork flew across the table completely of its own design. As if forks and rare roast beef are in cahoots. Or the time she sat at the table, rubbing her knife back and forth in that automatic way she does until she accidentally cut through the tablecloth her aunt gives her for the wedding. No one liked the fabric. Off-white, it matched nothing and was embroidered with hearts. What had been stitched together, now broken apart.

***

All the divorces are the same, too, except they unravel rather than ravel. Pieces begin to fly off. It starts with a dinner party. Too many people's expectations. Too much wine. Too many different levels of caring—who cares if the forks are on the left or the right? Who cares if there's a little piece of lettuce stuck to the plate or if the parmesan is grated with the big holes instead of the small holes or if you asked them if they'd care for a drink or if you'd taken their coats? The level of care is a hard equation. Two does not equal two. Sometimes the hole-size on the grate of parmesan does matter more than the promise of death do us part. Sometimes making your guests remove their own coats rather than taking them for them does suggest a lot about the potential of "for better or worse." Things fall apart so quickly. The stitch the vows tried to make doesn't always take. She asks him to come upstairs with her so they can have a little chat and suddenly she's brought the roast up with her and she's winging it at his head and he ducks but too slowly and now he thinks she's making fun of his manhood as if she cared about his manhood. She just wanted him to be a good host and make sure that everyone had enough to drink and didn't spend the evening draping their coats over their arms.

Thrown, a whole hunk of meat, unlike hamburger or shrimp paste or Arby's roast beef, is heavy and causes damage, no matter how clumsily thrown.

The food of divorce is the food of the climate crisis. Both will be good practice for the COVID-19 pandemic. The unpredictability of the future that reminds the divorcée that she's single again with a whole fridge and some nobody's fourteen kinds of salsa filling it up. Processed food is the go-to food while she tries to process where she went wrong. At first, she tries the nothing diet. Then there's the maraschino cherry and bacon diet, the popcorn and peas diet. There's the chips and one of the fourteen kinds of salsa diet even though the salsa had a bit of mold on it. There is no fundamental divorce diet. Eventually, there's Stouffer's and Lean Cuisine, but on the road toward that break, it's a hodgepodge of chocolate squares and orange slices, beef jerky and sautéed onion, fried bread and scrambled eggs with green olives in them. Because who knows when she'll be able to eat like this again? Eat cream cheese with her finger. Ball up Wonder Bread in her fist and eat it like the dough it once was. She eats ketchup on spinach. She dips pickles in Cheez Whiz. She bites chunks off of cheese and eats onions like apples. She puts mustard on rice and eats it with her fingers. She gives up on napkins entirely.

The end of an unproductive, meaning unsuccessful, meaning childless, marriage does have some benefits. She can eat what she wants. She doesn't have to eat just chicken. She can eat sweetbreads and steak tartar and garlic. No one chides her. She doesn't have to worry about who will eat what. She doesn't have kids maneuvering for mac and cheese. Her husband doesn't remind her that he doesn't like fish. Her husband doesn't tell her, after she's been slaving over the brisket for hours, that he doesn't eat beef anymore. That mad cow disease has turned him off of meat, for once and for all. He only eats unprocessed foods—kale, spinach, fresh-squeezed orange juice. She loves him just as much as she ever did. Almost. Although looking at an old photo of his bony face makes her hunger for a cheeseburger.

HOW TO MAKE
MOZZARELLA

TRYING TO GET PREGNANT IS a lot like trying to make cheese. Although with cheese making, you have a little more control over the outcome because you have more control over the equipment. You can clean out a nonreactive pan within inches of its life. Can you clean out a nonreactive uterus? Can you see right down into its spot-free shine? Even the HSG, or hystero-salpingography, the radiologic procedure that shows how your uterus is shaped and in what shape your fallopian tubes are, lighting your uterus up like a football field, only paints an image in shadows and light. It cannot reveal what nefarious, smirking substance might be clinging to the inside, preventing whatever would-be embryo from implanting into to the uterus with one of its dirty looks. Imagine the ovum is the milk. When you make cheese, you can choose milk that hasn't yet expired. You cannot choose the age of your eggs, which have been lined up in your fallopian tubes since the day you were conceived. Your eggs have an expiration date, and, like my sister once said to me, maybe your eggs are old and sour and curdled.

To impregnate a resistant egg is almost as hard as it is to change a planet's climate. The balance of the number of O_2s, nitrogens, carbons, had held stable for so long. Like the stubborn egg, there was no need, really, for the situation to change. Everything had been going fine for the egg. Everything had been going fine for the climate. Trees expired oxygen, they sucked up

CO_2. The creatures inhaled and exhaled. The sun beamed down in predictable measure. The plants grew in the summer, chilled out in the winter. The oceans held their pH levels steady. The egg was hanging out there in all the uncertainty with so much anticipation. But if an ecosystem tips out of balance, all the processes that run like clockwork stick in the wheels.

To make cheese: into the clean, endometriosis-free, nonreactive pan pour the fresh, whole milk. For conception: go ahead, pour in the substance. It's the same idea although, in the latter case, you may as well keep your eyes closed; you're working with product so small it's invisible to your naked eye. Imagine making cheese with microscopic curds in a completely dark kitchen. Would you trust that cheese?

Thank God for thermometers. As with cheese making, trying to conceive can be measured in Fahrenheit. With cheese, the temperature should reach 105 degrees. When you're trying to conceive, if, when testing to see if you're ovulating, you hit 105, you're already doomed. You're cooking those eggs, not hatching them. Go to the doctor and get that fever down. Try again next month. When trying to conceive, your body temperature should rise just slightly before ovulation. You have to map it out for months to see what your baseline temperature is. Cheese is less picky—let the milk hover around 105 degrees for a few minutes. Add the rennet. Stir. The curds will begin to separate from the whey. The curds will begin to cling to each other. Drain through a cheesecloth-lined strainer. Press with the back of a spoon and then begin to manually press the curds. Working with your hands gives a greater sense of control. Push the curds together like kneading bread, then pull them apart like taffy.

If you're trying to heat up a planet, 105 degrees will do. Tell Columbus, Ohio, that 105 isn't too bad for May. Tell Reykjavik. Oslo. Tell Melbourne it has a fever at 110. Turn the air conditioners on in March. Leave them running until October. Plant tomatoes as you usually do. Maybe they'll produce like that egg of yours, on time and at the end of the season. Maybe a cold snap will be a fluke of July. Try again with tomatoes next year. That mozzarella you can eat on pizza with canned sauce. Caprese salads will have to wait another day.

The cheese-making experience resonates with other foods you've cooked. You've turned out soufflés and candy and cakes. You've used your fingers to mold meringue into shape, dough into perfect rounds, shape cookies onto trays. If you could use your hands to organize things on the inside, fallopianly, do palpable guidance on the sperm, digitally direct the sperm into the egg, wouldn't you have more confidence? Perhaps it would take some of the magic out of "the birth story" but isn't there magic enough in turning milk into cheese? The miracle of life can sometimes be overrated and the miracle of cheese can sometimes be underrated. There's something to be said in being able to see and touch the efforts of your work. Cheese making provides great joy in that you don't have to wait two weeks to discover how things turned out, at least not for fresh mozzarella. Unlike climate change, the results are predictable, immediate, and satisfying.

WHAT THE DIRT
KNOWS

T HE DROUGHT MADE GROWING TOMATOES hard. Or made
the watering of tomatoes emotionally difficult—rolling out
the hose every day, imagining half the water evaporating into
the air. And there was something wrong with the ones that did
grow. In the backyard, I had layered newspapers, peat moss, and
compost on top of a small square of the quarter acre of grass
that came with the house my sisters and I had bought in the
Avenues after moving back home to Salt Lake City from Oregon. These layers would, in a year, turn to great soil. I was in a
hurry so I had planted tomatoes directly into the newspapers.
Paper makes good compost, adding the twenty-five parts per
carbon per one part nitrogen to balance the soil. Burying paper
would be a great carbon sink if the carbon stayed in the ground
rather than snuck back into the atmosphere, climbing molecule
by molecule, melting into the sky the other ethereal ideas the
inky letters exhaled.

There's a difference between live soil and dead dirt. Dead dirt
lacks the microbes and carbon to make plants grow. Drought,
deforestation, removing native grasses and planting imported
grasses—like the Kentucky bluegrass that rolled from the back
of the house a quarter acre toward the back fence—help kill the
soil. Tucking carbon back into the dirt helps restore life to the
earth.

This isn't only good for growing tomatoes. There's some
promise that soil could store some of the carbon that makes up

the greenhouse gasses contributing to climate change. Because a good portion of the dirt has been degraded, the opportunity for the dirt to "soak up" some carbon is pretty great. Researchers Ahmed Chinade Abdullahi, Chamhuri Siwar, Mohamad Isma'il Shaharudin, and Isahak Anizan, in a paper titled "Carbon Sequestration in the Soil: Opportunities and Challenges[7], assert that soil could sequester up to 1.2 billion tons of carbon per year. Rotating crops, planting cover crops, minimal-impact tilling, adding native grasses, even keeping goats or other grazers around the yard helps restore carbon. But keeping the carbon tucked away in the soil isn't so easy. Or rather, it's just as easy to release the carbon as it is to store it. For although plants inhale CO_2 and soil absorbs it, soil, microbes, and fungi also exhale carbon. Decomposition sends nearly the same amount of carbon into the air as their composition once sequestered. Perhaps we can get the dinosaurs to come back and lie down under a bed of ash that keeps them layered so deep their decaying bodies can't reach the atmosphere—until some constant-72-degree-temperature-loving beings come back to burn them into the sky. The planet loves a balanced chemical equation—it doesn't care if the balance happens in the ground or in the sky. The carbon we have is earth's forever. Maybe the next generation, or the next species, will be able to move these dinosaur carcasses around with more forethought.

For my tomatoes, I didn't think I would have to worry about chemistry. I had imagined I would just need to stand back and watch the plants grow, Jack and the Beanstalkian. I expected fully red tomatoes like my mother and grandmother had always grown in their backyards, but when I bent down into the small garden, my tomatoes were brown on the bottom. Usually that indicates overwatering, but the soil was as dry as bone that day. The tomato plant's leaves looked haggard, yellowed on the edges. Folded over on themselves, the leaves' cell walls looked like they had collapsed—texture kale turned texture Kleenex. I turned on the hose and tried to reinvigorate the leaves. Water should provide stiff cellular structure. I should be able to break a leaf like a stalk of celery. Crushed between my fingers, the leaf smelled of dry toast, not fresh-cut hay with hints of marijuana. Usually, when I put tomato plants close to my nose, I sneezed—but these dumb leaves catalyzed no nasal reaction at all. I could have called my grandmother, who had been growing tomatoes in Salt Lake Valley since she moved down here from Evanston, Wyoming, forty years ago, to ask if her tomatoes were, this season, brown on the bottom. I could have called my mom to see if she remembered what she and my dad, when they were married and gardened together, did about rot-bottomed tomatoes. Mom and Grandma probably would have both responded: "Miracle-Gro." But I wanted to be able to do this on my own—just me, some seeds, and some semi-fertile soil. I wondered, what would I have done for lunch if I had to rely on my own gardening skills? What if I had been one of the first white settlers in this valley, if I had been a Mormon pioneer? What would I do if there were no grocery stores to sell me tomatoes brought by semitruck all the way from Mexico? Thank God Smith's grocery store was only a couple of blocks down the street. I didn't absolutely have to have caprese salad for lunch, but now that it was on my mind, I couldn't think of anything else that sounded good.

I went to the store to buy the tomatoes and another pregnancy test. My period was almost late. I came home, dropped the tomatoes on the table, and walked to the bathroom, where I didn't bother to shut the door. I watched as the fluid flowed past the first window without passing go. No line. No color. In the second window, a pink line appeared, showing that the test was indeed working. No false negatives here. I added the stick to my collection, hidden inside an empty box of tissues in the back of the bathroom closet where no one could find out just how many of these tests I'd taken.

I was thirty-one years old, which was old for Salt Lake City. I'd had my period since I was ten. Something was off with me. Perhaps I'd taken the pill for too long. I'd convinced my endometrial lining to thin to a ribbon so thin it couldn't sustain a tomato seed, let alone a zygote.

It had been a year since I'd started trying to get pregnant. It never occurred to me that I wouldn't be able to accomplish this ordinary task. Although I'm not a member of the Church of Jesus Christ of Latter-day Saints my ancestors and grandparents were. My family was just as renowned for our fertility as the next Mormons. My great-great-grandmother gave birth to thirteen children, nine of whom survived. In Evanston, Wyoming, my great-grandma had nine children. My grandma, four. My mother gave birth to me plus my twin sisters. Perhaps there was a winnowing. Was it possible that my genetic heritage had reached the end of the line? Was I left with an ugly-ass tomato and an uncooperative uterus, thinking everything is drying up? Maybe my laptop constantly sitting on my lap had irradiated my uterine lining. Maybe my wine drinking had upset my chemical balance. Maybe I had decried overpopulation too many times and hypocrisy had come to bite me on the ass. Or, in the womb. Maybe the inversion that came to Salt Lake Valley in short, three-week increments when I grew up there and now comes for three-month stretches now that I'm back has rendered me toxic. Maybe I just am toxic. I have a lot of opinions. Maybe I'm just out of balance—too much Salt Lake, not enough Portland. Too much cheese, not enough tomato. Too much me, not enough someone else.

I had planned a caprese salad: mozzarella, basil, tomatoes. I should be able to make or grow all of those things. And yet the tomato, its brown bottom papery and fragile, threatened to dissolve into my hand. I had no cows to milk to make the mozzarella. The basil alone, though a little spindly, looked edible.

Perhaps there were some piñon pinecones in the foothills I could mine for pine nuts. I could make pesto instead of caprese, although I had no bread or noodle to spread it on. This desire to make things from scratch—did it come from the past, coursing through my ancestral blood, from when the Mormons landed in this valley and learned how to grow food in the desert? Or did it come from the future? From the thin pinch I felt in the air? From the sense of a warming climate and too little rain? The valley was hot and dry and dusty. As the waves of heat rolled north across the valley from the most southerly point of the valley, Point of the Mountain, toward my house at the far northerly end, a few streets up from where Mormon prophet Brigham Young made his home, nothing felt like growth or fertility. The blighted tomato I held in my hand made both the past and the future seem highly improbable. The tomato was an eight ball telling me tomato-growing- and baby-making-wise, I was no Mormon.

I couldn't even manifest destiny lunch.

When Erik came home, he found me surrounded by books—a book on how to drill a well if the plumbing infrastructure collapses, one on how to cure tomato blight, and a cookbook opened to a recipe for fresh tomato sauce. I cannot drill a well or, apparently, grow a red-all-over tomato, but I can make tomato sauce, even if I have to go to the store for tomatoes.

I poured a glass of wine for me and handed him a beer. "The test was negative. Is spaghetti okay for dinner?"

"Spaghetti sounds good. What test?"

I rolled my eyes. Sometimes, some people aren't as obsessed as they should be.

"We were filming in Weber County. Boy Scouts missing. Breaking news. Again. We stopped at a gas station. Totally eighties candy." Erik worked as a news cameraman. He and his reporter friend, also named Nicole, spent a lot of time together. They'd gone skydiving. They were the same age. They both liked the movie *Dumb and Dumber*. When I visited Erik at work, I squinted at the button of her fashion pants as if I could see through them. Her endometrial lining was probably rich as Pacific Northwest humus.

But he did hear me. He knew what test. What was there to say? Instead of patting my head or shaking his, he handed me a Garbage Pail Kid. The garbage pails were a perfect medium in which to foment a memory of riding my bike to the 7-Eleven when I was eight. I remembered youth! I could ride my bike again. I could eat pure sugar candies again! But when I took a bite, the candy was stale, reminding me and my eggs how long ago the eighties were.

I turned from his distractions to my distractions, dropping the Roma tomatoes into boiling water to peel their skins. Erik liked spaghetti sauce any way I made it, but tonight I needed something complicated. He touched my shoulder as I chopped garlic. He ate some garlic raw. When Erik and I met at the Zephyr bar, where many now-married non-Mormons met, I had only recently returned to Salt Lake from living in Portland. We took shelter from the commandments that hung thick as smog in the atmosphere of Salt Lake City by hiding out in the smoky, heathen-rich clubs and bars. I showed him how I could take my bra off without taking my shirt off.

"I have never seen anything like that before," Erik said.

"I am a magician," I told him as I stuffed my bra into my purse. Just like a proper magician, I knew how to distract. Bra removal is a great way to avoid talking about your boyfriend who still lives in the Pacific Northwest, who you might be breaking up with, if this bra trick turns out well.

Maybe that was my problem. Keeping the past separated from the present. Maybe Portland isn't so different from Salt Lake City. Maybe it wasn't so bad that I sort of started dating Erik before I fully broke up with Jonathan in Portland. Jonathan could have come to Salt Lake with me for graduate school. The

University of Utah admitted him. Perhaps I should stop imagining one life in Portland and one life in Salt Lake. Maybe they are all my lives, mushed up and messy together.

It was only a few days, plus or minus a few months of negotiations with Erik and now-ex-boyfriend, after we started dating that I started pestering Erik for help with the tomatoes. I invited him over to my house. I took him out back. I showed him the plants. They weren't doing so well in the clayish soil. They seemed stunted for mid-June without any yellow flowers on them at all. Their green tended more toward tree branch than leaf. Still, the plants were still alive. I considered this an achievement for me in the no-rain Salt Lake Valley. In Oregon, you had the opposite tomato problem—green vines from garden to fence but not a red tomato in sight. You need sun to convince a green thing to let go its abundantly moist soil deal and turn to seed-mothering fruit.

Erik stuck his finger in the ground next to the feeble plant.

"This dirt sucks." This was before the layering of newspapers in the ground, before I knew of the chemical difference between Portland soil and Salt Lake soil. Erik had worked for a landscaper during summers. He knew that Salt Lake subsoil was high on clay, lime, and salt and low on organic matter and nutrients.

"You need to amend the soil. It's all crusty dead stuff. Mix it with a bunch of organic matter. Maybe some manure."

Hence my mom and grandma's Miracle-Gro.

"It's not just water. It's the whole system. The dirt around here is clay. It would take years to amend. But if we build a raised bed, you can start your plants with healthy soil."

But at the moment, we were more interested in drinking another beer than adjusting the pH of the soil. And then we were more interested in rolling around on the crunchy grass.

Afterward, with sticks from the box elder trees in our hair and shaking the box elder bugs out of our clothes, Erik promised me he'd build me wooden boxes in which to grow my tomatoes.

✳✳✳

In Salt Lake, a temperature inversion sets in when a high-pressure system presses down from the mountains, creating a lid over the valley. Sunny at the ski resorts, the valley cups a soupy smog. Pollution from the oil refineries, the Kennecott Copper Mine, the magnesium plant, the emissions from a million cars finds particulates to hang on to. Under the lid, the skies turn grayer and grayer.

It's not only emissions and industrial pollutants that add to the layers of gray. Soil, once held down by plants and microbes, has been eroded by energy exploration, off-road vehicles, cattle over-grazing, and agricultural use. On top of that, a drought that's been in place since 2000, plus dam upon river dammed, has evaporated rivers and lakebeds. That unloosed dirt, stirred by wind and cars, combines with the pollution to add another layer to the thickening soup. I've overthickened soups before. They turn into porridge—thick enough to stand a spoon upright. I suppose the humans are the spoons of Salt Lake Valley in winter. But soup, even brothy soup, is notoriously bad to inhale.

In the backyard, though, I planned to nail down this soil thing. A few weeks after Erik mentioned raised beds, garden boxes emerged from redwood and nails, lined with weed barrier. He joined the edges and made a ledge to sit on. It was more a cabinet than a growing box. It was so beautiful. I wanted to take it inside. Perhaps I could doctor my uterus by sleeping in an indoor raised bed.

"It's for the tomatoes," he said.

Not that he didn't pity my uterus. He worried about all my body parts—even my ovaries. He just didn't think sleeping in soil was the immediate solution to the problem. He thought sex was. Because he's a guy. My grandma said, in front of him and my mom, "You have to have more sex!" My grandma loved to embarrass my mom. I imagined this whole "trying to get pregnant" phrasing embarrassed Erik. No one likes to try with-out results. We redoubled our efforts growing tomatoes. Little did we know, tomatoes would be one of the answers to our future pandemic lives. It was good luck to try to give ourselves twenty years to figure out gardening. Who knew climate change and the collapse of the world economy would make growing tomatoes more necessary than babies?

To thank Erik for building the raised bed, I cooked dinner. Tacos with ground beef and cheese. I'd been making tacos since I was eight when Mom's bridge went late. I checked in with her at the neighbors to see if she was winning. She laid down her cards and stood to go because my dad would be home soon but I said I could do it. I crossed the street to head home and waltzed into the kitchen. I took the ground beef from the refrigerator, added salt and pepper and a little chili powder. I tore up the lettuce with my hands and grated the cheese. Mom came home to cut the tomatoes and the onions right before we ate. I've eaten tacos at least one day a week since then, and I still loved them even though I ate the components one by one. Erik looked at my divided plate. I kept the meat separate from the cheese and the lettuce, from the avocado and onions.

"Don't you need, you know, like a holder to make it a taco? A base to keep it all together?" Erik said as he ate—tomatoes, hamburger, lettuce, onions, avocado, Cholula, and cheese all together—his third.

The tomatoes, store-bought, I kept away from the also store-bought onions since neither could I grow. I hadn't yet learned how to like traditional tacos, which I now eat once in a while, all compiled into one food bite like a regular taco-eating person. Perhaps it takes tearing down the borders between your onion and tomatoes, your cheese and avocado, to make a real taco. Maybe you have to take it all in together.

BEFORE TACOS

SOMETIMES, I THREW MYSELF INTO my Mormon heritage like a frog throws herself into the pond. Sometimes, you've got to jump all the way in if you want to catch a dragonfly. Right after I'd moved back to Salt Lake, by promising me fried chicken and rubbing in the I-never-see-you-guilt, my grandma convinced me, my mom, and sisters to go to the Durant family reunion. We met in Henefer, Utah, forty miles northeast of Salt Lake City. The sprinklers watered grass that never should have been planted there. The native grasses had long been overrun by Kentucky blue. My great-uncle asked us all to gather round to bless this meal: fried chicken (only one piece per person please), funeral potatoes (shredded potatoes topped with cream of mushroom gravy, cheese, and crushed cornflakes), and Jell-O salads—lime with pineapple, strawberry with bananas, mixed with whipped cream and a can of tropical fruit to make the salad portion of the meal more healthy.

JELL-O SALAD INGREDIENTS

- 1 cup boiling water
- 1 package (3 oz.) lime- or lemon-flavored gelatin
- ½ cup cold water
- 1 can (8 oz.) crushed pineapple, undrained
- ½ cup shredded carrot
- Mayonnaise or whipped cream, if desired

DIRECTIONS

Pour boiling water on gelatin in medium bowl; stir until gelatin is dissolved. Stir in cold water and pineapple. Refrigerate about forty-five minutes or until thickened but not set.

Lightly brush six 1/2-cup salad molds with vegetable oil. Stir carrot into thickened gelatin; pour into molds. Refrigerate about four hours or until firm.

To unmold salads, dip molds into hot water for ten seconds. Place salad plate upside down onto each mold; turn plate and mold over, then remove mold. Top salads with mayonnaise.

One of my great-uncles interrupted the swarming of buffet line to give the blessing. I tried not to look at my mom or my sisters. They would catch me rolling my eyes and then someone else would roll her eyes and one of us would laugh. We didn't believe but we also didn't want to be rude. We were already out of place, four non-Mormons at a totally Mormon event. In the Mormon Church, laymen are the preachers. My mom's uncle, Martin, as a bishop, and a member of the priesthood, gave the prayer. My grandmother, although older than he, the matriarch of the family now that my great-grandmother Minnie had died, and the person who organized all the food, sat quietly in her nylon-weave folding chair while Martin conversed with God.

"Dear Heavenly Father, we ask you to bless this food and the hands that prepared it. We thank you for bringing us together, especially Jan and her girls who are not so often with us. We thank you for providing this beautiful meadow upon which we may eat our meals and be with our family. We thank you for Grandma [who calls his sister 'grandma'?] who encouraged Jan and her daughters to come to join us for this delicious meal. Amen."

As if we didn't feel conspicuous enough, hiding our beers in can cozies and pretending to eat some of the Jell-O salads, Uncle Martin made clear in his prayer, in case God hadn't noticed, that we hadn't attended a reunion, let alone church, in quite a while. I felt guilty anyway, chewing on the second piece of chicken I'd snuck from the buffet line.

The fried chicken was not homemade. The fried chicken wasn't even from KFC. It was grocery-store fried chicken. Breaded and coated with at least five spices, it was still good. Even mediocre fried chicken is excellent fried chicken.

I swatted at the bees that had come to eat the chicken, not to be confused with the ones who came to drink from the sprinklers. Utah may be the Beehive State but the bees always seem thirsty here for irrigated water, piped in from Jordanelle Dam, as the sprinklers rata-ta-ted over the green lawn. Everything here had been imported. Even me, back from Portland. Still, this was home. Organized fried chicken. I felt embraced by the familiar. I felt at home enough to sneak one more piece of chicken.

When I read about the Mormon trek from Missouri to Salt Lake, I read for the food. I salivate over what they left behind in the Midwest: fruit pies and warm bread, chicken soup with dumplings, roast mutton and roast veal—and yet the list of provisions of dried fruit, jerky, and johnnycakes cooked on the open fire also make me hungry. I imagine a kid, walking alongside a handcart, sometimes pushing with his one free hand, gnawing on a piece of beef jerky. That kid didn't know salt was his destiny. His family had been given a list of provisions. Some of them made sense. Some were pie-in-the-sky suggestions made by people who themselves hadn't even crossed Nebraska's Platte River.

Those who brought cattle and other farm animals lost most of their stock, including animals needed to pull their

wagons. In spite of having to travel light, some immi-
grants succeeded in bringing cows, pigs, chickens, seeds,
and tree-root stocks to start their farms...Although game
and wild plants could be relied upon to provide some
nourishment along the way, the covered wagons were
loaded with enough food to last the journey. Food for the
trip had to be compact, lightweight, and nonperishable.
Each family brought along such staples as flour, sugar,
cornmeal, coffee, dried beans, rice, bacon, and salt pork.
Some also brought dried fruit. Mealtime on the Oregon
Trail was goverened [*sic*] by the sun...Breakfast had to be
completed by 4 a.m. so that the wagon train could be on
its way by daybreak. Beans, cornmeal mush, Johnnycakes
or pancakes, and coffee were the usual breakfast. Fresh
milk was available from the dairy cows that some families brought along, and pioneers took advantage of the
rough rides of the wagon to churn their butter. "Noon-
ing" at midday meant stopping for rest and a meal. Little
time could be spent preparing the noonday meal, since
the wagon train could only travel by daylight. Usually a
piece of meat was fried over the camp fire. Longer-cook-
ing stews were left for the evening meal. The women
made bread dough while riding in the wagons and timed
the rising so that it would be ready to bake when evening
camp was made...[8]

I liked the idea that even covered with dust, blistered by
shoes and sun, exhausted from walking hundreds of miles, there
was still something edible to look forward to. At least beef jerky
could distract you from the fact that the trek over the Rocky
Mountains was cold, uphill, and seemingly never-ending.

When the trek did end in Salt Lake, the first order of business to make this place their place was to guide the water out of
the mountains and into the reservoirs and canals. It may have

been arid in the valley, but the surrounding mountains sported hundreds of inches of snow a year, melting into tiny streams and then bigger rivers that heaved hundreds of cubic feet of running water in June. The Mormon settlers moved the water from those heaving rivers, stockpiled it in reservoirs, and then meted it out in good measure through irrigation ditches and channels. The water no longer trained into the barren Great Salt Lake but rather into square, food-making fields. They saturated the valley with the snow's measured-by-the-foot bounty. Thanks to that foresight, today I can hook a hose up to that faucet and water my tomatoes. Thanks to the cooperative efforts of a bunch of people I never met, faithful to a religion of which I was never a member, I can, supposedly, grow my own food, grow my own vegetables self-sufficiently, another latent family trait. And yet, when I went outside the next day to check on my tomatoes, they still looked withered, like they'd rather be back in the Midwest where the summers come with the promise of rain. It was 105 degrees and the afternoon thunderstorms of my childhood were now just legend.

Mormons must develop imagination fortitude. Members of the LDS religion don't really believe in the rapture—that their church members will be beamed into heaven, leaving behind the unbelievers. But they do believe they are living in the last days of this world. Hence the name, Latter-day Saints. They believe Jesus will return to the earth, restoring all that has been lost. Perhaps it gives believers an out not to worry about the climate crisis: the over-carboned atmosphere will be restored to Jesus's preferred setting. But it might also suggest a deep love for the planet. Unlike they who believe in the rapture, Mormons aren't going anywhere. They're staying in this place. The trees and water and air may be spoiled by their guns, cars, and toxic industries, but the substance itself matters. The earth, the place they live, isn't temporary, it's forever.

Knowing that they will be staying put, that the planet might suffer fire, locusts, burning seas, pandemics, it makes sense that they'd pack a deep store of wait-it-out supplies. And, in their move across the country, they practiced eating the kinds of supplies one might eat waiting for the time between disaster and Jesus's restoration. Is the food of a pandemic different from the food of the climate crisis? Mormons, their imaginations tied to earth and earthly bodies, practice for both.

The Mormon settlers couldn't have predicted this changing climate any more than they could have predicted the crickets that descended in clouds to eat their first irrigated crops. Nor could they predict the seagulls that flew in from the Great Salt Lake to save the crops by eating all the crickets. Prediction wasn't their forte, faith was. I have skills in neither. My skin feels dry. The tomato, hollow. I imagine being reduced to eating swarms of crickets. It was hard to believe a savior, in the form of gulls or other, was coming now. The air is getting drier. Fewer inches of snow accumulate in the mountains every day. What the early Mormons had been so adept at—turning dirt into fully fertile soil where the Mormons could grow Midwestern, familiar crops and alfalfa to feed their stock—is now turning back into desert. A desert of parking lots and freeways but also a desert of alkaline soil and parched trees. Mormons are masters of fertility, not only producing bushels of children, but also peach trees where no peach pit would be naturally or natively found. But something is shifting in the air. And now my tomatoes have something called dry rot or rot bottom that I cannot cure by turning on my faithful faucet.

There are many causes of infertility—polycystic ovarian syndrome, endometriosis, pelvic inflammatory disease, male-factor, secondary infertility, tipped uterus, hormonal problem. These are all internal problems. But what causes the internal infertility? External, environmental issues can play a part. Sometimes the body takes a direct hit like exposure to DES (diethylstilbestrol), which some women in the '50s and '60s took to prevent miscarriage and prematurity. And then there's the more indirect route: there is plenty of mercury-laden soil thanks to mining in this valley. It leeches into the water; the trout absorbs it. I eat the trout. The ovaries grow so heavy with the metal they drop the eggs right out of me. Pesticides to kill the aphids and whiteflies on the tomatoes, on the peas, on the peaches could easily warp a sperm or an egg much smaller than a crop-eating bug, even though not sprayed directly on the pelvis. Or perhaps global warming warms the ovaries—shirring the eggs, leaving them still soft but set. There can be no hatching of an even slightly cooked egg.

But I prefer to apply a model based on superstition and paranoia to diagnose my disease. The superstitions run like this: I started having sex too young; I had my chance to have kids when I was teenaged and fertile and lost it when I chose graduate school over settling down and getting married earlier, or maybe basic biological incompatibility when I did finally find a good person to marry. But the idea that I'd just been at this fertility business too long dominated. My sister said to me, "Well, you started your period young. Maybe your eggs are just too old." I was thirty when she said this. She, younger than I and having already successfully produced two kids, could administer diagnostic advice. I looked at my stomach, cursed my old eggs.

With persistence, knowledge, and a great deal of technology, you can make anything happen. You can turn an inhospitable uterus into a homey one. You can turn a desert into a garden. You can, with a similar magic, turn a liquid into a solid. Human progress can be measured by its ability to take a patch of dirt and rake it into a row of beans, pickax it into gold, level it and build a house. To everything turn, turn, turn it upside down. Turn the ground up. Make it into something new. The cook knows this best. He takes a green that looks like ordinary grass, possibly bamboo, cuts a blade off at the base, sticks the cut right into his mouth. It tastes like lemon and the cook's bravery has paid off. It's less fun when the cook sticks his mouth around some milkweed or dabs his finger in a bulge of piney sap but those are the drawbacks of being the family taster. But when he's successful! What luck. Being a pioneer of any sort isn't all hardship. On the culinary frontier, he discovers a sweet, citrusy bamboo. He takes the lemongrass home, chops it into squares. He soaks it in some coconut milk. He pairs it with galangal root. He remembers lime leaves and flicks his tongue against his teeth to remember chili flakes. The lemongrass is no longer grass but a cloud in the sky from the beach of your fertile imagination as you lie there with a piña colada in your hand, your skin letting the sun abuse it.

If you think that's impressive, think of what a cook can do to a tiny kernel of wheat by just grinding it up and adding a little yeast, turning it into an entire balloon and calling it bread. Cooking is never simple, as Grant Achatz from the restaurant Alinea writes: "Manipulation is not a bad word at Alinea. Food is constantly being modified wherever it is cooked and presented and changing forms, textures and temperatures is the goal of every recipe. Some presentations are just more familiar than others."[9]

The early Mormons and Grant Achatz could get along. They liked to make the unlikely happen, turn something ordinary into eighteen separate recipes for one complete dish of opah braised with apples or into a multimillion-large following. I, however, couldn't make the most natural of manipulations go.

The Mormon settlers manipulated their environment into a midwestern oasis in the middle of the desert. Although now, half the winter, it's a soupy bowl of smoggy air on par with Beijing's and Delhi's. "The Greatest Snow on Earth" is only great about once every seven years. Five days of over a hundred-degree temps aren't uncommon. If the Mormons were so good at convincing the desert to bloom, perhaps they could devote as much energy to finding a way for the smog to clear, the snow to fall, the temperatures to regulate. They're good at regulation, Mormons. Perhaps chatting with the carbon dioxide puffing from the refineries in North Salt Lake would prove as effective as talking the peach trees into growing in a land that was once peach-tree free. My inheritance of regulating temperatures, getting pregnant, and growing edible plants did not manifest as promised in this new millennium. Three years later, the tomatoes were sucking again.

The first year Erik built the grow box, problems with my tomatoes disappeared like fried chicken at a family reunion. The next year, the tomatoes grew as luscious and balanced as a homemade taco. But again, just like before I met Erik, I looked down at my composted dirt plot, puzzling over the tomatoes, wondering why they had so much blight. I checked on the ones in the grow box. They, too, had papery bottoms. It was a sign, I could tell. An over-hot summer coupled with a drought meant the end of times. I wanted to take one to a Mormon bishop or even a stake president and ask, what do you make of this? He would tell me it was a sign of judgment day and then he would ask me to convert because the end times are good times for Mormons. But I didn't want to convert. I just wanted the chance to marry my latent Mormonism's contagious, overabundant fecundity to my uncooperative eggs.

INSUBSTANTIAL

GRANDMA AND I WERE SHELLING peas on my sister's back patio when she asked, "Why don't you have any babies yet? You're not getting any younger."

"Grandma! You can't ask me that. I'm finishing school. PhD school!"

"I had most of my kids by the time I was your age. And your grandfather's mother, Grandma Durant, had thirteen kids. Nine lived. Of course, she didn't have to take the time out to get a PhD."

My grandma was simultaneously proud of me and mystified that I would go to school for so many years. I was similarly mystified, especially now that I am thirty and my eggs seemed like they were already too old. I'd be on child number four by now if I'd followed my grandmother's path. "My mother had a baby every three years. Get pregnant, give birth, breastfeed. She nursed her babies so each of we kids were spread nicely apart. Not me. I had two in a row. Your mom was born in June, I was pregnant again by August. The doctor threatened that if I didn't get an IUD, he'd sew me up with barbed wire."

Overabundance. That was the uterine history from which I descend. I'd spent years taking birth control pills, trying not to get pregnant, trying not to be like my grandmother, pregnant with her first baby at nineteen and married to a man who disappeared while she was pregnant with her third. You'd think going to graduate school would make you feel like you could determine your own fate, but my inability to get pregnant made me think perhaps my life was unfolding in ways as determined as hers, just opposite. I looked at Grandma, picturing barbed wire as vagina sutures. I wish John McPhee had written about fertility as much as rivers when he wrote his classic, *The Control of Nature*. The Army Corps of Engineers might find fallopian tubes a harder challenge than redirecting the Atchafalaya River system. I thought of the years of birth control pills I'd ingested for no good reason. With a bucket full of fresh peas and a tinny womb.

For my grandmother and my great-grandmother, conceiving kids was easy. Feeding them, however, was not. Some of the houses they lived in had floors of dirt. Most of them had regular hardwood floors, scraped raw by men's work boots, dogs' feet, the angry strokes of hard bristles, the sometimes-shod feet of children. Most of the dirt was confined to the outdoors and the cellar. In the cellar, in crocks and bins, my great-grandmother kept cabbage and onions, turnips and beets, potatoes and squashes. The cellar was never empty but beef was hard to come by. Especially fresh.

My grandma told me back when my great-grandpa hadn't been able to find any other work and had to settle for WPA work and WPA pay, he took his pay from the commissary. He came home with a big can of meat—the most meat the family had seen in a single setting in a year. Minnie opened the can, took one whiff, and set the can down on the floor. The dog took his own whiff, tucked his tail between his legs, and ran out the door.

But for people who were sometimes so hard up for protein, they never once went up to the Bear River to fish. Granted, they didn't have a car, but they were descended from pioneers who trekked from Missouri and Iowa. Surely a two-mile walk to the river to catch fish shouldn't have been the problem. No, the problem was my grandma was a city girl—as much as Evanston, Wyoming, could be counted as a city. She was used to food from the grocery store not the high plains wilderness. Cans of food and butchered meat. Even in 1930. Fishing was a sport or a side-line or something people from the country did.

Years later, when the pandemic hit, I looked around Flagstaff for fishing rivers. How far would I have to walk to reach one? There used to be at least a golf course lake down the road but even that's been drained. Erik teases me about my peas—"I'm sure we'll be fine on five pods a day." It's summer and this is as self-sufficient as we can get. We hoard paper supplies instead of tomatoes because this pandemic began with a rush on toilet paper. Each disaster has its own personality, but in the end, toilet paper would be the least of our concerns. We should have moved closer to the creek.

When I asked Grandma the first time she had eaten fish, she said it wasn't until Wally, her third husband, my step-grandpa and the only grandpa I ever knew, took her fishing that she even thought about eating fish. But the fishing had been just a ruse. He brought only one pole and no bait. He drove her to the bank of the Bear River where, from the car, they watched the water flow. Even then, 1960, Grandma said, the river was stocked by Fish and Wildlife with rainbow trout, which decimated the indigenous cutthroat species. Rather than catch fish, they sat in the car, ate sandwiches with bologna bought from the store. Grandpa told Grandma that he'd like to marry her but no more kids. He already had three from a previous marriage. She already had three. He told her he had had a vasectomy. But men will say anything in the front seat of a car to get into the backseat.

Grandma, persuaded by the idea of no more kids, let Wally kiss her inside that car, in front of that river where the original fish swam the original cold waters. Vasectomy or no, Grandma gave birth to my aunt Michelle nine months later.

In the 1980s, finding fresh fish in Salt Lake wasn't easy. Native cutthroat and farmed rainbow trout swam in the nearby streams but no one I knew fished for them. The seafood my family ate in

Salt Lake primarily consisted of fish sticks from the frozen food aisle of Smith's or Albertson's. The Oyster Bar restaurant that my dad took us to was an anomaly for the Intermountain West. Or at least for Salt Lake.

I think that's the reason my dad liked it. In 1986, it seemed distinctly not Mormon to order oysters by the dozen and salmon with a sauce other than tartar. But by the time I'd returned, in the aughts, Aquarius Fish Market had set up shop across from Pioneer Park. Erik bought me *The French Laundry Cookbook*. I could follow Thomas Keller's recipe for black cod with vanilla bean and mussel reduction. "For the mussel stock: Place the mussels in a pot with the garlic, shallot, thyme, bay leaves, and wine. Cover the pot and bring to a boil: remove each mussel as soon as it opens. Reserve the mussels for another use. Strain the mussel stock through a chinois" (73).

Thomas Keller has much advice about how to cook the actual fish: "When the oil is hot, add the fish fillets, skin side down. Press a lid or another pan down on the fish to flatten the fillets and keep the skin in direct contact with the skillet. Cook this way for a minute, or until the fish is 'set.' Remove the lid and continue to cook for another 2 to 3 minutes, or until the fillets are almost cooked. Turn the fillets and 'kiss' (briefly cook) the flesh side of the fish. Remove the fillets from the pan" (147).

The last bit of advice? "Always keep in mind how delicate fish is. Cradle it like a child" (121).[10]

A desert is still a desert if your only child is a fish.

Some things you think your body can do intuitively. Some, you have to practice. I practiced my straining skills. My kissing skills. I learned to reserve completely good mussels for another use (eating them out of the fridge, cold, dipped in crème fraiche). Since my body wasn't listening to me, I practiced doing what I thought I could control. I cooked fish for Erik. I cooked fish for my friends. I cooked for my famous poetry professor,

Donald Revell, and his famous poet friend, Dean Young. They came to my little house on G Street. Dean helped me flip the fish as I turned tiny bits of chilled butter into the red wine and raspberry reduction. I hoped the sauce would hide the slight undercookedness of the opah. The rule for fish, according to Thomas Keller, is two minutes on one side, one on the other, but this apparently did not apply to chunks of Hawaiian moonfish. At least the sauce was kind enough not to separate. The chanterelle mushroom soup I served as a first course was the best he'd ever had, my professor said, which, one hopes, makes up for undercooked fish.

While I washed dishes in the kitchen, Don and Dean and my fellow grad school mate, Derek, talked about Kenneth Koch's posthumous book. While they worried at the possibility of Koch slipping into obscurity, I got mad at the fish. Actually, I was distracted by the whole dinner. There was something so inauthentic about serving mushroom soup with opah, red wine with raspberries, too-pink-on-the-inside fish. Everything was out of season. In the Northwest, chanterelles are an of-course menu item but almost nowhere in the world do chanterelles and raspberries grow at the same time. There was a habitat problem to the dinner made more obvious by the fact that I thought you pronounced Koch's name like the New York City mayor and my guests kept saying Coke, Coke, all night, proving to me I was out of my element.

Where was Erik? He avoided these dinner parties. Not because he didn't like the poets and not because he didn't like poetry but he didn't like how they made me second-guess myself, wondering if I should have become a chef instead of gone to graduate school in English, wondering if I wrote more like Kenneth Koch, the poets would have stayed for one more drink.

By the time Erik did come home, I was exhausted. He'd been out at the Twilight with some friends. He smelled like smoke and beer. I smelled like fish and wine. We went to sleep on opposite sides of the bed, which is no way at all to get pregnant.

I caught my own fish once. Deep sea fishing with my family, on a trawling boat, I was out of my element. At thirteen, I shouldn't have stood so near to the man who drove the boat or the man who helped me guide the reel. I was young enough to take his hands on my ribs as gestures of guidance. I was old enough to want them to stay there. When, in pulling the barracuda to the surface, his hands slipped and glanced against my breast, I turned to him and laughed, not grasping the idea of accident at all. I did grasp the idea of flirting. I didn't stop him. I didn't say anything. In fact, I might have tipped my hip toward him. I was thirteen, old enough in some countries. Old enough in some offshoots of the Mormon Church. When we, more he than I, landed the forty-eight-inch barracuda, I was hypnotized by the fish's tiny sharp teeth. They reminded me of my dad's automated sprinkler cogs or the derailleur on my boyfriend's bicycle. I bent down to touch them and the reeler-man moved my hand away. I should have been flattered by his concern but instead I thought he was being condescending. It was my fish, wasn't it?

I look at my then-self and think, how transparent. Thirteen years old in a yellow and black bikini. I did not want the fish. I did not want the kudos for catching the fish. I wanted reeler-man to find me more attractive than the fish. I wish I had wanted something more substantial. I wish I had known what to do with a forty-eight-inch barracuda.

Now, here I was, able to do many things with a fish and absolutely nothing with my own body. I felt reeler-man's eyes on me. I felt Kenneth Koch's eyes on me. I felt the eyes of men and how I had wanted those eyes. What did all that wanting get me? Their eyes on me were like scales. They made my body now impenetrable, unhookable. Nothing could get in here now.

I blame myself. I should have learned to say "no" at twelve. I wouldn't be here, empty-uterined and hard as overcooked fish now. Bodies are not supposed to be overcooked. They become brittle then flake away.

Rebecca, Emily, and I started cooking two days before the New Year's party. My hands hurt from chopping and from turning meat into wrappers. We were not accustomed to this much food manipulation. I made a test pot sticker. It should have been delicious. All those scallions I'd sliced and mashed into the ground pork. I'd tucked that meat spiced with ginger, mirin, and soy into those wontons. I thought, if I can make Chinese food, what is there I cannot do?

I seared the wontons in hot oil and then added water and covered to steam them. The crunch of the crispy bottoms and the scallions foils the softness of the steamed dough and fleshy pork. Pot stickers are testament to two cooking methods, two textures, and three food groups—bread, vegetable, and meat. But when I tasted it, it didn't taste like the delicious ones from the Hong Kong Tea House, my favorite dim sum restaurant in Salt Lake (and also, at the time, the only dim sum restaurant in Salt Lake). Mine was kind of bland and a little mushy. I'd never seen anyone make wontons. No one taught me how to make them; I'd only read the instructions. I must not have cut the scallions precisely. I must have over sesame-oiled the pork. I must not have asked for help from either Rebecca or Emily.

I tried dunking them in more sauce but the oil and soy just slid off the over-steamed wonton wrapper.

Although Thomas Keller gives precise directions in his cookbook, he also believes one can become an intuitive cook. Not everything has to be so mitigated with perfection. It's not how small the brunoise is cut but how the final dish tastes.

5 Steps to Becoming an Intuitive Cook by Thomas Keller

1.   Start with your all-time favorite recipe from your favorite cookbook. Cook it by the numbers, following every instruction.
2.   No more than three days later (so you don't forget too much), take out a piece of paper, write out the simplest version of the recipe that you believe you can work from and cook from that.
3.   A few days later, write an even less detailed version—a few sentences at most—and cook the dish again.
4.   Over the next few weeks, cook the dish entirely from memory at least several times, but make a small change each time (swap out a spice, change a vegetable), so that the recipe becomes a rough template, not a fixed set of rules.
5.   As you repeat the process with other recipes, experiment with skipping Step 1 and then, later still, Step 2. 7

Intuitive means, to me, to know it in your body. I practice on wontons later. I practice pinching the corners by pinching the flesh between my thumb and finger. I make another batch. Still, flavorless. I think my body will have to go to China to intuit how to make these pot stickers taste right.

Everyone was dancing. My sister and her husband were making out in the corner. Emily was kissing her boyfriend. I felt conspicuous and out of place, no partner of my own. I wondered where my husband was. It was almost midnight. I'd been in the kitchen most of the night, abandoning him to the work of making drinks and talking to strangers. I found him outside, smoking.

"I thought you quit."

"It's a party."

"But, the doctor said…" I stopped myself from finishing the sentence. I did not want to turn into those women who needed to control everything their husband does through the lens of "trying to conceive."

Still, when I kissed him, the smoke tasted bitter.

When, two weeks later, my sister told me she was pregnant, that she'd probably become pregnant on that New Year's Eve, I recalled that acrid taste of smoke. I hugged her hard—half in congratulations and half in the hopes that some of that fertility would rub off on me. I said the word "congratulations" out loud. And in saying so, I meant it.

I don't like to use the telephone. I don't like to go to the doctor. I don't like anyone to know I've failed even though I know how deeply I've failed at this uterus business. My grandmother didn't know fish even though she lived next door to a river. She could have been eating meat all the time. But if you're not used to a thing, if fishing is not part of your skill set, then how are you ever going to catch one?

It took me a while to get it. There are many kinds of intuition. Some have to do with your body, some with your words. I had to do the hardest thing with what I wanted. I had to say it out loud. If I wanted this, I would have to say something. I'd have to admit I wasn't, even with all the instruction from Thomas Keller, going to be able to fry this fish myself. Sending wishes telepathically to my ovaries wasn't going to work. So, with a false kind of confidence, I picked up the phone and said, "I can't get pregnant."

And by saying what I wanted, maybe I did a little work to make it real.

ANTI-BODIES

MY SISTER VALERIE WAS CONVINCED by the backbend I was making in the hospital bed. My stomach nearly stretched flat as it reached toward the ceiling. A perfect Urdhva Dhanu-rasana, which I could never do properly in yoga class.

Pain is inspiring. The way you try to wriggle out of it. The way your body can move to get away from itself. The way another life can inspire that body to move to get outside of you. If I had been more conscious, my feelings would have been hurt. I hate rejection. Here was my firstborn, already trying to get away from me. My mom, who had been folding towels near the edges of the room, not wanting to look, not wanting to see me turn inside out, said, "I'm going to go get us lunch at Arby's."

At least, if the baby came now, the nurses would let me eat delicious, re-formed meat.

Valerie went to get the nurse. "She is practically upside down. I'm pretty sure she is having a baby in there." The attending physician came in with a herd of nurses and told me to lie back. She inserted a speculum.

"I can't see anything in there."

"Will you please use your fingers to check?" I begged. In a normal labor, the doctor feels with her fingers to see how wide the cervix has opened.

"You know I can't. The risk of infection is too great."

"But what if I'm in labor?"

"I don't think you are."

"But it hurts. Why would my uterus hurt if I weren't in labor?" I wasn't even a PhD yet, let alone a real medical doctor, but still. I'd read about the waves of pain. The convulsions beyond control. The shaking of the core. The volcano on the verge.

The doctor was the kind who believed in instruments, like divining rods, Geiger counters, metal detectors, and fetal monitors. The monitor wasn't registering any contractions even though I felt them low in my back. It wasn't fear. It wasn't hope. I wasn't imagining things. It just was the way things were. I tried to say so—I tried to make it clear that something was happening inside me and they should listen, but what was happening wasn't visible, so they didn't believe it. They couldn't hear me because they couldn't see what was going on and if you can't see it, it is hard to prove it is happening. And upside down isn't listed as an indication of labor in the National Institute of Health's *Preterm Birth: Causes, Consequences, and Prevention.*

Botulism is also invisible. The botulism bacterium grows in most soil. Botulism is a rare but sometimes lethal nerve toxin. Because of soil and high altitude, the western United States has one of the highest incidences of botulism in the United States. Besides thriving in western soil and altitude, botulism also thrives in high-moisture, low-salt, low-acid environments. Trying to keep out botulism is not an unrealistic fear. Believing you can prevent microorganisms is one of the ways humans are particularly foolhardy. But with enough attention to detail, you often succeed. Of course, you'll still worry incessantly about the botulism invading your tomatoes. You can't help it. It's just the way things are. Most of the time, one is warned about botulism when one is canning fruits and vegetables at home. But botulism can be controlled in home-canned foods if home canners are aware of the dangers and take steps to prevent it. When I preserve tomatoes, I try to be as sterile as possible. I wash the jars in the dishwasher, rinse them at "high temp." I scrub my hands, scrub the pots, boil the lids. But when I peel the skin from the tomatoes, I use my fingernails. Even scrubbed fingernails harbor some kinds of microorganisms. The tomatoes themselves are full of microorganisms. How much boiling of jars, lids, tomatoes, jars again can one person do?

From earth we all come and to earth we will all go, so doesn't that mean earth and all its microbes should be good for us? But not everything that's inside the body of the dirt is good for us. In terms of climate change, soil sequesters carbon through many of its microbes, but some microbes might kill us. It's not that the microbes want to kill us. In fact, microbes and viruses prefer a live host. But as we will find out during the coronavirus pandemic, sometimes viruses miss their mark. Sometimes, the body overreacts to a tiny thing. Sometimes, the body revolts. In terms of bodies, inside the pregnant woman is a fetus, dying to get out, which may kill her in doing so. I think of the song "My hat it has three corners, three corners have my hat. And if it had not three corners, it would not be my hat." If everything that was good on this planet was 100 percent good, well, this wouldn't be our planet.

Here on our mostly sweet planet, the permafrost, which kept so much carbon tight between its moss and its microbes, has begun to melt, releasing even more carbon into the atmosphere so then more permafrost and other frosts will melt, producing less ice, more dark ocean waters, which will absorb more heat instead of reflecting heat like white snow.

Positive feedback loops should be more positive. The feedback I'm getting from the soil is: hey, I might kill you if you don't boil me for a thousand hours. The feedback I'm getting from this fetus is: hey, get me out of here before more infection sets in. The feedback I'm getting from my writing about climate change is: hello, it's already hot in here.

***

The first seven months had been uneventful. Pregnant, I was happy as a cow. I grazed vegetation as if I were a cow. Spinach, Swiss chard, and whole milk, cream-on-the-top yogurt. Folic acid, folic acid, calcium, was my mantra. Lynn, my friend from graduate school who had a baby a few years before me, told me that it is out of fat that a gestating baby's brains are made so I supplemented everything I ate with an extra tablespoon of butter. I ate pies with double crusts. I followed Joël Robuchon's advice to use a full pound of the best quality, unsalted butter to every two pounds of potatoes to make mashed potatoes that float on your tongue as they coat the inner trenches of your arteries. I ate English muffins with butter for breakfast and buttered noodles for lunch and a pad of butter on top of a filet of salmon for dinner. I didn't think about my thighs or my cholesterol or my blood pressure. I ate butter like it would bear me into a happy, fat-baby future. I sautéed mushrooms in butter and ate them straight out of the pan. There were pinkie-fingernail marks on the stick in the fridge and butter on the corners of my mouth. I made roux for gravy and beurre blanc sauce for black sea bass. And, although I couldn't have known it, all that butter did amount to something. My baby grew big. My body, like any storage pantry, looked like abundance in times of plenty. That same pantry, though, looks like rations when times get hard.

Your body will do anything to make a baby. It will make scarcity out of your abundance. A fetus will pull calcium from its mother's bones to grow its own. When you're pregnant, it isn't just your stomach that billows out. Your whole body changes. This vampire embryo, having injected its villi—fine, cellular fronds—into your uterus, begins to suck your blood. Blood vessels grow on the villi. At first, the embryo receives its nutrition exclusively from these but then the villi grow to become the placenta. Spiral arteries bathe the intervillous space with the mother's blood, providing nutrients to the embryo.

The villi dangle in the intervillous space waiting for glucose and amino acids to stream by. The very thin membrane villi catch what they can, passing nutrients onto the fetus through the umbilical cord. The image of tiny fronds, waving their arms like sea plankton, hoping to gather enough protein to grow a whole person, made me nervous. If you've ever tried to devein a lobe of foie gras, you know how precariously the liver is held together. Each time you remove a vein, you risk turning solid mass into a pile of liquid.

Botulism will do whatever it can to colonize a jar of tomatoes. The proteolytic type A, B, and F strains of botulism are very heat-resistant spores—the major concern in processing of low-acid food. These types digest proteins in food and produce a foul odor that warns consumers of spoilage. This is why you boil everything. This is why you add a little citric acid to your medium-acid fruit—to reduce the chances. But, just as the baby co-opts the villi, so might the botulism co-opt your tomatoes. Nature constructs as it destructs. Babies are cute. Botuli? Probably not correct and probably too small to count, anyway. But both become something out of almost nothing. A microorganism on a speck of dirt. A sperm on a speck of egg. Be fruitful and multiply, says every living creature on earth.

The body responds to infection by marshaling its antibody forces. The body acts against an invasion like it is war. The immune system is called into battle. Bone marrow sends out white blood cells to try to conquer. The cells target microorganisms and viruses as the invaders they are. It's often a one-on-one battle and the bacteria or the virus lose. But sometimes, the virus or bacteria blooms, forcing the immune system into more nuclear response. The immune system sometimes launches an all-out assault. Cells go into battle, fighting off the bacteria or the virus. Soldiers are wounded. The dead cells die, causing severe irritation. The body responds to the irritation by inflaming other cells. Fluids accumulate. In gastrointestinal situations, it can lead to sepsis. In respiratory situations, the alveoli in the lungs are too wet to inflate and you drown in your own fluids.

A planet acts like this, in defense against ecosystem disruption. In the case of temperature fluctuations, it masses tornadoes, hurricanes, droughts, floods. A body will hurt itself, trying to reestablish some kind of balance.

Heat is life. Also death. To boil the hell out of the jar of tomatoes means the tomato-eater lives, the botulism dies. The husks of dead microorganisms might be healthful for the eater. The biotics that grow in the gut might be happy to meet new cousins in the belly. Some biotics may allow the botulism not to get too excitable, keeping it in good balance. Another microbe, salmonella, only kills you if it reproduces too abundantly. A little raw chicken? A little salmonella? It's keeping things in check that matters.

If things get out of balance, that's when the stomach throws up its hands and says, "Burn it all down." Then you throw up or worse and then you can't eat. If it's really too much, your body will shut down. When everything is out of balance and no way forward seems to exist, that's when the botulism says, "Burn it all down." When the seas rise and the ocean acidifies and Australia burns and Sydney sees nothing but pink skies through black clouds, "Burn it all down," may have been taken too seriously. We didn't mean to burn down the whole planet but if you start bringing the combustibles up from the underground and light a match—you get what you deserve. But with pregnancy, no one made it clear that abundance was a danger. My understanding was to eat all the blueberries. To eat all the butter. I didn't know about microorganisms breaching my cervix, effectively telling the amniotic sac to "burn it all down." "Burn it all down" is not a thing you say to a pregnant woman or a baby. And yet, here I am, in the hospital, where it burns.

At our house on G Street at two in the morning, I was surprised by wet sheets and wet underwear. I had to pee a lot when I was pregnant, more than usual, nearly every hour. But I always made it to the bathroom. Was it possible I had wet the bed?

I woke Erik up and asked him. Did he think it was possible I wet the bed?

He thought it was entirely possible that I had wet the bed.

I didn't know he had so little confidence in my bladder sphincter.

But wishful thinking takes you far. I would much rather believe that I had peed the bed than that my water had broken at only thirty-two-and-a-half weeks pregnant. I got a towel, covered the wet spot, and went back to sleep.

When I woke up to a towel soaked and sticky, all the wishful thinking in the world couldn't make me believe all that water was pee.

We drove the four blocks to the hospital. When we arrived, I was admitted to a room with a window pointing east. I could, if I stretched my neck, see the back of my house. I wanted to go back there, to an hour ago when Erik and I were asleep and the baby was asleep and the water was not leaking. The attending physician and three residents came into my room. I took off my pants so they could quickly check me out and send me home.

They swabbed to see if the fluid was amniotic. I felt fine. The fetal monitor showed the baby felt fine. I did believe that some water had broken, but that it wasn't enough to be worried about.

But between none and some is the point where they don't let you go home.

The primary concern was infection. "Infection" sounded more innocuous to me than "preterm baby." But I was wrong.

The risk of infection was worse than having a baby early. I could go septic. We could both die. Although neither situation was a good one: If I remained pregnant, I ran the risk of infection. If I didn't stay pregnant, I would give birth to a too-small baby.

The resident prescribed fat doses of ampicillin and erythromycin and nurses told me they hoped I could keep the baby in for another week and a half, when she would be thirty-four weeks gestation—that's usually the age where babies do fine without extraordinary measures. The longer the baby stayed inside, the more likely her lungs would grow strong enough to breathe on their own. But despite their wishing, the medical team operated on a "this baby is probably coming now" program. I didn't believe in now. I believed in nine months, like the book told me to expect. I told them that since we lived only a few blocks from the hospital I could go home and if my water broke any further or if contractions started, I would just come back. But, despite all protestations, I was booked into labor and delivery with a nice view of my block-away house.

It's not that the botuli hate you. They love you. They love you as much as they love tomatoes inside a Mason jar. So once they're inside you, they do what they do naturally. They multiply. This is bad for you but good for the botuli. Still, you might suffer from symptoms of foodborne botulism, which usually appear within eighteen to thirty-six hours after the contaminated food is eaten, although the time can vary from six hours to ten days. The most significant symptoms are blurred double vision and difficulty swallowing and speaking. Fever is absent early in the disease. For some types of the disease, early symptoms may be gastrointestinal (nausea, vomiting, abdominal pain, constipation, cramps, headache, fullness) and lead to a false diagnosis of appendicitis, bowel obstruction, or heart attack. Again, the point is not to blame the botulism. It's just doing what it does. You should have washed your hands better. You should have boiled those lids the full ten minutes. Did you process those tomatoes as long as you could have? Why did you turn the stove off at sixty-five minutes instead of seventy? Actually, for the altitude at which you live, you should have boiled all the tomato products for eighty full minutes.

It was hard enough listening to the *What to Expect* book and avoiding sushi and luncheon meat and making sure I had four servings of calcium a day and three servings of vitamin C, which I could procure in these exciting ways: oranges, grapefruits, or their juice; cantaloupes; honeydews; mangoes; peaches; papayas; kiwis; strawberries, blackberries, or raspberries; bell peppers; tomatoes; broccoli; cauliflower; spinach; avocados and six to nine servings of grains. You'd think with all these choices I'd be happy, but I found the list limiting. I wanted, knee-jerkily, everything not on the list. I like to make decisions, even bad ones, for myself.

Somewhere in my head, I knew that being in the hospital was good for me, like an abundance of vitamin C was good for me. But I wanted the opposite of being confined to a hospital bed.

I thought, I could break out of here.

I told myself, I could walk home. If I were home, this wouldn't be a bad thing.

If I were home, this wouldn't be happening.

If I were home, I could make something edible and amniotic-sac-sustaining like chicken noodle soup with extra butter.

I tried to imagine how I could fix this with food, even though my body already felt heavy with fear. I lay in the hospital bed willing nothing to happen. I tried to make my body even heavier. I wanted to weigh down my uterus. With the power of fat and muscle, I could round out against water breakage. With more muscle mass, I could clench my cervix closed. I wanted to eat. Fattening up was the only control I could think of to slow things down. To keep that baby in long enough so her lungs could develop. For her to breathe on her own, she required more mass.

Some forms of botulism, nonproteolytic B, E, and F strains, do not give off an odor. Sometimes, you can't see or smell any changes in the food. That doesn't mean change hasn't happened. Of course, nothing seen or smelled may mean nothing has changed at all. Nature plays her hand close to her chest. Or it might mean imminent danger. You think she is beautiful in her mystery but you know mystery can be deadly too. Is it good news that the lethal type, type A, is the one you can detect by smelling? If you smelled and ate it anyway, does it matter what precautions you took? Now you're in the hospital and you have to admit that you're an idiot with a poor smeller who isn't 100 percent convinced rank odors were proof of anything.

According to the social worker from the NICU, all that butter-eating hadn't helped at all.

"This is your first baby, right?" Like if I'd done this before, I would have done something to stop this. I was too afraid to ask, what should I have done?

"I'm working on it. I'm keeping my legs closed." It is a family curse, trying to be funny in hospitals.

The look she gave me was hard. "Thirty-four weeks is good. Thirty-two-and-a-half is not."

I chanted "thirty-four, thirty-four, thirty-four" in my head but felt a twinge of contracting muscle in my back. My inability to stop the tide meant the baby was in imminent danger.

"She will probably live, if her lungs inflate." For that, they would give her artificial surfactant, derived from pigs, to make up for the fact her lungs could not yet make their own. Surfactant works like dish soap, to bubble the air sacs, to keep the air sacs, when she exhaled, from sticking together, to keep the lung from collapsing. That was the first concern, but then there came the list: RSV. RDS. IVH. ROP. PDA. A life of messy letters. "Your baby, once she's born, will be taken immediately into the NICU. That's why you'll give birth in the operating room—it's attached to the Newborn Intensive Care Unit. After her Apgar is taken and her breathing is confirmed, she'll be put in a warming bed. Her blood pressure, her breathing, her pulse, will be taken. They'll insert a needle into a vein."

Am I glad to learn these letters? Is it good that I know how lungs work? I tucked words like *ventilator*, *oxygen saturation*, into my brain like so many microorganisms. Microorganisms, like in your gut biome, do a lot of work to keep you healthy and sane. Microorganisms like botuli can destroy not only your tomatoes but the sense that in an end-of-the-world-type situation, you can rely on your own food preparing skills. Little things reproduce.

"We want to prepare you. Sometimes the best veins are in the head."

I didn't want to be prepared. Why was she being so dramatic? Babies don't die. Not with NICUs and CPAPs and IV fluids. Not with teams of nurses and neonatal physicians. Not with antibiotics and microsurgery. Babies don't die in the United States, in this day and age. At least, I thought that to be true.

You most likely won't die of botulism, these days. In the United States, between 1910 and 1919, if you were infected with botulism, the death rate was 70 percent, usually from respiratory paralysis. When the toxin is absorbed into the brain, the neurotoxins dissolve the proteins that take plasma to neurotransmitters, which leads first to nausea and diarrhea, then to droopy eyes, then difficulty swallowing, and then other kinds of paralysis. Then death. That rate dropped to 9 percent in the 1980s and 2 percent in the early 1990s, mainly because of the development of artificial respirators like ventilators. Up to 60 percent of botulism cases are fatal if left untreated. But "thanks to the development of artificial respirators" isn't the ending you had hoped for those canned tomatoes. It isn't the dream you had for them at all.

The dream of being born alive shouldn't be a dream. In a developed country, you think the basic standard of "development" would be low infant mortality. But no, it's not so great in the US. Compared to the UK at 3.8 infant deaths per 1,000 births, the US, at 6 deaths per 1,000 seems a little surprising. Compared to Japan, at 2 deaths per 1,000 births, the US rate seems a bit astonishing.

African American infants and infants born in the South are most at risk in the States. Respiratory problems like the above-mentioned RSV and the not-yet-mentioned pneumonia are a leading cause of infant death. Studies have shown that children born near high-emissions industry[11] and in high-traffic areas are more prone to respiratory issues. In the South, where the airborne particulate matter can be particularly severe because of low regulation of power plants and other industrial emitters[12] the effects of global warming feel slightly less severe. The black particulates help block out the sun. But they also help block out the oxygen the lungs of the tiny baby needs. Thicker air—good for filtering sunlight. Tiny alveoli—not the best at filtering the residue of burned dinosaurs. Because of centuries of inherited wealth and/or social capital, white people are able to leave neighborhoods near refineries and industrial emissions, neighborhoods with nonstop traffic driving through them, neighborhoods near Superfund sites where funds, let alone super ones, may never be spent.

A nurse came in and gave me a shot of corticosteroid to speed lung growth. If I didn't deliver the baby first, they could give me the other shot in twelve hours. With both shots there was a good chance that the baby would be able to breathe on her own.

I asked her why this happened. She shrugged. No acronyms as answer this time. She said sometimes it's something introduced—an infection, or something environmental. Even a yeast infection can lead to preterm labor. The amniotic sac collapses from foreign invaders.

"Sometimes it's something internal, like a funky chromosome that makes the sac weak."

I don't think *funky chromosome* is the technical term but I wondered about trying so hard to get pregnant. I wondered if by maybe forcing the issue, like whenever you're in a hurry and, because you're in a hurry, you can't find your keys, I might have left some of the important parts of getting pregnant, like a resilient amniotic sac, out. Perhaps it was just fate or, rather, the meddling in thereof. If you push the fates and say, let me conceive, they push back and say, conceive this.

When I screamed, "I am going to push right now," at the top of my lungs directly at the doctor, she gave in and checked me with her fingers.

"Nine centimeters dilated," she announced to the nurse. They told me not to push as they moved me into the OR that was adjacent to the NICU. The resident who made me feel like it was my fault for dilating to almost ten centimeters without keeping her up to date by making my cervix more visible (perhaps by wearing it on the outside), told me to expect the baby would spend the first six to seven weeks of her life in the hospital. "She'll be released when she reaches normal gestation." I hated this person who I just met and would never see again. Who introduces more bad news at the edge of an operating table?

The lights were bright in my eyes. Erik wore a plastic outfit. Infection still threatened. My midwife rushed in, also suited up.

The midwife, whose blond hair had been pulled into a ponytail and hidden behind a plastic cap, but whose hair I had loved because it reminded me of a more beautiful version of mine, told me I was doing well. I nodded and pretended that this was fine and that I was fine. So fine, if not normal.

"Fine" is wishful thinking, spread like mayonnaise over bread on a sandwich heading for an arid picnic. We'll try to keep the bread moist, say the little mayonnaise particles, struggling against the nearly impossible.

I dreaded pushing. I wanted to keep her inside. Once she was out, it would be all up to her. It was hard enough to expect a full-term baby to carry the weight of the world, but one born almost eight weeks early?

I had no choice. My body pushed without considering how tiny her lungs were. When she made a whooshing sound with those seven-week-early lungs, I let myself hope, for just a second, that everything would actually be fine.

They took her away from me and to the warming table so quickly that I couldn't be sure what I heard. Maybe the sound hadn't been air but had been water instead.

I was still tied by my IV to the bed. I couldn't get to her to see whether she was breathing or drowning, but Erik told me her lungs were inhaling air on their own. A step toward fine.

The NICU doctor pinned her to her warming bed with an IV that ran through a vein in her skull, another IV that wove up through her arm to her heart, and a cannula of oxygen taped to her nose.

They say in the future, humans and artificial intelligence will merge into one being. They say in the future we may all have to wear gasmasks. They say in the future, they'll find a way to kill all microorganisms. Life as we know it will end, but no one will have botulism and certain amniotic sacs will stay structural and sound. They say in the future, we'll be lucky if we can produce one live baby per thousand. But as much as a baby embodies all the hope for the future, I didn't want my baby to be of the future. The future seemed so obvious before. Now it fractured into so many possibilities, they were impossible to count. Imagination, which seemed to be a good thing, back when I was trying to will pregnancy, incant a baby, chant thirty-four weeks, now seemed like the most dangerous thing in the world. When you open a jar of tomatoes, you can wish all the best things in the world, you can even smell the contents before eating, and you still may end up back in the hospital again.

VEAL

L
ISTEN TO THESE THREE WORDS: *delicate, tender, low-fat.* These
are qualities you're looking for in meat. You want the meat to
give easily at the bite. You want the flesh to float lightly on your
tongue. You don't want to be reminded of tongue—you want to
be reminded of meat that is not quite like meat—meat that has
barely had the time on earth to gather up the electrons necessary
to put together a carbon muscle.

Delicate, tender, low-fat are not words you want to apply to
a newborn baby.

The process to get from abstract idea and self-supporting
meat involves suspension of disbelief for a specified duration of
time. It takes forty weeks of mother-dependence for a human
baby to get meaty enough to unplug itself and support itself on
its own. Not that that support means the baby doesn't need assistance. Although the heart beats, lungs respire, mouth sucks, the
baby still needs someone to feed it, hold it, keep it warm. After
nine months in the womb, although a baby can't survive on its
own, its body processes no longer require the direct blood support of the mother.

A calf's gestation is 265 days, or nine months, about the
same as a human baby. However, the actual length of gestation
varies depending on the cow's breeding and age. The thinner the
cow, the shorter the gestation. The older the cow, the longer. Paradoxically, at least in my experience, which, I admit, is limited,
the poorer the fertility, the longer the gestation.

In humans, there seems to be a correlation between poor fertility and short gestation. But the outcome in the variation of gestation of cows and humans is different. A short gestation for a calf probably does not indicate poor lung activity. It probably indicates that the calf takes longer to stand up, an hour or two, than a cow gestated longer. Humans are more particular about time than cows.

It is difficult enough for any mammal to leave the safe space of the womb. That first gulp of air inflates flat air sacs. Like any hard stretch, there is resistance. To a baby born early, those air sacs aren't meant to expand yet. There is not only resistance, there is inflexibility. The air sacs are cheap balloons—you stretch them before you even try to blow but instead of expanding, your eyes bulge and you blow a few brain cells. The sides of the sacs stick together. There's not enough fat in them to allow them to slip apart and expand and inhale.

A calf is born folded and collapsed, covered in vernix caseosa. He should be able to stand and nurse within one hour. If he is lucky, he will be born into a dry spring. The rains that come will leave just enough water for the grass to grow thick and tender green. The mother pulls her lips back to get at the roots. Pulling the milky stub from the ground, the cow transforms cellulose into rich cream. To be a calf and drink that first spray of almost-butter.

A human baby is born stretched and red, covered in vermix caseosa. She should be able to crawl up her mother to reach her breast. The birth matter still stuck to her helps her slide uphill, towards those monumental breasts heaving toward her. They've been waiting all these months, actually aching for this moment. The baby should know how to turn her head, how to open her mouth as wide as the nipple is large. The baby should be born with the talent to suck-swallow-breathe. It sucked coming out of that warm, quiet place into this field of noise and light but the milk makes it go down a little easier; she swallows the warm quiet in.

To turn a calf into veal, you must first separate it from its mother. The calf drinks a formula very similar to Similac, the formula given to human babies. Milk proteins, vitamins and nutrients concocted. It's a small pen he's introduced to, a small crate too small for the calf to lie down, stretch, or turn around. It's important for him not to move, otherwise muscle builds up, culminating in a toothsome resistance. He doesn't resist. He's an hour old. Then, he's three months old. He faces forward, staring at the same motherless wall.

To turn a premature baby into a regular baby, you must first separate it from its mother. To ensure the pulse-ox and the heart-rate monitor leads stick to her nipples, she is quickly stripped of all birth matter. She makes no noise as the cold air blows through her too-thin skin. Intravenous fluids, made from saline or electrolytes, gelatin or sugar water, replace what milk she would get, if she could digest milk yet, if she could swallow yet, if she could master the suck-swallow-breathe on her own. She isn't on a ventilator or the CPAP machine so she's better off than many preemies, although the oxygen cannula hooked into her nose is pushing almost a liter of oxygen. The cannula bugs her nose. She'd like to scratch it but even if she could make a fist and bring her arm that far northward, the IV in her arm keeps it pinned. She stares through the ceiling of her see-through incubator like plastic is her favorite mother.

It takes a lot of design to make these babies better. In the calf's case, better tasting, in the baby's case, better living. It makes you wonder, isn't veal better than beef because of all of these ministrations? Isn't Zoë, this prematurely born daughter of mine, more miraculous because of extreme intervention? Human-made, mostly, these creatures are an art as much as medical success stories. Veal, after years of scientific experiment, by crating sooner, by injecting them with antibiotics more often, by skinning them half alive, has been made tastier.

Preemies now can survive births as early as twenty-four weeks' gestation by infusing them with surfactant made from pig fat to make their air sacs inflate earlier, by injecting them with antibiotics more often, by surgically closing their PDA ducts regularly.

Both veal and premature baby are miracles of human desire made real and regular. But the end results aren't quite the same. The sound the veal makes as he's prodded from the crate isn't a cry that lasts very long. His mother, in her own feed-lot pen, waiting for the truck to drive her to a Nebraskan slaughter, can't hear a sound. I, on the other hand, pick up that baby and have the luxury of listening to her, once she's detached from monitor and tube, yell and yell and yell.

MOVE OUT

1 SALT LAKE CITY IN A bottle:

The valley. The mountains. The snow. The Great Salt Lake. Salt Lake City is its own microclimate. I have lived in that climate for most of my life.

Stand on the bathtub ring where Lake Bonneville once crashed its waves against these foothills.

From here, on a clear day, you can see the LDS temple, the Wells Fargo building, the Oquirrh Mountains, and the Great Salt Lake, the watery remnants of the lake upon whose ancient edges you're standing. You can see the oil refinery and the coal plant, the smokestack at Brickyard Plaza, Kennecott Copper Mine. You can see I-15 running straight through the middle of the valley and I-215, the belt route, circling. However, a clear winter day doesn't last long. A high pressure has settled in. The city starts to disappear. First the Oquirrhs. Then the refinery. Then the temple. Your own feet look hazy. You're not sure which way to walk. You're stuck now in the foothills of a mountain. Below has turned to murky soup. The big lake has returned but in the form of soot instead of sea. The emissions from the cars, from the oil refineries, from the coal-burning plant have billowed up from the tops of buildings and settled in a layer of atmosphere that will continue to collect particulates until a storm comes in and flushes the haze out.

Stand at Primary Children's Hospital. The view is the same.

***

2

I sat on the couch with Zoë, dressing her up in her snow-suit with lamb ears. We planned to meet Erik for lunch. At eight months old, she'd survived the worst of cold season, which the doctors had warned, because she'd been born prematurely, we'd have to take extra caution against. We'd survived a trip to New York. She just had a cold. But her cough hacked as if through walls.

You could see her ribs as she tried to inhale enough air. I thought that maybe we could stop by the pharmacy after lunch and pick up some decongestant. I didn't know what kind to get for an eight-month-old.

I called Dr. Feldstein's office to ask if he could prescribe something.

"Is that sound I hear her breathing?"

"Yes. That's why I called. I wanted to get something for her cough," I said, cheerful and hopeful as anyone with an eight-month-old dressed in a lamb costume.

The doctor didn't sound cheerful. He sounded mad. Like I was an idiot. "You need to take her to Primary Children's. Right now."

Doctors boss me around a lot. I'm short and I'm a woman. I did not know to what degree his command should scare me. I did not know how nervous to be. I did not know whom to call. I did not know how fast to drive. I tried to do everything right. I did not know where Primary Children's was, really. There are a lot of hospitals in my neighborhood because it's close to the University. I drove to a hospital. It was Shriners. They told me to keep trying. Next hospital on the right. Does one park in the regular lot? Should I run? It's hard to move fast with a baby-bucket car seat hanging from your elbow. I limp-ran to the intake station.

At the ER, Zoë stopped coughing entirely. She smiled from her car seat, batting at the animals that hung from the handle.

Her cheeks were pink. She was honking in her normal goose noise. And yet, they admitted us on the spot. The number of breaths per minute, the amount of oxygen in her blood, the way I must have looked unsure about how serious to take this situation must have made the intake nurse rush.

I still didn't believe babies in this day and age, or in this baby-loving city, might die. I didn't know any that had died. It seemed very unlikely that babies got colds, let alone died from them. But I'm naïve. I don't know many babies. I barely know my own baby.

The nurses whispered nervously under their breath. "A baby died in their ER. They sent the mother home. Kid had RSV. Died in his car seat," they said as they put a pulse oximeter and a heart-rate monitor on Zoë.

Their ER was not this ER. In this ER, they would never send you home.

3

There are some things you know and other things you have to figure out. There is a difference between sour cream and bad milk. When you dip a celery stick into sour cream, you expect some degree of acidity. Perhaps the delight is in how the creaminess stops the acid at the just-too-far-gone point. And when you push back the triangle of cardboard and put the milk to your lips, you expect smooth, tongue-coating, mostly-bland-a-little-hint-of-vanilla flavor. When you get any hint of acid, a chunk of proteins, a texture where there should be none, you don't reach for a stick of celery. You run to the sink to spit. There should be no globules in your refrigerated, pasteurized milk. When milk begins to separate, it does not make you think of creamy cream. It makes you think of things expectorated—mucus, vomit, slurry.

***

1

In the valley, in the bowl of smog, in that layer of air, particulates hang. They're called PM2.5 particulates because they're 2.5 micrometers in diameter or less. A micrometer is tinier than a sperm. Smaller than a woman's egg. An order of magnitude smaller than a human hair.

The humans, and other lung-equipped creatures, are good at inhaling tiny things.

Inside the lungs, PM2.5 particulates get stuck. Easy to breathe in. Hard to breathe out.

2

Here is where they undo my daughter. She's lying on the hospital bed, happily staring at the monitors. She looks at me like "aren't you glad we're having one more adventure?" And then the respiratory therapist approaches her with a tube. She loves tubes or, like other cats, all string-like instruments. She opens her eyes as wide as she can as if to welcome him to her world of upside-down fun.

She startles when the respiratory therapist takes hold of her shoulder. She looks over at me, when he asks me to hold her other shoulder down, with hope. But when the tube goes up her nose and the RT turns on the pump, her look changes. She doesn't open her mouth to protest. Her eyes roll away from me. She cries but not to me. I can't stop this. I'm afraid my hand on her shoulder will never be anything but a bad sign again.

As the machine pulls gunk from her sinuses, her face muscles clench up to scream but she can't get enough air what with the tubes and the layers of gunk. They pull the tube out and Zoë and I both relax a little until the RT shakes his head in my direction. This time, my hand on her shoulder makes her scream. He digs in again, winding the tube as far into her sinus cavity as it will allow. He thinks maybe using a larger size will pull more mucus. He pulls out the narrow tube. He goes in again with a fatter one. Her nostrils strain against the plastic. She must feel like she's underwater. I feel like I'm underwater. I think, it's so unfair that I know how to swim and she does not.

When he's finally done, he says I can pick her up. I do. Not that that necessarily helps. She's crying so hard she can't catch her breath. I wonder how good can this practice of nose-suctioning be if it makes her cry so hard she makes new mucus? How useful can it be for her lungs if, after the gunk-suctioning, she can't catch her breath? I walk her around the room, naming the faucet and the rocking chair, the phone and the window. I pretend this place is a place she knows, that she doesn't have to be scared. She has these same things at home, I explain. Sink. Faucet. Chair. I do not point out the pulse oximeter.

I look at the pulse oximeter. Ninety-three percent. Holding steady. I look at my baby, laid waste, purple eyes, blue skin, shadow baby. She is heaving on her side, trying to sleep. She won't be able to. The cough will keep her up. I look at the pulse-ox again. Ninety-three percent. Holding steady. I look at my baby, the color of the sky outside, as gray and as entrenched as the winter smog.

She is stuck in here. I have to get out.

I leave her, in her bed, in the room, in the hospital, trying to sleep, struggling to breathe.

But outside is no better. The valley is socked in. When a flake lands on my hand, I think, thank God, the snow is coming. That will move this junk out of here. But when I look up, it isn't storm cloud. It is smog. The air has turned solid and now little particulates are falling on my head, making me feel heavy, making even my healthy lungs ache.

3

Fat globules in milk are lighter than the plasma phase, and hence rise to form a cream layer. The rate of rise of the individual fat globule can be estimated using Stokes' law, which defines the rate of settling of spherical particles in a liquid. In cow's milk (but not all milk), the cream rises to the top because fat globules are far less dense than water. In cow's milk, globules cluster. Upon clustering they rise faster than the cream of any other milk, faster than goat's, buffalo's, or sheep's. Their quick rising makes it easy to take the cream and turn it into solid. Milk will always stay milk. Cream becomes butter, yogurt, sour cream. Cream, once the fat globules are stuck, can't go back to milk.

1

Eventually, a storm will come in to dislodge the smog. "The Greatest Snow on Earth" comes from the unique climate event of cold air traveling over the warmer Great Salt Lake, gathering up water. Lake effect sends the dirty air up into the mountains where snow pummels down on the ski resorts. Eventually, the snow melts, and the water is returned to the Great Salt Lake.

The air seems clean after a storm. But those particulates haven't gone far. They're tucked into the snow. The snow will melt. The melt will flow into the Great Salt Lake. The water will fill with soot.

The clouds will take up last year's particulates from the lake, combine them with today's smog, and snow them down onto the mountains and the ski resorts again.

Sometimes things stay. Sometimes things move. In the Great Salt Lake, as well as in all of the other bodies of water in Utah, the nitrate, sulfate, and mercury levels are extremely high. High enough fishermen are cautioned against eating the fish. Some of that stays in the lake. Some of it rises up, falls in the form of snow, melts back down into lake again.

2

I was rocking Zoë in the chair next to her hospital crib when the chair of the English Department called. My mom was sitting with me, offering me sips of smuggled-in wine, watching me rock. She handed me my cell phone. The area code was Michigan's—616.

While we had been waiting to get out of the hospital, I had also been waiting for this call. Waiting to find out if I wouldn't be calling Salt Lake home anymore.

"The faculty unanimously voted to offer you the job yesterday." He seemed ebullient.

"That is great news." I tried to make my voice follow the bubbles in his—I let it rise higher and higher until the voice wasn't in the room with me anymore.

It was great news. Jobs are good. But Grand Rapids, Michigan. My mom's face fell when I said Michigan.

I called Erik.

"We have to sell our only home."

"They have houses in Michigan," he said. "How's Z?"

"The same. They're coming to suction her again in an hour. Come after that."

I let Erik off the hook from watching the nurses thread the tube down Zoë's nose since he would be the one sleeping over, listening to her cough through the night.

I had to feed her before the suctioners came. I untangled Zoë from the tubes, stretched them as far as the oxygen tank and the monitors would let me. The cannula in her nose, plus the mucus, plus the exhaustion in her cheeks made it hard for her to swallow. But we tried this manner of breastfeeding, every three hours except at night when we would pretend she slept and didn't need any milk.

3

The point of making sour cream: Sour cream is not better than milk. Sour cream won't soak your cereal or thicken your soup. It won't fill your baby bottle—or, it will, but it won't come out the hole in the nipple. Sour cream is heavy, full of fat.

Like yogurt, sour cream has all those probiotics, acidophilus, ensuring good microorganisms in your gut, but no one eats sour cream for one's health. You eat it fully for its full-fat mouthfeel. You put it on potatoes. On spicy soups. No one eats sour cream by the spoonful. And yet there's something fundamentally alluring about sour cream. Stay here, it seems to call. You don't need to go anywhere. Everything you need is right here. Why leave such thick tanginess?

Zoë's RSV must have thought the same things about her lungs.

1

The mercury levels in the Great Salt Lake are higher than in any other body of water in the United States. Mercury is a heavy metal. It sinks deeply. And yet, it's not above being whirled into clouds, dissipated into snow, dripped into rivers. Small birds eat heavy brine shrimp. Big birds eat heavy, small birds. The birds, it is surprising, are still able to fly.

2

This doctor was not making my kid any better. She walked in wearing scrubs and surgical gown. She put on a mask before she looked at Z. I could tell it was to protect herself, not Zoë.

"She's getting worse," I said. I could still see Zoë's ribs when she breathed. Her lungs couldn't catch enough muscle to help her cough. Her mouth bobbed back and forth as if she was trying to bite the air.

"She has atelectasis. It's like pneumonia." Later, I looked it up: Atelectasis is deflated alveoli complicated by pulmonary consolidation, or edema, fluid-filled cavities. The layman's term was collapsed lung. By 2020 we would all know this term. We would all know that fluid fills the lungs, forcing an adult body to lie prone on a ventilator, while we the family stay isolated at home, praying for the fluids to run dry. Collapse suggests an ending, buildings pancaking after earthquakes.

Nothing gets through a collapse, not light, or hands, or air. The water from the fallen levies surges in. What had been in the service of air had turned into the service of solid.

The doctor said, "Touch her fontanel. See how it depresses. The striking thing about collapsed lungs is that yes, the air sacs are heavy with proteins and those proteins are taking on water. But it takes more fluids to separate them. You can tell by the way her fontanel is concave that Zoë's dehydrated."

I'd been breastfeeding her regularly. We'd been weighing her diapers to ensure she was excreting a reasonable amount of urine. The numbers might have been off. Or, it just might take a lot more fluid than we knew to make the tiny air sacs shake off the hanging-on proteins. Either way, I brought in pumped milk I'd saved in the freezer. I gave her a bottle. She drank it like we'd been starving her. Thankfully, I'd kept all that milk I'd pumped when she was in the NICU after she was born so early. I gave her another. She drank that one down too. I swear I saw the top of her head fill like a river fills a dry lake bed.

After another two bottles of pumped milk, she was coughing like a regular baby, meaning productively. Meaning getting the gunk out of there on her own. By the next day, we waited for our regular doctor, Dr. Feldstein, to measure how much her ribs retracted when she breathed. He could count only one rib when she inhaled. He counted only fifty-five breaths per minute. He forecasted with these numbers we'd be discharged the next day. Instead, she drank so much milk and coughed so cleanly, the doctors let us go home that afternoon.

***

The nice, new thing was I could give Zoë a bottle. She drank from it happily while we drove home. The radio told us a big wind was coming, hopefully strong enough to blow the smog out of the valley.

"At least Michigan won't have the inversion," Erik said.

"And it will be full of water," I said. "Think of how easy it will be to grow lettuce. Spinach. I bet the ground is as fertile as Oregon's."

"The economy isn't so good there."

"But at least we won't die of thirst," I said. "They have big lakes there. Great big, unsalty ones."

Perhaps Michigan's water currents are strong enough to drag me there, without my having to willfully leave this place I usually call home.

3

Say that one day, you have to leave the place you had lived for almost forever. Say that to leave that place felt like you were leaving everything you knew. The streets would turn differently in Michigan. The trees would smell differently, deciduously. At least in Salt Lake City, even in the smog, you could feel your way to the grocery store. You could have, if you'd had to, find piñon pines to pull pine nuts from. You knew how to grow tomatoes, in Salt Lake City. How much Miracle-Gro to use. How much sun they could tolerate. Where to curl the hose. You knew where your grandmother stashed the peaches and where your mother kept boxes of granola bars from Costco. You knew where the hospitals were.

But there are other foods out there. You can make them from scratch. Notice the breast milk. You saw from the way you handed your daughter a bottle, you can transform ordinary, kind-of-milk-you-know into miraculous, foreign, surprising milk—that the vessel might be the important thing. Get yourself into a vessel and drive.

It's easy to make sour cream, just like it's easy to stay put. Open up some windows and let the lactic acid in. But here, you've got to do something harder. You've got to take that sour cream, turn it back to milk, ride the car east, the other direction from the one your ancestors trekked, the way against open spaces and wild animals. You've got to turn against your own nature, your own desire to stay, your own love of what you know. You've got to turn that dam to stream, virus to new host, and get out before you get stuck.

DISSOCIATION (THE NATURAL ORDER)

A T THE HOUSE ON G Street, I made beef Jell-O for our last dinner before we left for Michigan. My mom and sister Val liked to challenge their taste buds but neither my husband nor my sister's husband thought eating organ meats or strange amalgamations of regular meat was a delicious idea. I promised them transubstantiation. Thanks to the bones the butcher down the road gave me, I would make a cow turn into complete liquid and then I would reconstitute her as aspic. The husbands made me promise pizza if everything went wrong.

But everything did not go wrong. We ate the aspic with crème fraiche, or fancy sour cream, as Erik called it, out on the back patio. The sun beat warmly enough to continue to grow the tomatoes and make me feel a little bad about my brown, water-conserving lawn, but not so hot as to melt the aspic.

"This is actually good," Val's husband said.

Erik nodded, saying, "And I don't even like Jell-O." I had procured all the ingredients in nearly-culinarily-sophisticated Salt Lake. I had won the husbands over. Now that we were leaving. I tried not to think too hard on the fact that we were leaving. If I had fully understood that I would not be coming back, I wonder if I would have managed to leave that patio, my tomatoes, that family, that house.

I tried to focus on all the good things I'd heard about Grand Rapids, Michigan. I'd heard the Upper Peninsula, the UP, was full of wolves, lakes, and snow. One of my best friends from graduate school, Julie, had described Alaska like that. I pretended we were moving to Alaska, doing the hard work of settling a new frontier. It was a new frontier to me. I'd lived as far away as Portland, but I had never lived so many miles from home.

I told Julie that unlike the West where we watched as our childhood foothills were bulldozed and open spaces filled with chain stores, Michigan had already done all the nature-destroying it was going to do. Michigan was recovering. The wolves were coming back. The lake was being rehabilitated. The buildings were crumbling and native grasses were growing back in their place. But when I visited, Grand Rapids didn't look renewed. It looked old in some cool and some dilapidated ways. When we went in May to look for houses, I saw that the roads had potholes the size of my head. The grasses that were retaking the buildings looked scraggly and weedy, not wild and lush. But the buildings they'd carved from the first clearing were ornate with Craftsman-style windows and doors and light fixtures that cost more than my car was worth. The house we found had been built with architectural details in mind, like a vestibule and a thick wooden front door, dormer windows, ornate window trim. It was similar to the house on G Street—brick with good hardwood floors but the moldings were thick and the windows leaded glass. The fireplace made me think the house would be cozy in the winter, but from what we'd been hearing, sometimes even the summers were too cool for tomatoes. We should plant cold-weather plants. It's a good thing we didn't pack the wooden boxes Erik had built. In that backyard, there wasn't anywhere to put them. It was all deck. No room to tuck warm-weather-loving plants anyway.

Tomatoes would be fine to grow, it turned out. August was hot and humid. When we arrived at our new house, our furniture hadn't arrived. We lay on the carpet in the family room that had been converted from a garage and tried to sweat out the night. Zoë would arrive the next day with her grandparents. Her body, born in high mountain desert, had only learned to cool itself by letting dry air blow over sweating skin. In Michigan, wet air does not cool by drying hot sweat. As I lay there on the floor, watching strange stars through the skylight, I thought, I don't know how to cool myself either. I consoled myself with reminders of my car and how fast I could make it back to Salt Lake, even by road, if I had to.

Zoë had survived the worst of the RSV. She hardly ever got colds anymore. I could relax, teach at my job, see if I could find a way to make a new place feel like home.

It took us a while to find a good grocery store. The D&W in our neighborhood had good produce but no sesame oil or panko bread crumbs. Meijer, which was like Super Walmart before there was Super Walmart, had sesame oil, panko, and sriracha sauce, but their meat was mostly prepackaged and I could not find boneless, skinless chicken thighs.

I was going to try to make pho in a town where pho was even harder to find than it had been in Salt Lake City. I stocked the cart with rice noodles and basil leaves. I asked the butcher to slice the meat thinly but to him thin meant a quarter-inch thick. That thick of cut would never fully cook in hot broth the way beef is meant to cook in pho. Thick is bad both for pho and the environment. I run a calculus in my mind that bears in no way upon reality: the thinner the beef is sliced, the less the beef contributes to climate change. It should have been the thickness of carpaccio but I didn't want to sound like a snob in front of the butcher. Besides, Zoë was being weird; in the baby seat in the cart, she leaned over the handle and let her head fall toward her toes.

"Bob, bob, bob, bob, bob," she kept saying.

"What are you doing?"

"Bob. Bob. Bob," she said back.

I was thinking maybe tonight wouldn't be the night to have something as complicated as pho. Head-bobbing isn't conducive to trying to get marrow out of bones to make a great broth. All that skimming. We went back to the meat section of Meijer to find some chicken drumsticks, both of us head-bobbing all the way. I didn't give it a second thought. Maybe my calculus should include sticky lungs as much as sticky carbon. But again, my math and my reality do not often align.

As if thinking the worst will stave it off. As if making a list of bad, worse, and worst will in some way hedge your superlative bets against the poles of news. I'm interested in the politics of thought. In the methodology behind wishing. In figuring out how to go against nature. In figuring out how to let nature run its course. The difference between right thought and right action.

There is chicken on the bone. There is chicken off the bone. Chicken on the bone is all the chicken I'd want in all its decadent renderings—by all I mean one. Fried chicken. There are many bone-in chicken recipes like chicken hindquarters in port and cream, barbecued chicken, buffalo wings, though they may be a kind of fried. But fried chicken is a testament to the beauty of the disarticulated chicken. Every piece a handhold. Every piece its own integrity. The coating wraps a thigh like snow, a breast like a scarf, a leg like a stocking to protect it from the cruel world of hot oil. Frying chicken is the nicest thing you can do to a dead chicken.

But there are some who cannot eat the chicken on the bone. Breast of chicken, boneless thighs, cubed in korma, rolled cordon bleu, that's doable. At the bar, spicy drummette in my right hand, hot sauce on my cheek, a pile of bones in front of me, I turn to my friend Ander, who will not eat the boney chicken but is currently eating chicken tenders. I do not comprehend his reluctance.

"It's the same thing," I argue.

"It's not." He pushes my plate of sticky bones further away.

"But you eat meat. Chicken. Steak," I say.

"I prefer hamburger," he says.

Perhaps he does not like the resistance of muscle.

Hamburger is muscle turned to vegetable. You don't want to think muscle. You want to chew very little. You want to swallow before you can think about the sad doe eyes. In the face of the accusing animal, you can solidly deny you knew what you were doing.

But what's worse? Finding joy in licking the rib clean? Of polishing the bone? Or letting the process happen behind closed doors for you by a grinder, a man in a once-white apron, by knives and forks not your own. You brought only your mouth to the table but it masticates to the same beat as mine.

I stream bad thoughts. I try to see how much I can take. I put into my head images of my hip blown open by a land mine. I see myself apart from myself. I can see the wide-angle lens version of the bomb. I can see the close-up of the wound. I think about the splat sound my body makes as it hits the concrete from a hundred stories above. I think plane crash. I think explosion. I think burning skin and how it might smell like frying chicken. I think these thoughts to get other worse thoughts out of my head. I don't want Zoë to get sick again. I don't want her to be in the hospital. I don't want her to be in pain. I don't want her to cough. So I imagine the insides of my body turned outside. My femur open to mercurial winds. An open wound, seen from above, is a bloody version of a daughter. Didn't you always want to see what the inside of a chicken looked like anyway?

My imagination is not as strong as it could be. I look only to my body. Only to my child's body. If I could have had a less myopic vision, perhaps I could have envisioned whole hordes of humans, sick, prone, ventilated. I could have imagined the cruelty of letting some people die so others could pretend nothing bad ever happens at all. Perhaps I could imagine how many people have died so the façade of the White American Dream could be perpetuated. But I kept bargaining for a worry-free life. I should have bargained for a bigger brain with a bigger imagination in order to avoid pity. To stave off self-pity. Here's what should have been the method: think the worst first.

There are many degrees of vegetarian: no meat can ever have touched that pan to a little chicken broth won't kill me. The first kind of vegetarian matches up nicely with the carnivore who avoids bone. The second kind I can invite to dinner.

When Zoë is scheduled for an MRI, I stop talking to her. She's one and a half and doesn't talk much anyway but, before they scheduled the MRI, when I changed her diaper, I used to tell her about the hawk that sometimes sits in the tree outside her window. It's one of the only words she's learned to say. At one and a half, she should be able to say something like two hundred words. Maybe even to make a sentence, "there hawk" or "hawk flies." I used to tell her, between naming her elbows and her knees, about the time there were so few hawks the squirrels overran the park, that even the dogs were scared to run loose for fear the squirrels would gang up on them and attack. I used to tell her, in between naming the zipper on her sleeper and button on her shirt, about how a chemical they sprayed to keep mosquitoes to a minimum ended up poisoning the hawks too. I told her, between trying to convince her to say the *k* sound of sock rather than just "saw, saw, saw," that now the birds are back and so are the mosquitoes. I used to tell her, between buckling her shoe and picking her up to look outside for the red-tail, that now the mosquitoes will probably bring us down with their West Nile or the hawks forecast an avian-flu-infected chicken, which will topple us quicker than any invading army. I used to tell her about the way an owl can turn his head almost all the way around, the way the peregrine falcon flies faster than a cheetah can run, that the big brown girl hawk in that tree is being chased by the smaller boy hawk because he loves her but they'll never be together because he's red and she's all brown and they just don't match, a lot like her socks.

But now I can't say any of this—even look her in the eye. It's better this way, I figure, if she is already lost to me. If I am already lost to her. If this magnet that determines her brain is not normal human we will have to move to isolate poles where the only bird that will trouble her will be the penguin and the only bird to trouble me will be regret. So I button her shirt and smile but I cannot bring myself to say a word.

Nobody told me about the toxins in meat. I learned it by watching TV. The TV doctor tells a man with severe cirrhosis that he couldn't eat meat—his liver couldn't handle the toxins. That's a lot of meat toxins—to be as bad as alcohol for a cirrhotic liver. I wondered if it was only red meat or if chicken and the other white meat(s) are included. I didn't do any research because I really did not want to know.

I did know several bad things about the ways cows are toxic to the environment. On the eastern side of Oregon, closer to Idaho than ocean, cattle graze on open range. Fences are built to keep deer out of cow land even though, of course, the deer were there first. It's another kind of disorder.

My friend Misty and I go camping on this side of the Cascades in the winter because although it's colder on this side, it's less wet. Near the John Day River, we pull into Big Bend to pitch our tents. The pine trees here are short, and truly pine not fir. There's juniper and piñon and the whole place reminds me of the southern Utah desert except for the rocks are yellow and tan rather than red. The green, the number of trees, and the gigantic river running through the pine remind me how much Utah it isn't.

We pack lightly. We're just going for a day hike. Granola bars and nuts and sardines plus half a gallon of water each should be plenty for a few hours. Misty wants to take more water but I promise her, this isn't Utah. We will never run out of water. Not in Oregon. Our packs are heavy already. She goes ahead and agrees. Heavy steps. We head north, away from Portland, away from our campsite, not toward Utah.

We should have turned back when we saw the first dried cow pie. But I'm from Utah. Cow pies practically lined my backyard. Or at least I was familiar enough with them from the rodeos my aunts took me and my cousins to. We didn't turn back because how bad could one cow pie be? Or even twelve? Or, as we were counting a bit later, a carpet of manure. The methane pumped into the sky. The carbon dioxide counter ticked. We watched every step as though we were walking through land mines. We looked down until we couldn't stand it anymore. And then we were in real danger. A wall of cows stood in front of us. Up to their shanks in a little creek, the cows wended for a while. For as long as the creek went, so went the cows. Their hooves stamped into the mud. The mud grew thicker. So thick, what was creek was now just mud. Whatever salmon might have wanted to spawn there in the fall would have to turn back. The stream was gone. And we were surrounded by an uncomfortable wall of beef. We tried to turn back, just as the salmon would have tried, but the cows flinched when we did. One black cow in particular, perhaps a Holstein, perhaps an Angus, I didn't remember from my rodeo days as much as I thought, was looking at us with savory eyes.

Were her eyes savoring us or were they looking edible? Cows are vegetarian but they can kick a dog to death if they feel threatened. Misty and I weren't that much bigger than dogs. The order of the universe seemed to be reversing. Here we were in the middle of Oregon. There were no salmon. We were surrounded by cows more than stream. We were running out of water. The cows, though perhaps not predatory, were not letting us go. Corralled we were. We were not them: waiting to be branded, Burdizzo'd, taken to the feedlot, but we waited nervously just the same. Misty and I stood there like chickens for what must have been only an hour and a half but what felt like three until the cattle moved off to find another salmon stream to stamp out. By the time we could move on, we'd polished off our water.

I want two drinks a day but I want the days to be twelve hours each. This is a joke I tell my doctor who is also Zoë's doctor. He says women don't metabolize alcohol as well as men. He tells me not to drink. I tell him I just want that number of drinks per week. I would never drink that many! I lie a little. He is the one who has ordered the MRI for her extra-large head. If she could say some words, he says, I wouldn't be so worried. But maybe it's hydrocephalus. Water on the brain. I wonder which part of this makes me a bad mom. That in the hospital, I couldn't hydrate her enough to flush the pneumonia from her lungs. I couldn't pop her fontanel convex until the very end of the hospital stay. And now, it's possible I've overhydrated her brain. At least with alcoholic drinks, I do a better job of balancing.

I try to talk the doctor out of the MRI. Her dad has a big head. She knows all the words, she just chooses not to say them. She can say *box* and *socks* and *bottle* and *salsa* although those words sound like "bah" or "sah" and it takes a bit of pointing to fully elucidate her point. Her tongue is long, I mention. Perhaps it's unwieldy. I try to tell him about semiotics and the signifier and that with her, the signified is never separated, that when the idea of milk emerges so does the word and she always wants a lot of milk so she knows what she wants concretely, abstractly, and pushes her bottom teeth forward to make the sign for *milk*.

It doesn't take smarts or thought or anything. It's an automatic process, slightly better than pointing. If it's effective, it's language. She knows the word, she's not dumb in either sense. The doctor doubts my argument and possibly also my grasp of semiotics. He might be impressed if she could spell. I tell him my joke again about the drinks a day and he tells me again not to drink so much. Again, I tell him I don't, I just want to when Zoë might have RSV again (I also repeat myself when I want things to go a certain way they are not going)—it's a good way to think about something else. He doesn't believe I'm joking and tells me that drinking too much can lead to cirrhosis, which can lead to hepatic encephalopathy including such troubling symptoms as

- impaired consciousness (drowsiness),
- monotonous speech,
- flat affect,
- metabolic tremor,
- muscular incoordination,
- impaired handwriting,
- fetor hepaticus,
- upgoing plantar responses,
- hypoactive or hyperactive reflexes,
- and decerebrate posturing.

I tell him I have none of these things except the impaired handwriting and possibly "upgoing plantar responses" since I don't know what that is. And why are we talking about me? In my broken imagination, he tells me to stop being reactionary. *Reactionary* does not mean to overreact. It means to be so conservative that you never change your ways. Maybe he does mean that. I choose to think he means hyperactive reflexes. I do respond quickly to his insinuations.

He's still talking about me instead of Zoë. He says to stop eating red meat. The toxins in red meat can kill someone with cirrhosis. I don't even have cirrhosis, I say. I'm the doctor, he says. You have no idea how bad things are going to get. You have no idea what's going to happen in the future. You cannot will away bad news with steak and wine. If you don't listen to me, I'll write the word *noncompliant* in your chart.

I open my mouth and squawk at him. No no no. He has no idea what I am saying. I feel a little bit like Zoë must feel when she's pointing at her socks and saying "saw" and I bring her a salad.

Erik takes Zoë in for a pre-MRI doctor's appointment. Zoë starts coughing. The doctor makes Erik take her to the ER, which is not MRI related. I am at school in a faculty meeting, dressed in my only suit. Navy. Polyester. In my mind, this meeting is important. In my mind, I think the doctor is crazy. She gets sick. She coughs. She gets better. But now I'm at the ER with Erik and the attending doctor is saying that they must admit her and administer fluids. I know from when she had RSV that her lying down, being trapped on the bed, being suctioned through her nose means that she will get sicker. But of course, I don't know-know these things. Of course the boundaries between what I want and what I know slip and slide. Am I being selfish? Do I just not want her to be in the ER? Or am I right, that she will bounce back in a couple hours? Am I saving her or saving me? It's the IV that makes me believe I'm right. No one who coughs wants to be tied down. But I cannot know who is right. I cannot know if it is Zoë's nature that makes her fight these colds off better than the doctors believe she can. I cannot know if it is natural to let the cold run its course or if it's natural to listen to the doctor who went to medical school. I don't know and yet I have to decide. I know that if I give her milk, she will drink it and drink it and get as better as she would with intravenous fluids. I pretend that I know things for certain. I walk out of the hospital with my kid.

***

Later, our regular doctor is railing at me while still trying to convince me she needs the MRI. Words and phrases like little bombs set me off: *Noncompliant. Against medical advice. IV antibiotics. Chest X-ray.* And now *magnetic resonance imaging.* They aim-shoot-fire-destroy a little bit of my heart and so when the results turn out fine (don't they turn out fine, dear God? They turn out fine. Don't they?) my heart doesn't grow back and when Zoë says *hawk* to me I have to shake my head and say, I don't see one. I'm not sure what makes me so badly not want her to have the MRI. To some degree, it's an antiauthoritarian stance—I don't want him telling me what to do with my kid. But I recognize that quickly enough to realize that it's irrational. Rationally, I really don't think there's anything wrong with her. But I'm good at lying to myself. How should I know whether I'm protecting or condemning her to a life of water on the brain and other cephaluses by not letting them anesthetize my baby, pump contrasting solution and hydrocodone into her veins? I don't. So I take her to the place that will strap her down and hook her up. The contrast flows in. The veins in her brain light up like a winning slot machine.

Is it necessary that the food I love most in the world be the most inhumanely prepared food? Does it follow necessarily? Does cruelty taste good? Or is it the way we don't think about it? I see a flock of geese fly over my head as we're driving by the manufactured pond and they honk and I wave and I point them out to Zoë, to whom I can speak again because I believe the MRI will be normal. The word *normal* puts words back in my mouth. I say *geese.* I say *goose.* I do not say *foie gras.* Like all animals we eat, in preparing it, you destroy the animal. If you don't prepare it right, you also destroy the meal. It's a fine line and many of those lines are the veins you have to slide out from that bulged out, fattened liver. To cut the two lobes, you have to be quick with the knife. If you cut too slowly or the kitchen turns too warm, the liver can turn into pure liquid.

The liquid cannot be made back into a solid. Once you've turned the goose inside out, you cannot restuff him. You have to work quickly and use a sharp knife, not only to kill but to cut. To devein. You must use a sharp knife to separate the part from the whole even after the liver has been cut from muscle and ligament and artery and skin. Cutting foie gras takes as much care as crossing a minefield. Like any minefield, one false move, and all that's left is blood and veins and solids seeping into your cutting board.

But if you cut it right, slice it fast, make your careful moves as careful as a stitch, you can slice the foie gras into perfect rounds. You can sear it in a white-hot pan. You can top it with a sauce of wild cherry and demi-glace. You can eat it. You don't have to think about it. When she wakes up from the MRI, she seems the same as she did going in. The little cotton balls over her eyes are still taped on. There is more tape holding in the earplugs. Tape on her arm in case she needed an IV, which she didn't. The brain highlighted just fine. Her dad and I watch her lying there. She is like a mummy, ancient, wrapped. The veins run across her forehead like a map. If only the doctor could have read that cartography rather than the behind-the-skull map of the frontal lobe that the MRI has infiltrated and detonated in her head.

I am told to get the nurse when she starts to wake up. The minute Zoë moves, I want to go to her and pick her up and take her away from the people who discriminate against big heads and babies who say "hawk" both for bird and sky and sometimes chicken but I do what I'm told and go get the nurse. She comes in with rubbing alcohol. She runs her fingernail under the tape, moistens the glue a bit, pulls a bit more tape back. This will take hours, I think. It's more important that we go home, I think.

I go up to the baby. I put my dirty, alcohol-free finger under the tape and pull it off. Quick. Like a Band-Aid. She cries. To hear her resist, to come back into full voice, fills me with a little bit of joy. I pull the other five strips off fast. My method is painful but quick and I can pick Zoë up now from behind the white sheets and take off the pulse oximeter and put her in her shoes and let her walk out the door. The MRI comes back clean and all I can think is how many more hours of her life have to be associated with hospitals and X-rays and needles and being stuck some place she doesn't want to be. I ask for the slides. There are over a hundred images of her brain—slices of the shape of her head. As far as I know, they didn't break anything taking the picture. She won't remember this as cruelty. She won't remember this at all. And I will forget this just as quickly as I forget the goose when I eat his liver.

Leaving the doctor's office makes everything okay. Just as the taste of foie gras makes whatever you imagined painful to the goose entirely palatable.

Instead of going home, which we were told to do, we defy the doctors. Zoë is walking and she hasn't eaten since last night at eleven and it's four-thirty now and what better time for dinner at Rose's.

I order one of the twenty-eight glasses of wine I more than want.

Erik orders a beer.

We look at the menu and although there are several good vegetarian options—pizza with goat cheese, portabella sandwich, fettuccine alfredo—what I really want is some meat. I order a steak. Rare. Cold in the center. I want to feel the smooth pain of the cow who suffered quickly with the bolt through his head. I make myself think of the bolt as it explodes into the cow's brain. I think of it and make myself eat a bite of meat. We don't have the results from the MRI yet and it's time to face the facts. The brain may be faulty. The method may be cruel but the answers are abundant—I will force myself to think of it and do it anyway. I will take her to the machine that tosses magnets at her brain. I will pour the medicine down her throat while she screams. I will hold her legs apart and keep her arms wide for the X-ray like so many chickens. I will eat the steak and think of the cow's eyes and I will say the word *hydrocephalus* while looking at my daughter and pass her a glass of water to hold between her little hands and tell her to drink carefully as if spilling cold water on her pants could hurt her. She drinks the water, compliantly, carefully. Raising kids is its own kind of cruelty. Thankfully, I've recently practiced by eating liver.

The food comes.

We've ordered grilled cheese for Zoë. She'll have to get a little older before she can practice any cruelty by ordering for herself.

MAKING IT PALATABLE

I SPILL APPLESAUCE DOWN MY shirt while trying to shape it into something palatable for Zoë. This little baby will not eat. Or, she won't eat anything as perimeter-defying as applesauce. She will not eat anything that isn't square, so I'm always sticking macaroni and cheese into the refrigerator in a Rubbermaid container. When it's cold and hardened, I pop it out of the plastic and cut the newly formed mass into squares. Everything must be made square—because she likes the pointy edges or because I am limited to squares by my sculpting skills, I'm not sure. Mashed potatoes I take between my hands, pat into a square, and fry. Cucumbers, cut down the middle, edged, and quartered, she'll eat. It looks strangest on the meats—chicken squares, steak squares. I try to resist taking her to Wendy's daily for the pre-squared hamburgers. If you take the tops and bottoms off Wendy's fries, they are practically Pythagorean.

I wonder at her need for this distortion, this manufacture. She deems it safer because it's been gutted, rendered, turned inside out by her mother? It has been vetted by an adult and now is deemed safe? Or taste is already too much to take in, let alone all the shape and texture. Let's make it through savory and sweet, salty and sour first and then perhaps we can move on to smooth, crunchy, balled-up, or flat. She probably mostly likes it because I'll do it, letting me be pleased by my patient, considerate mothering. The time I spend transforming the food into something perfectly unnatural lets me transform into a mother that I am not always, but always want to be.

*

They say for toddlers, what they choose to eat is the only choice they get to make so they take that choosing seriously. How do you convince a baby to eat something she doesn't want to? (Form it into squares?) How do you convince someone to turn off their engine instead of leaving it to idle, spewing carbon into the atmosphere, as they pop into the store? (Hop in their car and drive it away?) I pull into a parking stall. Parked next to me is a woman in a thick coat, chatting on her phone, car idling away.

A car idling for ten minutes puts one pound of carbon into the air. I want to knock on her window and tell her that. I want to say, do you know that the arctic ice is melting? The permafrost is thawing? Even though it's cold right now, you're wearing a coat. You don't need to be that warm.

We've only had gas furnaces and oil-burning stoves for two hundred years. In 1950, there were 280 parts of CO_2 per million. In 2013, CO_2 levels reached 400 parts. In just sixty-three years, we thickened the atmosphere to a level where dinosaurs, not humans, were most comfortable. How do you convince someone to do the smallest thing to protect themselves, like stay home or wear a mask?

How can you convince someone to be uncomfortable? How do I tell the woman to let the cold in, feel the chilly air? To be grateful for cold? But I can't tell her because this is the United States and it's her God-given right to be warm and idle. And it would make me uncomfortable, commanding someone to do something that they don't want to do. There are so few choices, even for adults. At least Zoë lets me think it's my idea to form her food into perfect squares.

***

Jodie climbs up onto the bed where I am already sitting and holds the strange globe out in front of me. The way the skin slides from dusty pink to dimpled red to dot-splatter reminds me of granite. And then like magic, she pulls the halves apart. Inside it's rock again, now not granite but geode—an explosion of shiny stone.

The rule of this game we've invented is that if you pull a pomegranate seed out whole, you have to put it in your mouth. If you eat the seed, biting through its glistening skin, you have to tell the darkest thing you know. I know that whatever secrets I keep are far darker than whatever dark secrets Jodie keeps. My fingernails are long and sharp. I dig a seed out from the honeycomb webbing without dripping juice everywhere and pop it in my mouth. I keep that seed rolling in my mouth, tasting exactly like what a ruby jewel should taste like. As long as I keep myself from spilling any juice, I keep myself from spilling any secrets.

I roll the pomegranate seed from one side of my mouth to the other. I'm only twelve years old but I know the purpose of suspense. The story I had planned to tell is one that I shouldn't and I really don't want to tell it. But this pomegranate seed has busted, so I had better think of something, if not that. It's important with this story that I tarnish neither my reputation nor the idea that Jodie is the most beautiful girl in the room. It's her job to be the most beautiful—she wears Jordache, she looks like Madonna with a bit of a more upturned nose. Everything about her seems to me to be perfect—her hair, her skin, her cheekbones. When I look at pictures now, she's still cute, but not that much cuter than I was. She had one fewer bad perm than I did, fewer pimples, but overall we could have played for the same cuteness team. At the time, it was my, and the sixth-grade boys', opinion that she was the most beautiful girl in the world. I would sit here on her bed and tell her stories all day long if I was allowed to be best friends with the most beautiful of all of us. It wasn't entirely a matter of my low self-esteem. At the time, I thought it was a most adult and considered stance. Objective. Also, she and I were teammates in the torture-the-boys game. She kicked the boys in the shins with her clogs. I scratched them with my long fingernails. Our boys-should-be-attacked belief trumped whatever beauty-is-power belief. At least through most, if not all, of the sixth grade.

Still, I had to earn my spot on the bed. Her mom did not really like me to come over because I might be a bad influence. My family wasn't Mormon like the rest of our neighbors. My parents drank wine. The wine was a large signpost that we weren't Mormon and an indication of our unstable status—that we could maintain this suburban family fantasy for only so long, that we could live in this suburb for now but were on the verge of transforming back to our hedonistic, non-suburban selves and would slide back down to Heathenville. I wasn't sure where this Heathenville was, possibly Denver or Las Vegas, but it made me feel like I was always grasping to stay in Salt Lake, in the mountains, while the Mormon kids and their parents kicked at my hands. I hold on to Jodie's bedframe to buy me time.

The transportation industry *is* our food industry. Food comes to the suburbs from elsewhere. Pomegranates come originally from the Middle East—Afghanistan, Iran, Pakistan. But, as does most winter fruit, pomegranates find their way to Utah from California. You can get almost any foods in Utah. You can get sushi in the high-desert mountains. It's flown in every day from the distant southern seas as well as from closer, western ones. When I was pregnant with the "only right-angled food for me, please" eater, I wasn't allowed to eat sushi. The prohibition wasn't just against me, it's not recommended for any pregnant woman, but I thought the edict, like all the other restrictions against eating and drinking particular food and drink, sanctioned me particularly, personally.

The chance of ingesting a tapeworm is the happiest bad end to an anorexic but is truly contraindicated for a pregnant woman trying to grow an extra body from her own. The larvae of the cestoda worm are invisible. They hide in the muscle of animals, turning fleshy food into poison and in turn, will turn you, fat, pregnant lady, into skinny, unpregnant lady in no time.

Even cooked fish, when you are pregnant, is recommended to be eaten only in small amounts. Fish, though potentially troubled by tapeworms, is, in its pure form, a perfectly perfect protein. But what looks like a piece of perch on your plate may really be a square of PCBs, filleted to expose more Cs than Bs or with a pink-ginger sauce to showcase its Ps. That coating of black sesame seed protects your tuna from overcooking on the edges but no arsenal of *Sesamum indicum* will protect you from the mercury that finally found a home in that fish. It's not the fish's fault the mercury ended up in its flesh. Burning fossil fuels releases mercury into the air, combining with water molecules. The molecules fall down in the form of raindrops. The raindrops slide downhill, gather in waterways. In the water, where the fish live, the mercury saturates.

Reducing carbon output isn't going to be enough to stop climate change. We're going to have to completely cut ourselves off. Our infrastructure will have to change. Our habits and proclivities will need to be rethought. We imagine we're taking steps but those steps are baby. Hybrid cars still rely on gasoline. Natural gas, though it burns into less CO_2, is still a fossil fuel. If we want to stop, or reverse, climate change from causing worldwide drought and flooding, we are going to have to decarbonize.

But I can't even explain to my neighbor that his leaf blower is not only loud, it also adds pounds of CO_2 to the atmosphere. I can't convince him to invest in solar power. I can't convince him to vote for politicians who will shift us from the current fossil fuel funded power grid. Heck, I can't even get him to take his reusable grocery bags to the store. Of course I can't convince him. He hasn't even bought any yet. His garbage can is filled with layers of those thin-skinned plastic bags.

It's going to take a big mental shift, or some stark image, for him to be able to see. But maybe not even that will work. In a few years, we'll see people lying prone, attached to ventilators, and that might not even persuade some people to stay at home. And if eventually he does see, by then it might be too late. I could take comfort in waiting for his old ways to die and a new vision to take over but I realize then that he is not much older than me.

*

While I was pregnant, I wasn't allowed to eat sushi but sushi as metaphor was permissible. My sister and I went overboard and made reservations at the most expensive restaurant in Salt Lake. For the dessert portion of the prix fixe, the pastry chef made a map of sashimi on a square dinner plate. He candied the ginger, making it as pink as pickled but more sweet. He sliced a strawberry so thin and so red, it marbled into ahi. The chef wrapped the tuna in a chocolate ganache as thin and dark as nori. A thinly sliced mango became hamachi and bright green pistachio cream stood for the wasabi. The dish was all concept. It tasted fine—clean and simple and the pistachio cream offset the sweetness of the fruit in the exact opposite way the spice of wasabi sets off the sweetness of fish. A purely intellectual enterprise—we weren't surprised that the fake sushi tasted like chocolate. The mango did not even hint salty fish. And yet the act of substitution allowed for us to exist in two places simultaneously—one at this fancy dining place eating dessert and another in NYC being fed slice after slice of ahi, crunching salmon roe against the roofs of our mouths, taking daredevil bites of wasabi that the sushi chef tossed our way for free. Now, here, it was no challenge to gobble down the whole of the pistachio cream but our tongues burned a little bit anyway. If sushi metaphors can transport us to New York City via pistachio wasabi, what can't metaphors do?

*

Who is going to give up sushi to save the ice? We won't give it up for the ice or the permafrost, the polar bears or the over-fished ahi themselves. Unlike metaphor, we don't get two for one. It's either sushi or ice. It's either coal-burning power plants or polar bears. Our air pods come from Shanghai, China, just in time for Christmas, thanks to UPS and Amazon Prime delivery.

Like trying to adapt to wearing masks during the pandemic, to opening up and closing down, to imagining the number of deaths would be greater than a hundred thousand people, it's going to take a revolution in the human brain to decarbonize our infrastructure. Maybe there is hope in animals adapting to climate change even if humans don't adapt away from it. *Smithsonian Magazine* writes, "Zebra finches feeling the heat from warming weather may be able to give their offspring an early weather advisory right through the eggshell—which could in turn help baby birds prepare for the forecast."[13] We could learn from the bird. Take what you have always known and turn it into something else.

The man with 23,083 plastic bags waited for the woman who crochets plastic mats for the homeless to sleep upon to come to his house to pick up the bags.[14] She's crocheting as fast as she can. There are ways we can think of others first. The woman who sews masks for people on the Navajo Nation. You may not believe it, but people it is possible to give up driving a car. You will see, in the future, carbon outputs will fall by 17 percent in one month. There is evidence we can give up a lot to save a lot. Now, if we can only find a way to do it for a long time. Or better yet, to realize that doing things to help the people and the planet feels better than feeling good yourself. But we need a metaphor for that.

And neither polar bear nor garbage patch nor dust storm makes the picture big enough for all.

*

As for Jodie, if she couldn't persuade me to tell the real story, I'd have to tell her a good substitute story. I had to shape it into something she wouldn't notice as an untruth—a stretch—to keep me up there, high on that bed. The ruby seed had popped and I was going to want another one and then I'd have to tell the real story and who knows what sort of gravitational force would take over in this basement room and drag me off of this canopy bed.

So I came up with a secret to bide my time. "Have you ever been to school at night?"

"How could I? I live too far."

"It's not such a long walk."

I did my part to lend some credence to the thought that my wine-drinking parents were more permissive than her Mormon ones.

"David White met me last time."

"David White?" I forgot David White was her latest favorite crush.

It's easy to avoid offending the most beautiful person in school when you're making things up. I changed his name. "I mean David Burris. We were trapped in the tire." Our school playground had huge tractor tires embedded upended in the sand for us to play in. They provided shelter and privacy to kids who really needed neither.

"We pretended we were trapped in a snowstorm. We had to keep warm. David lay down and put his head in my lap. It's usually the girl's head that sleeps in the boy's lap but not David. He kept his head there for a long time. We didn't leave until nine. It was cold by then. We could have stayed but we didn't have any blankets."

Jodie had to think about people in blankets. Under blankets. She popped another seed but didn't offer any stories of her own. I dug another one out of the comb and held it in my mouth as long as I could. It got warm but it was still intact and lolling.

*

Food, in the form of vegetables and meats, bread and cheese, comes to the restaurant in its original form, intact. In the chef's kitchen, that food is deconstructed, reshaped and delivered restructured, restacked and re-tact. *Culinary* seems to mean substitution and transformation. Lobster corn dogs seem to marry the highest and lowest of food cultures—until one remembers that there were rules in New England that prohibited feeding servants more than two pounds of lobster a day. Or that once upon a time, so many lobsters abounded that people called them bugs. Dogs and bugs. One hopes that a hot dog is as far removed from dogs as lobster is from bugs. But why are we such snobs about bugs?

To make a lobster corn dog, take a three-ounce lobster tail. Turn it upside down and rub your finger along the ribbed underside. Feel the expanse of the ridges. Imagine how the seams bind the tail. Cut down the center of this tail; make a zipper. Click the carapace back. The flesh will seem to pop out. Pull it from its shell and dip it into a wash of cornmeal, milk, tempura flour, salt and pepper. Then dip it again into a vat of smoking hot oil. Unlike your everyday corn dog, these imposters come out all light-colored and tempura'd. It takes an expert from Hot Dog on a Stick to darken the cornmeal without burning it, to give the outer edges crunch, to make a forgiving meaty center, to make the corn dog magically encased in natural perfection, as if never touched by human hands. Still, the lobster dogs are tasty with a smidge of wasabi ketchup on the end.

In eating the lobster corn dog, you bridge the gap between two worlds—the carnival and the Four Seasons. You are at once comfortable everywhere and nowhere. The reality of the situation is, you really like corn dogs. The reality of the situation is, you really like lobster. Wasabi ketchup? You can take it or leave it but the way the desires press upon each other: wanting to be at a carnival, tossing a ring over a Coke bottle, wanting to order that bottle of wine from Bin 108, wanting to bite the burned cornmeal off the stick, wanting the hard crunch of deep fry against the soft butter of lobster. For some reason, when you make a lobster dog, the resulting dog comes out looking angular, nearly square, instead of cylindrical. Transformation is just a kind of substitution—turning more and more into ourselves as we ask which one's the mask, which one's the real? Perhaps it is more a matter of the cornmeal reaching for its square kernel than the lobster trying to return to its rounded shell. At the Ionia County Fair, I tell Zoë we're going for the petting zoo but really, we're going for the corn dogs. I've kept my habits from the NICU and, after petting the alpaca and other animals, we wash our hands with Purell. Hand sanitizer would stay my closest friend, next to the baby goats. We search out one of those deep-frying trailers that roll from fair to fair—the kind where the vegetable oil is changed only twice a season, the kind where the cornmeal that coats the hot dog is of the same corn that was fed to the pig that became the dog—and buy a corn dog. I peel the coating off, making the edges as perpendicular as I can. Zoë eats most of the outside I've successfully squared. She even tries a tiny square of dog.

*

Lie to me. Tell me that the predictions aren't true. Tell me the ice sheet grows back at night. Tell me what I put in my body doesn't have a physical connection to what happens to the ice's body. Tell me the permafrost rebuilds. Tell me the reed warbler comes back. The saw-whet owl. The Pico ground beetle. The Bermuda flicker. St. Helena's heliotrope. Even the Rocky Mountain locust that once swarmed and now may be found as a solitary grasshopper. No one's seen a locust since 1902. Tell me it all comes back. I'll give you a pomegranate seed for every lie you tell me and then, when Persephone takes me to meet her mother in hell, I'll let her convince me it's cold as ice there too.

*

It doesn't matter how many pomegranate seeds she eats—she's not going to talk. Jodie is going to sit there and pick her pomegranate seeds and bite them thoroughly and give nothing up. It is her house. Her pomegranate. Her willingness as the most popular girl to let me, the non-Mormon girl, sit on her bedspread gives her the prerogative. Her prerogative turns my words projectile. I eat the warm seed and then take another. I blather more story.

This time, I don't use names she knows. Although I'm not Mormon, I do go to church with some neighbors across the street. A really liberal church that sings Simon and Garfunkel songs instead of hymns. I tell her about the coffee in the basement. Shocking enough to a member of a church that frowns on either caffeinated or hot drinks—it depends who is drinking what when you get the low-down on the edicts—but coffee is both hot and caffeinated and therefore strictly prohibited and to allow this in a church is the height of heresy—or at least a worth-noting phenomena. I overstress her surprise a bit. She's actually pretty sanguine about all the stories. Perhaps because they don't really shock or perhaps because they're too far-removed from her experience to bear on her existence at all. Or maybe the lie is coming off just as that—ill-formed and overly detailed.

Still, I try again. It was in the basement of the church while the adults were having coffee that a group of us kids snuck off into one of the bible-study rooms. The older kids goofed off on the chalkboard, drawing pictures of Jesus upside down, of two well-hung boy camels getting on the ark, of Joseph touching a very bulbous version of Mary's breast. Then, they sat in a circle and pretended to drink coffee like the grown-ups. I just watched. The girls mimicked the women by laughing too hard at the boys' jokes. The boys mimicked the men by accidentally walking by the girls to pour more "coffee" and brushing against our sweatered chests. I told Jodie about Stan, who got a little crazy with his walking by, a little forward with his brushing. He went so far as to stick out his hand when he passed Sarah. Sarah pulled her arm back in reaction. She kind of got him in the crotch.

"Got him?"

"Rubbed him. He turned around but we could still see it."

"You could see it? What it?"

"He was wearing sweatpants."

"What it?"

"A boner. You could see it. Joe told me later that it happens quick like that. The blood just rushes there."

"Who is Joe?"

I swallow my pomegranate seed. "Just a guy from church," I lie. "Give me another one."

"You can wear sweatpants to church?"

Maybe I will get an extra pomegranate seed for this story.

*

In the kitchen, necessity and invention are nicer ways of saying substitution. Yesterday, I was making chipotle ranch dressing for a southwestern salad. I had no buttermilk. But I faked it with homemade buttermilk (milk and vinegar), a little mayo, scallions, lemon zest and garlic and a chipotle. The other day, my sister used Worcestershire rather than soy sauce for a pepper steak marinade to a relatively successful end. I've used baking soda for baking powder, mint for basil, chicken stock for beef, all to varying degrees of success. My husband Erik tells stories of his grandmother substituting ketchup for tomato sauce on spaghetti. She sliced hot dogs into Jell-O instead of mandarin oranges. The vegetarians have soy-matter for chicken nuggets. The carnivores who won't eat vegetables have carrots and beets and broccoli stuffed into sausages. You can use oil and water for eggs. Cornflakes for breadcrumbs. Milk for cream. Cream watered down for milk. Who really cares if you can't taste the difference? Even if you can, the taste can be washed away. Erik's grandfather dutifully ate every bite of the dinner Erik's grandmother made him. He turned hunger into thirst. He chewed quickly, swallowed fast. Then, he would drink, slowly, sixteen ounces of Coke. He'd swish the Coke around his mouth, each pop of carbonation scrubbing clean his offended mouth.

*

There have been successful revolutions of human mind and behavior. Those Mothers Against Drunk Driving did a good job. The people who convinced us to cut up six-pack holders to save the turtles ran a strong campaign. Regulations did a good job getting rid of the aerosols that bore the hole in the ozone. We ride in cars with seatbelts. The Humane Society began as an organization to prevent child abuse. When child abuse moved from the normal to the prosecutable, the Humane Society moved on to protect animals.

Change can happen. Too slowly for some of the dead by drunk drivers and murderous parents but fast enough for the majority.

What we need is a big metaphor—the biggest kind to perform a little switcheroo. Layer the parking lots with solar panels. Install photovoltaics inside roofing tiles. Sit outside in the summer, store up the heat for winter. No, bigger. *Waterworld* the movie did a good job having the Universal Studios logo swallow all the land and ice. Perhaps we should make people live under glass like a greenhouse for one year? Perhaps we will one day quarantine ourselves for a year and the picture of downtown Los Angeles will lead everyone to do what they must to tackle the particulates, seek the CO_2, give up plastic. If we just had one image that persuaded people to do what they could to be more like a tree, well, I would make that image.

Maybe Zoë intuited something about the importance of squares. Luana Steffen, writing for *Intelligent Living*, reports that planting trees in square holes is better for the tree. And, what's better for the tree is better for the climate, since trees might be our only hope to stop climate change.

> The chances of your tree surviving will increase dramatically by merely digging a square hole instead of a round one when you plant the sapling. The roots won't develop a circular root system because, as systematic planting trials have shown, the roots are not good at growing around corners. When the roots hit the 90-degree angle of a square hole, rather than snaking around to create a spiral, they spread out of the planting hole to colonize the surrounding native soil.

> Not only does the tree have a better chance of survival, but the speed of growth will drastically increase, and the tree will become more resistant to environmental challenges, like droughts.[15]

If you want your tree to survive, plant it in a square hole.
If you want your kid to eat, turn round foods quadrilateral.
If you want to tell your story, take the real version and stretch it out long enough so that no one, except maybe the pomegranate seed, gets hurt in the telling.

*

She presses me on who Joe is. I don't want to answer. But I want to stay in that cool basement bedroom, everything laid out in white. I want another pomegranate seed. The rules of the game are to tell, so I tell a crosswise story and eat another bit of the fruit.

"He's a guy from church."

"I got that. Why is he telling you what a boner is?"

"I asked."

"You asked?"

"I read it in a book."

"What book?"

"One of the Judy Blume's." Or from *Playboy*. But I don't want to tell her that I have rifled through my dad's magazines. I don't even want to tell her my dad has magazines.

"And what did he say?"

"We played a game. We played truth or dare." We did play truth or dare. Outside. Under his parents' balcony.

"He said he'd tell me what a boner was if I'd tell him what a uvula was." More show than tell. More dare than truth.

"Uvula?"

"Well, it's not what he thought it was. He was asking something else." I had opened my mouth, showed Joe the back of my throat. Close but no cigar. That was not what he wanted.

"What else did he ask?"

"He asked if I'd ever been naked outdoors."

"What did you say?"

"I thought we were playing story, not truth or dare."

"You have to tell me. I gave you my fruit."

"I have been naked outside." I don't say when. I answer her question. I don't say what I answered and I don't tell her when.

"What else did he ask you?" She is leaning toward me as intently as he had when I'd shown him my uvula. I show her the inside of my mouth, too. As he had, she comes closer. She, however, just looks.

I try to show off the pomegranate—that I can hold it intact in my mouth—that I don't have to tell any more stories. But as she looks inside my mouth to see the seed, I try to hide it against my tooth and I push too hard and it bursts. Inside, the pomegranate berry explodes. A little bit spills out of my mouth. The thing nobody wanted to happen happened: pomegranate juice on the white bedspread.

I wonder what would have happened if I'd told her the truth. If I'd gone so far as to explain the nakedness. She probably would have done the same thing. Told me it was okay but then the next time I wanted to come over, told me I wasn't allowed because her mom found out about the pomegranate stain.

Now that we've tasted everything—kiwis and tangerines, bananas and pomegranates—and bitten into the authenticity where we expected travel and transportation to take us, maybe we can move past the authentic thing itself to the thing that is close enough. Like they do with plant-based meat, we can substitute far-flung fruit for homegrown. Instead of pomegranates shipped from the Mediterranean (or Arizona), perhaps take an apple from your backyard. Use a tiny melon baller. Make perfect rounds of apple—unless you're baby Zoë, then feel free to cut the apple into tiny squares. Polish the skin of the apple until it shines red. Hold it in your mouth for a long time. At least until it feels real. What is the point of authenticity if someone is going to get hurt?

*

It is the middle of winter and I'm introducing Zoë to red bell peppers. I slice them down the vertical into strips and then crosswise to make them square. The skin side is dull and opaque but the inside gleams. I tell her the squares are jewels, candies, squares of imported sunshine, full of vitamin C. She's eating the rest of her lunch, squares of turkey and Triscuits, and she asks me where the sunshine went. February in Michigan. No one knows where the sun is. So I tell her about summers in the desert—how the sand sticks to the sweat in the fold of your elbow, how even your eyebrows get hot, how there are no carnivals and no sushi but there's a waterslide made from the one river that runs over those baked rocks. All the while, I'm thinking how to convince her, when, in the near future, she finds herself under a balcony or in a dark basement, to turn the lights on, to keep her mouth closed, to keep the bedspread clean.

She asks for a slice. I tell her to finish her turkey. She points to the red bells and says not jewelry. Not candy. She wants to know. I dare to tell her what they really are. I say peppers. She says "pepper" for the first time, making with her mouth a perfect square of the *p*'s and *r*'s. She eats another bite. Red bell pepper squares don't spill and even if they did, they don't stain. I don't tell her then about how the edges of a whole pomegranate may look angled and the honeycomb that holds the seed may look quadratic, but a pomegranate's true form is round. Some circles cannot be squared.

OUT OF PLACE

B IRDS OF PREY WEREN'T NEW to me. I'd seen them from
the car, driving through southern Utah, sitting on posts
of fences put up to keep the cattle from wandering onto I-15,
now providing perches for red-tailed hawks. On the way home
from Torrey that one pretend-apocalypse winter, I saw five bald
eagles, standing as tall as fence posts by the side of the road.
On the ground, they were undignified, tearing at a deer roadkill.
But when, in my rearview mirror, the head of one eagle turned
nearly all the way around to make sure the car moved on its way,
the eagle's white head eclipsing the thin, exhaust-dirty snow, the
eagle made it clear that I had interrupted them. On the side of
the road, tugging meat, was where the eagles were supposed to
be. I, in my car, driving with salmon through the desert, was the
one out of place.

Compared to southern Utah, western Michigan seemed like
the last place you'd see birds of prey. Once, Erik and Zoë and I
tried to go camping. We drove and drove until we found a campground far from the city. As we unpacked the car and began to
set up the tent, I spied a basketball hoop hanging over a concrete
driveway. The campground was in the neighborhood. Or the
neighborhood was in the middle of the campground. Basketball
hoops do not make the outdoors feel wild.

And, no matter how hard I tried, I couldn't make Grand Rapids feel like home. Grand Rapids was not Salt Lake, where I had

lived for most of my life. I'd left for college, stayed in Portland for a few years, went back to Salt Lake for grad school. Now, in Grand Rapids, having moved for a job, I wanted to go home. In time, I would get used to this place, I hoped, in the same way one gets used to oneself: you learn to like the way your hair parts on the left, the way your left eye is smaller than your right, the way you bite your pinky fingernail just like your mother. You learn to adapt to the place you live. But as the climate changes, as even your native land changes—butterflies in November!—I wonder how anyone is supposed to get used to that. Maybe Michigan would always feel like butterflies in November.

But I also felt like I should stay away from Salt Lake. That place has a way of domesticating even the most wild child and Zoë, three years old, though stubborn with her love of square food and rabbit-like dialect, wasn't particularly wild. She liked her face and her hands clean, her hair brushed. She folded cloth napkins straight from the dryer. She suggested that we get out the iron before company comes, like my mom does. I wanted her, even if it was a pain in my ass, to be more stubborn, less acquiescent. Fierce. If we went back to Salt Lake, I was afraid my daughter would follow my path, would fall for boys who said they liked the way she laughed at their unfunny jokes, the way she asked which way to turn, right or left, although she knows full-well which, the way she puts her pinky finger in her mouth just like I do. Just like my mom does.

We shall go a-wilding, I promised myself. Grand Rapids, April 5, and this was the first time Zoë and I, since one freakishly warm week in January, had seen the sun. Finally, there was only residual snow on the ground. We could see grass. We looked for early flowers over at the small college across the street from our house. The college's budget was hemorrhaging but the hemorrhage had spouted beauty. The unfunding let these typically manicured lawns and flower beds turn back into wild.

On the campus, we found purple striped crocuses. Zoë

wanted to collect all this newness. She said, Let's pick the flowers. I told her, No, the flower lasts longer in the ground than in
your hand. Not much longer, but longer. Is it wild or domestic
to curtail someone's dream to collect flowers? Either way, I distracted her from picking flowers with a stick that had fallen from
a sycamore tree and the promise, as I pointed to a little boy's Big
Wheel, that we would get her a Big Wheel. Keep her moving, I
thought. A kind of wild.

The little boy's dad, who saw us pointing at the Big Wheel,
asked if we had seen the owls.

I had been satisfied by crocuses and promise of daffodils. I
had never seen an owl.

"Come on," the dad said, "I'll show you." We walked across
the Catholic college campus, past the Jesus sculpture, toward the
middle of a tiny parking lot. The kids followed us—his on the
Big Wheel, mine mastering the art of curb-walking.

"Look at the 'no parking' sign, then look straight up," he said.

In the branches of a sycamore—still dry with winter and
bare of leaves—sat two gigantic owls. They looked like snowy
owls. They were so big and so white and soft, the size of a big
cat, maybe a raccoon. But they are just chicks, the man told me.
Owlets. Babies.

"Look at the daffodils, already blooming. Usually owlets
aren't born so early. They shouldn't even be hatching yet. These
ones are premature."

I believed him. He had probably lived in the Midwest his
whole life. He knew where nursery flowers and wild animals
collided. He even knew the type of owls these were, barred, not
snowy. He was half woodsman, half gardener—a species we
all aspire to be, someone who knows and who cultivates that
knowledge. He said that barred owls try to get a jump on other
species and lay their eggs in late March or early April. It was
early April just now and these eggs had not only hatched, but
these birds were halfway ready for flight.

The winter had been hard. But that one warm week in January had confused fertility hormones, leading animals to believe it was spring when it was still deep winter. Instead of waiting for March, the parent owls must have mated in January. These snow-colored owls are not the breed that usually matches snow-colored ground. But without this weird weather, I would not be looking at these owls now. The tree's foliage usually hides the owl's sunlit feathers. It was only thanks to the freak change of climate that I could see them on the bare branches of winter.

Like all people who hate change, I read a lot of studies about global warming. When Zoë had been born seven weeks prematurely, I looked for anything that would explain what had gone wrong. Her early birth had led to chronic cough and a battery of MRIs. The *American Journal of Epidemiology* published an article correlating climate change in California with human preterm birth. A significant positive association was found between apparent temperature and preterm delivery during the warm season in California. Mean, maximum, and minimum apparent temperatures all had significantly elevated associations for lag days up to one week. When they considered vulnerable subgroups, all studied showed increased risks regardless of maternal age, racial/ethnic group, level of educational attainment, or infant's sex.[16]

The study also commented on other studies that had shown that environmental factors such as air pollution and high ozone levels contribute to preterm birth. And further studies have shown that the smaller environment, that of the mother's body, when infected with bacteria or suffering from high stress, sometimes explains early labor. It depends on what lenses you want to look through to see how to explain the growing trend of premature babies. I tried to look through both. Self-blame plus entire species blame was my favorite way to go. Neither the global lens nor the personal one made her cough go away. Neither one prevented a visit to the emergency room. And, apparently, neither one provided cover for these chicks from the brazen sky.

Climate change seemed the most likely indicator for the owl's prematurity, but maybe the cause was something else. Nesting on a college campus, even a Catholic one, might do weird things to hormones—oversexed teenager owls. But these naked-in-trees owls, born early too, would have a hard time of it, at least for a while, if they even made it through spring, whatever the cause of their prematurity.

The owls, big as preemie babies, stared back with wild eyes. One, smaller than the other, nudged its sibling's wing, like it wanted to tuck under, like it wanted its mother. They looked caught, trapped somewhere they didn't want to be. Normally, they'd have unfurling leaves to hide behind. Shadows of bigger trees should, in May, conceal their furry heads, making them look not so big, not so obvious. In early April, their white down matched the color of the naked sycamores. But white is never camouflage against early spring blue sky. One owl stretched its tail out, full-fan nervous. I wanted to stop looking at them. I was making them anxious. We were all making them anxious. But how do you stop looking at something you've never seen before, even if it shouldn't be seen?

"The mother owl must be off hunting," the man said.

I looked around for her but I couldn't see anything with the sun in my eyes. Zoë, complaining about the sky being too bright, only looked up at the owls for a second. I thought she saw them. She blinked a few times in their general direction. She takes birds in stride. Like the crocuses, she thought she'd see another one around the corner.

"Leave them there," she said, repeating what I'd said about flowers.

We left the owl-man and his son and headed toward home. I hated leaving the owls. They looked hungry, but I had my own kid to feed. Maybe the humans leaving would convince the mom to return. The sun, still crooked so early in spring, reminded me it was time to start making dinner.

Zoë's face looks like mine only in a certain light, but when she heads right for the kitchen at exactly 5:30, her dinnertime, announces she is hungry, her heredity is confirmed. Any enthusiasm or excitements lead her, just like they did me, to the refrigerator. When something good happens to me, I want to commemorate the occasion with some fancy cheese or thin slice of prosciutto. When she says, "Can I have some blueberries or something," the word *something* inflects upward. My voice, when I'm unsure about what I really want to eat, ticks up too.

When we got home, I did what I could to find something that tasted like summer berries. I settled on "something" like grapes, which you can get all year long. I wondered what the owls would eat, born out of season. Can they substitute mouse for squirrel? Maybe the owls could get back on discarded dorm food and French fries spilled and forgotten in the parking lot.

I laid the chicken breasts between wax paper and got out the rolling pin.

"Where's the pizza?" she asked. She was used to rolling out pizza dough with me.

I showed her the chicken breasts and pointed out how fat and uneven they were.

"We've got to pound the breasts thin," I told her. "For chicken parmesan, they need to be half an inch thick. Do you want to try?" She said yes but she hit the breasts with no force at all. "You have to hit them hard." I took the rolling pin from her and gave the breasts a whack. They submitted, flattening out, becoming more dough than flesh.

In the middle of the next swing, Zoë yelled for me to stop. "That hurts the chicken."

I understood her point. It was an odd thing to do: take these round breasts and make them flat. Chickens, factory-farmed to make their breast so fat and thick, topple forward with the weight, their beaks nailing the ground. It's ridiculous, I thought, as I continued to pound the yellow flesh into smooth medallions, that the chicken-growers spent so much time, energy, and DNA manipulation making their chickens grow their breasts unnaturally fat and here I am, just thinning them out again. But that's the only way I knew how to make chicken parmesan.

We, cooks and raisers of children and chickens, think we can control the way things turn out but this determinism will disappoint. We establish boundaries between I and you but what if there really is no separation? The fetus, in utero, interplays with the mother's bodily chemistry. The mother's food feeds the fetus. The fetus, not wanting to be rejected by the mother's body, sends some of its DNA back into the mother's body. The process, called microchimerism, takes from the Greek word *chimera*, meaning two beings fused together. The *micro* stands not for the size of the beings but in the way the beings are connected. Through the tiny works of cells, molecules, and DNA. It's an ocean of balancing. The villi inside the uterus suck calcium from the mother's blood. The bones deliver. But the mother's body has some resistances of its own. It doesn't want to reject the fetus outright, but it can't die trying to help it grow either. So the mother takes some of her own nutrition first. The more calcium she eats, the less the fetus is likely to pull it from her bones. The fetus, not wanting to be rejected, sends some of its DNA into her blood so it recognizes the fetus. The mother halves her DNA and replicates it line by line. This takes a lot of energy. Running a marathon is second to the energy it takes to build a fetus from scratch.

A chicken scratches against the floor of the coop, then hops up on a roost of straw. She broods to make the egg. Or perhaps the egg makes her brood. Either way, here the two of them are, stuck together for a while and then in each other's DNA forever.

Which came first, the DNA or the DNA? Classic chicken-and-egg problem.

We used to believe that the only code was the DNA code and replicate and rinse and repeat and one could make a cell of a hamster into a baby hamster with a little splicing and some warm sperm and the kind real estate of a surrogate womb. You could grow baby hamsters in the uterus of a rabbit without turning the hamster into a rabbit. We believed DNA predicted and predicated. Dolly the sheep was born a 100 percent replica of her mother. Except her mother lived a long life. Dolly lived only briefly. She was sickly. Even though identical to her mother, she was not the lamb her mother had promised her to be. DNA is not everything.

Chickens are both adapted and adaptable. Back and forth, the chickens adapted, then we adapted them, then they adapted to that adaptation and here I was, adapting them back into their original skinny selves. Adapting to a new situation is one thing. The owls. They adapted to a new climate. At least they had lived from hatchling to downy-feathered branch-sitters. Adapting the situation to suit your chicken parmesan needs. That is another kind of adaptation entirely.

It is strange to me that humans have been such successful survivors. Their DNA adapts so slowly compared to, say, a virus. A virus can fully mutate in one year. But then again, who am I to argue humans are more successful than viruses. Viruses and microorganisms will be here long after we're gone. The villi in the human mother's body will be just an added tool for a bacteria's next phase.

Since I had forgotten to buy mozzarella for the chicken parmesan, I tore up string cheese and layered the threads across the chicken breasts that I'd oven-fried at four hundred degrees. I topped the chicken with Prego. The string cheese, arcing under the heat, melted more like plastic than cheese. I hoped dinner didn't end up tasting like cheap, burnt polyester. Adapting a recipe to suit your unwillingness to go to the store doesn't always turn out for the best.

The next morning, I went over to check on the owls. I told Erik I was going running since it would sound weird to say I was going to stare at tree branches in the hope of seeing birds that weren't supposed to be there. But weird was why they were there in the first place. I was sick to my stomach thinking they would be gone, that their mom had been driven off by smoking college students and their loud cars, that someone had seen the babies and knocked them down, wanting to take them home as pets, that they were born too soon and the mother wasn't ready to feed them and they were starving up there in the tree and I wouldn't be able to tell because the downy fur made them look so soft and fat but even if I could tell, I did not know how to grind up raw squirrel with my teeth and regurgitate into their mouths.

When I got to the sycamore trees, I couldn't see them at first. But then, suddenly, there they were—their little white bodies two halves of one moon and I was happy for a second until I thought of all the falling down that could happen. If I could have seen the mother for just one minute, I would have faith that these little chicks would not break my heart. But there was no mama bird swooping in with half-digested vole in her gullet and I was unsure about the role of mother birds here.

I'm unsure about the role of mothers anywhere. I wanted Zoë to be fierce but I also wanted her to be polite. I wanted her to be strong and yet forgiving. I wanted her to have all the friends and a best friend, to be the smartest in the class but not too aware of being the smartest, to feel free and yet rooted. I wanted oxymoron after oxymoron just like my mom had. My mom wanted her daughters to know proper etiquette—we knew which fork to use when—coupled with feminism that insisted we take what was ours and not be demure. To this day my sisters and I can eat more ounces of prime rib than any guy we've known, with the correct fork and knife handling. Am I more of a feminist than an environmentalist? Or just more of a hypocritical hedonist? Dissociation may be my best skill. A cow is not a steak if I'm eating it. What happens to the body happened some other place, some other time.

Later, though, when my mom and I were talking about Joe and how I couldn't find the right word for too-early sex and she was telling me she was sorry, that it was her fault, that she shouldn't have let me hang out at a house where the parents weren't home, she explained why she did let me go over there so often. She didn't want Joe and Jenn's mom to think my mom didn't approve of their mom's working. My mom did approve. She had wanted to work outside of the house. She should have known better, she said. Insides of houses were the places where real danger happened.

"I should have known. It was obvious growing up in Evanston. Men take girls into the bathroom and use them like tissues," she said.

"You can't generalize. Not all men do," I said.

She scoffed. "In our family, it's genetic." Instead of going on about the family history of girl-breaking male behavior, she changed the subject. "I think Zoë needs some new shoes," she said.

I didn't tell my mom how often I let Zoë go barefoot in her own backyard. As a mother, she would have been okay with it. As a grandmother, she'd think it was too uncivilized, or too dangerous. But I believed that you have to explore a wilderness, sometimes, in order to discover something new, to start a new cycle, even if you get hurt. Unless you're an owl in the middle of the city. Then you should be very, very careful.

***

In the April 2007 issue of *The Economist*, the author of an epigenetics column reported on a study about free-range versus caged chickens. Free-range chickens born to mothers raised in cages behave like their caged mothers. Cages appear to physically alter the brain cells of domesticated chickens. Chicks of caged hens, walking freely, still act like their caged mothers—shy, ducking. The chemicals in the brain cells of domesticated chickens alter a chemical in the ovaries of the hens, sealing the fate of those free-range baby chicks. They cluck around like they're in cages anyway, scooting to corners when they're nervous, waiting for someone to feed them rather than pecking the ground for seeds.

Imagine your future mapped chemically and genetically even before you were conceived, regardless of your new circumstances. Things must be alterable. You pray there is something that will counteract whatever stress your mother may have experienced when young and trapped and domesticated by the overly familiar touch of an uncle or best friend's brother. You don't want to "adapt to" in this case. In this case, you want the situation to change. Adapt the world. Stop hurting girls. Stop hurting owls.

I lie on the bed with Zoë who is asleep and smell her hair and think, it's because I'm her mom that I can do this. I can stroke her arm. I can kiss her neck. There is a reason I can do this, I justify. I'm her mom. But that thought makes me dissociate. I hover above and see myself kissing her and it looks weird: too intimate. I scoot over, move away. Was this moving away the beginning of the gap? Is it my own nervousness that this is where there would be space enough for someone else to move in and make her body familiar? Her familiar body was mine, cultivated by me. But someone else will find it wild and want to make it theirs. I would have done anything if she would stay three years old and under the crook of my arm forever but then my arm cramps or her head itches and we both start talking about our favorite foods and get hungry and have to get up. Our bodies usually win these arguments. Between this wild rolling and that future, someone will move in to fill that gap, which, I guess, at some point, is natural too. I hope not a boy, not too soon. But I hope against history. I fear I've infected her already with this need to have somebody close to me. What if that need was in my breast milk? What if it is in my DNA?

But even now, already, when she kisses me, she holds me behind the neck and practically dips me, then kisses me fat on the lips. Even though she is only three years old, I see the sex approaching her. I recoil and recoil and then recover by talking to her like a mother. Reset the environment. "What should we eat for dinner?" I ask. Food puts us back in the realm of mother-daughter.

"Not chicken!" she answers.

When she talks to me she is herself, not just body. When she talks, she signifies her immediacy, not her future what-might-be.

Awake she is the funny baby who says "I need to talk with you" when she means "to you" and motions me over to hear the big news about what she's making me for dinner. "I'm making you some oats." She pinches her fingers together and hands me a single oat. She sings "I love Mom and Dad and the couch and the chair" and I think if she'll talk and sing always no one will put her in that place where her mother was put, and her grandmother before that and her great-grandmother before that: where the guy keeps telling her to be quiet and for some dumbass reason, she is.

Strands of ghost DNA follow our DNA like tracers. No geneticist could map it but it is as predictable as blond hair and blue eyes. This future is not predictable but it is traceable in hindsight: the tsk tsk my mother makes that I also make after someone suggests a heresy like putting ketchup on their scrambled eggs or spritzer in their wine. Identical eye rolls, my mom and I. If you could stop the DNA in its place and take an echo of those strands, you would see the T clutching the C and the A commingling with the G but you might also see the future: an aunt who won't look her uncle in the eye, a mother who glares at that same uncle at every family reunion, a different aunt pregnant and married at sixteen to the janitor who worked at the elementary school across the street from her house, bile in the back of your throat after having gotten drunk the night before not because you like beer but because it distracts you from what the guy who gave you the beer's hands are doing, a neighborhood boy telling you you're pretty, well, pretty enough to lead down to the unfinished basement where a mattress lay like it was expecting you, a friend who watched, a dare to go out to a boy's car who you didn't know and just "see" what happens. I can hear the echoes in my body echoing in hers. I close my ears.

How to spare Zoë? Cluck around like a real wild chicken, Z. Not a free-range bird borne of a caged hen, I should tell her. Or maybe I should stop calling her chicken and call her some wild bird instead. I should make wild noises. Adapt her world. Keep her moving. Keep her away from cultivated ground.

Could the owls, living in what might have once been their native space but is now space claimed by the city, hear what they needed to hear? I worried, late at night, that the owlets couldn't hear the sound of crickets, the chirping of frogs over the sound of I-96 as it sped along. Fulton Street, a main artery that runs into downtown Grand Rapids, bordered the college. In the way bats use echolocation to find their food or their way back home, owls use auditory space maps to hone in on their prey, to find their way back to the nests. How could the owlets learn to use that map if they couldn't hear their mother over the noise of the cars as she folded her quiet self around the noise of a mouse?

When I was pregnant, my food echoed in my body. I was gassy and bloated. I could feel right below my abdomen the round of the apple I'd just eaten. I could almost see the nest of spaghetti underneath my skin, just to the right of my uterus. And the food echoed to the baby. Every bite of red leaf lettuce, full of folic acid, was ammunition against spina bifida. Every glass of milk grew a bit of femur, a centimeter of ulna.

Every meal is special when you're pregnant. You're all nurture now. Nature has done all she can do with the making of the zygote and your job now is to support that—not screw that up by neglecting your folic acid or your calcium intake. Everyone watches what you eat, what you drink. If I had a French fry, I'd worry: What is this building in the baby? If I drank too much carrot juice, I wondered if the beta-carotene turned the baby, however briefly, orange.

Unlike eating for two while pregnant, breastfeeding balances nature and nurture. The milk flows, it matters that you ate breakfast but not so much exactly what. As the baby sucks, you stroke the side of her head. You watch with awe the fingers as they press on the side of the breast instinctively. You see how the dimple in her cheek matches the one in yours. Supposedly, breastfed babies learn to know when they're hungry and when they're full. Even if I end up giving Zoë some mediocre DNA and some inherited baggage, I hope by breastfeeding I gave her a sense of food as nutrition and food as love without one ever having to trump the other.

I think teaching her to cook nurtures Zoë more than feeding her does. I try to get her to eat nine different colors of vegetables and fruits a day but when we're cooking, things aren't as serious. If she pokes a hole in the pizza dough, we press the dough back together. If she adds a little too much salt, we add a little more water. If she adds too much cream, it probably just tastes better anyway. Cooking requires some precision and control, but cooking is mostly a forgiving sport—there are always ways to mitigate mistakes.

I take great heart in just the title of Ethan Watters' essay "DNA Is Not Destiny." The article describes studies done on agouti mice. These mice are fat and yellow. Their parents were fat and yellow. It seemed likely that their children would be fat and yellow too. These fat mice are susceptible to cancer and diabetes, as were their parents, as would be, so goes the thinking, their children. Two scientists, Randy L. Jirtle and Robert A. Waterland, designed a genetic experiment around these mice. They produced mice that looked nothing like their parents. These mice were thin and brown. Regular mice. Did they splice the gene, fix the broken DNA? No, they changed the mother's diet just before she conceived the would-be fat baby mouse. So while she still handed down those same old lousy genes, the genes reacted differently to the brand-new diet:

> Starting just before conception, Jirtle and Waterland fed a test group of mother mice a diet rich in methyl donors, small chemical clusters that can attach to a gene and turn it off. These molecules are common in the environment and are found in many foods, including onions, garlic, and beets and in the food supplements often given to pregnant women. After being consumed by the mothers, the methyl donors worked their way into the developing embryos' chromosomes and onto the critical agouti gene. The mothers passed along the agouti gene to their children intact, but thanks to their methyl-rich pregnancy diet, they had added to the gene a chemical switch that dimmed the gene's deleterious effects.[17]

By changing the mama mouse's diet, the scientists changed the mouse's body response to this gene. The call-and-response that usually goes fat-and-yellow echoed back brown-and-thin. Epigeneticists argue against the idea that genes determine fate. They see applications for cancer, rheumatoid arthritis, neurodegenerative diseases like Alzheimer's, and diabetes.

Eat more onions, garlic, and beets before you get pregnant. Signal to the future that DNA/nature isn't everything. Signal that long-time-lived environment isn't everything. You can change the soil you're standing on. Environment can change things. Food is one's primary environment. "Life-long 'methylation diets' may be the trick to staying healthy," Watters writes. Genes aren't deaf. They listen to the surrounding sound. This is good news I think, for the agouti mice and for me and for Z. It becomes less about how we cannot control our DNA or our inherited baggage and more about how we can control our environment. We can change, or at least influence, the DNA. Zoë loves onions. As I roll out pizza dough, she eats a whole Walla Walla sweet onion like an apple. Imbibe those methylenes, little Z, I tell her. Defend against your mom's predilections and habits, her distractions and substitutions, her thick waist and her short legs.

I think back. I ate a lot of onions before I got pregnant. Countries of them. When I was pregnant, my friend Matt made a four-onion soup and I didn't let a single *Allium cepa* escape.

The climate crisis is changing the songs birds sing. Finches, to prepare their babies for a warmer world,[18] sing different songs to their eggs. If the parent sings what scientists named "a hot call" to its chick, the chick adjusts its growth—it asks for food differently and grows a little more slowly. The smaller the bird, the easier it is to distribute heat through its body. The birds also tended, once hatched and making their own homes, to prefer slightly warming nesting sites.[19]

What if I had sung to Zoë in utero to convince her to stay womb-bound for another couple weeks, thereby shaving off the risk of her contracting RSV and pneumonia? What if I'd sung to her about loving round as well as square foods? What if I'd warned her about coming pandemics, saying, you're going to need the full capacity of your lungs to breathe through this hot world full of so many people eating so many animals, the future a grapple with zoonotic disease? What if I'd sung to her about the climate crisis? "Dear little baby, you should buy a house in the Northwest where there will be less drought." Or, "Little baby, please be born with a love of planting trees. Because it's going to take a trillion to save the humans and the chickens and the baby owls."

Erik and I had decided to move closer home—at least back to the West. We were leaving in a couple of days. I went one more time to check on the owls. I couldn't find them anywhere. I wondered if their attempt to make a wild place in the city had failed. Maybe the owls had died or maybe they found a wilder wilderness. Should I hope that they've learned to adapt? That this city environment could work for them—students throwing out burned French fries, half-eaten sandwiches, healthy snacks from home, bring squirrels. Every square foot, you saw a squirrel. Maybe this place was the exact right place for two barred owls. Positive thoughts, I told myself. I looked further.

The canopy of trees never appeared as thick and green as when I scanned them for something small and feathered. I looked through the branches into the sky breaking through. The sun was so bright it blinded me. I looked up and saw sun. I looked down to any still, dead owl bodies. But when I looked up again, I saw flashes of white everywhere—owls on every branch. I looked straight ahead. Don't look up. I don't try too hard to verify what I think I saw. I let myself believe that the trees were full of owls. Owls. They live here. There are plenty of squirrels. Maybe even owls can adapt the world to them, can make their own Edens.

Zoë won't eat the chicken. She says, "It's not square." As I jump up to cut the chicken into the square shape she likes, for fear she will decide to eat nothing at all, something a preemie can't afford to do, I can see who has adapted to whom.

She still won't eat it. I try to reframe the issue for her. "The owls would eat it."

I can tell immediately I've said the wrong thing. I've reminded her of the owls, of the bird-like nature of chickens. She pokes at her mozzarella. It's stringy as plastic. I go to the fridge to get her something, anything, to eat.

But she's not a preemie anymore, although we'll always have to worry about respiratory illnesses. Sometimes, you have to learn to adapt to what you've got. The owls, still surviving in their downtown habitat, too early in the spring, are doing it. Urban life is an owl's pandemic. Their immune systems adjust.

I sit back down in my chair, take a bite of my chicken.

I look up at her. She takes a bite of her mozzarella. She is at home in her body, eating what she likes, eating what I like, eating what I don't like. She holds her ground. I get up, tear her another bite of chicken. She takes another bite of plastic cheese, putting me in my place. I look at her and the lens through which I see her agitates. You don't have to move often or a lot, I think. The world shakes of its own accord, makes space between history and future, between strands of DNA. She is me and she is not me. In the gap between her chair and mine, she does not fall. In the space between she and me, I see displays of branch, the shimmer of light, the forest that, even though in the middle of a city, still finds a way to feed a couple of baby owls, born too early. Zoë, her eyes wild and fierce, chewing plastic-y mozzarella, defies her mother's desire for her to eat chicken, but concedes, as her mother does, to eat a bit of the cheese. Going further than her mother goes, trying a taste of store-bought, jarred Prego, she adapts to her own, shaky ground.

A PERMANENT
HOME

THEY'RE TEARING DOWN OUR OLD house in the Avenues where we had lived for eight years in Salt Lake. We had been in Michigan only five months when we heard the people we sold our house to had decided not just to remodel the old structure. They were starting completely over.

Erik had painted every wall of that house. He painted the moldings with enamel paint—hard enough to last forever. It's the house where Erik first brought me oysters and the house where I first made him tacos. It's the house we brought Zoë home to—where I first nursed her and where I first fed her puréed sweet potatoes. That house was where I learned to make cassoulet and where I made my mom's favorite, vichyssoise.

Every bit of evidence of that life is gone—it has been carted off to the landfill in dump trucks—the hard, glossy paint, the wallpaper under that paint, the countertops stained with beet juice, the hood filters shiny with frying grease, drywall where the smell of seared meat lingered.

We tried not to take it as a commentary on our life—that it was somehow worthless and disposable. Where do memories go when the thing that held them is gone? They seemed more in danger of being blown away like so much gypsum from broken sheetrock. What do I remember now about Z's first year? What do I remember about Erik's first visit? Less and less, and now I can't drive by the old house in order to jog the memory.

***

Perhaps it is hard to electrify people to climate change because it's something they can't see. Smog, garbage, algaed rivers, slag from pit mines, is visible. A political fight can be mustered against the visually apparent. Hence, the Clean Air Act, the Clean Water Act, Woodsy Owl's anti-litter theme song to Help Keep America Lookin' Good—these government programs and regulations transformed the air, water, and land before our very eyes.

The winter is colder. Or warmer. The summer is warmer. Or colder. Drier. Weirder. Everything is weird but nothing looks that different this year than last. The shoreline creeps imperceptibly. The buds bloom a day or two earlier. Climate moves by eons and human eyes move by minutes. Time-lapse photography is a human invention to try to make our vision move more like geology. A photographer would have to speed things up fast enough to fling herself into the future, and time-lapse the planet's melt and catapult it back to us in the present to make it matter in our lifetime.

The house the new owners demolished had not been perfect. At nine hundred square feet it was barely big enough for the three of us. The basement had been finished but was too cold from October to May to spend much time in. The driveway was narrow. The kitchen small. But it was our house and the yard was deep and the garden grew perfect tomatoes, eventually. Salt Lake is the perfect place to grow tomatoes—the summers are long and dry. The water piped from reservoirs and mountain springs was hard and mineral-filled, giving the tomatoes a specific Utah flavor. When I had lived in Portland, wet, short summers made for green, soft tomatoes. Oregon is great for growing mushrooms but not so ideal for tomatoes. Where we had moved—Michigan—we wouldn't end up staying long enough to plant tomatoes. And where we moved to next—Flagstaff, at seven thousand feet elevation, with windy days and freezing nights, even in the summer—made tomato growing difficult.

So I missed Salt Lake—for the tomatoes, the hot summers, garden hoses, and the fact that that's where I had lived most of my life. It's also the place where I learned to cook and, possibly more importantly, learned to shop for food. Walking in the Avenues, just a year or so before we moved from Salt Lake, when I saw the brick building, I assumed it was just an empty relic. I must have walked by it a hundred times and driven by as many but it never caught my eye. A cinder block structure with 1950s font letters attached to the side doesn't call attention to itself, but this time, I noticed. I expected to see boarded up windows or, in front of the door, a gate like those steel contraptions from old elevators that fold up like a bellows.

There was no metal or plywood barricading my entrance. Still, I was not sure if this place was open for business. But inside, a light—fluorescent and flickering. An automatic door sign cautioned its entering shoppers, "Caution Automatic Door," just like my regular grocery chain store but this door swung rather than slid. In fact, it swung so fast that it already opened, like it sensed me coming from far away. Like it could snap me into the building and make me inhale the Aqua Net from a thousand housewives ago. Through the open door, I saw aisles, stocked. There was someone standing at the bagging station but she looked out a window instead of through the door at me. I tried to remember if my regular grocery had windows. No, it didn't. The window the bagger stared through looked out toward City Creek Canyon—the tops of the brown hills turning green in the narrow V where the river ran. To imagine a view from within a grocery store made me feel like I was someplace else—out of the city, in the mountains, near a river, although in my imaginings the river was wide and the hills alongside were not parched brown. Maybe the bagger in her black sweatshirt and lip ring was also imagining the mountain greening. She smacked her gum. Maybe not.

Still, I was in the store now. If nothing else, I could buy some gum so I didn't look like I was casing the joint or staring at the relic as if I were visiting a museum. I moved from the soft, rubber pad welcoming me in and put both feet inside on the scratched Armstrong tile and I suddenly remembered the IGA my grandma worked at in Evanston, Wyoming, before I was born that managed to survive oil booms and busts until the third boom came and brought Walmart. In fact, this place smelled like my grandma's house—a little like her bathroom, a little like the old Freon that's escaping from her refrigerator, but also like saltines and Jell-O, foods I ate when I was a kid only at her house when she was watching me while my parents went out for steak dinner. Pectin and freezer burn. Like my grandma's, these floors had been washed cheaply with ammonia. The Pine Scent sat pristinely on the shelf. Pine Scent was for other houses. Not this place.

Walking the aisles was like walking through my grandmother's pantry and my mother's childhood. Among the Total cereal and Oreo cookies, Cheetos and Rice-A-Roni, I found packages for foodstuffs I vaguely remembered: Mister Salty Veri-Thin Pretzel Sticks, Postum, Carnation Instant Breakfast, Tang, Royal Shake-a-Pudd'n, Ovaltine, Spam, Mother's Cookies, Chef Boyardee, Knorr Beef Noodle Soup, as well as all the mixtures of Knorr products like hollandaise and hot & sour I used to find so easily and sometimes liked to pass off as homemade. I didn't have a cart so I loaded my arms with Knorr. Knorr made a beef gravy that rivaled my grandmother's, an au jus that tasted like prime rib. Knorr, I asked aloud, where have you gone? How could McCormick's brand beat you out? I asked the aisle. No one was there with me. I could talk to the groceries all I liked. I clutched the packages tightly to my chest, taking my haul, planning to find my gum, and headed to the cashier before anyone questioned my looting of the ready-mix department.

I looked at choices of gum—Extra right next to Bazooka, Orbit next to Chiclets. I jumped when the man behind the meat counter asked if he could help me. I jumped because at the Smith's grocery store down the road, I had to practice my semaphore skills to get the butcher to notice me. This butcher saw me first. He waved me over, asked what I needed. His voice sounded gruff. He didn't smile but since he went to all the trouble to see if he could help, I felt compelled to order something from him. I tried to think of a recipe for which I already had all the ingredients except the meat, even though I was suspicious of the would-be quality of the beef in this heretofore unknown, at least by me, store.

But I took a chance that the meat might be good. This guy reminded me of my mom's old butcher when we lived on the far end of the Salt Lake Valley, between the mouths of Big and Little Cottonwood Canyons. We could ride our bikes to the rivers that supplied more than half of the city with drinking water and the water for my dad's tomatoes that he watered with a garden hose, although that ride was straight uphill. In the summer, to shop for something to go with those tomatoes, my mom would take me to Meijer's meat market. Where, after bypassing the aisles filled with packages of Knorr, Rice-A-Roni, Postum, Carnation Instant Breakfast, Spam, Mother's Cookies, Chef Boyardee, my mom would approach the meat man who would wrap in pure, white butcher paper packages of hamburger, of sirloin, of chicken breasts, of cube steak. We went there weekly. My mom knew the butcher's name. This meat counter smelled like that meat counter—clean, a little metallic—which meant there was a chance the meat would be good, although I wasn't sure. Meijer's had closed years ago. For a meat market to survive in the big-box making of grocery stores, it seemed quality would have been the first thing to go.

"Do you have any tenderloin?" I thought that would be a safe bet because I was pretty sure that store would never have tenderloin—the only other people in the store besides me, the bagger, and the butcher were a man in a hard hat buying a single onion and a woman in a hair net comparing the boxes of Wheat Thins and Triscuits. They're both past their sell-by dates, I wanted to tell her. If he had no tenderloin, I could shrug and walk away and not have to tempt fate by ordering meat.

He asked me what I wanted the tenderloin for.

I was dismayed. Who cares what I want it for? I told him anyway. "Stroganoff."

"You don't want tenderloin for stroganoff," he said. He threw down a slice of butcher paper and slapped a tenderloin up on the metal of the display case. "See here, the sinews. They're short. Good for quick cooking. Stroganoff, it stews a bit. It lets the collagen melt, turn to gel." The meat on the counter made my mouth water. I'd never seen meat this color—not the red of oxidized meat. Not the pink of plastic-wrapped. It was almost blue, like the blood just barely left it. When the butcher pressed his finger into it, the muscle snapped back like it still had some reason to stand up straight and get itself together.

"Sirloin's good enough for stroganoff. Stew meat would work too, but you look like the type that only trusts an upsell." It was true. I would rather buy up than down. I realized I knew little about meat except for perhaps the cost per pound.

"Come back next week. I've got an order for skirt steak coming in. It's like flank but better. I promise I'll charge you too much for it, if price is the only way you'll believe it's good meat." He wrapped me up some sirloin and tucked the tenderloin away for someone more aware of the relative merits of long and short sinew.

When I got home with my Knorr products and neighborhood-market-bought sirloin, I realized I didn't have any shitake mushrooms. Or cream. Or tarragon. The Martha Stewart recipe called for tenderloin and shitakes. She also wanted me to use saffron in the noodles. Martha is, sometimes, a bit extra. And since all I had was sirloin, sour cream, and button mushrooms, I threw Martha's recipe out the window and tried to remember my mom's. I pictured her at Meijer's meat market, buying stew meat, checking the date on sour cream. I knew the recipe from her shopping list. I ran into a syllogistic problem though: If tenderloin is already tender and therefore, unlike a more sinewy cut, doesn't need to be stewed or marinated—in fact, Martha said to brown the meat one minute per side—then should a less tender cut like sirloin be cooked slower or faster? Or must I be resigned to toughness? Or would the acid in the sour cream work to loosen the collagen? Was the butcher wrong? He did not look like the Martha-Stewart-cookbook-reading type. I was pretty sure my mom used stew meat. Did she cook the stroganoff all day? Wouldn't the sour cream curdle?

In the end, I salted and peppered the hell out of the sirloin and seared it in a gallon of butter. Adding half a pound of butter to a sirloin does a tender loin make. The sour cream did its part too and the whole thing was melt-in-your-mouth goodness that made me thank the butcher on 8th Avenue for saving me seven bucks a pound and reminding me of the power of butter, sour cream, and mothers' shopping list and recipe. The nice thing about my mom's recipes—I can take them anywhere. They're indelibly printed on my brain—a recipe I can take out of my memory to read at any time.

If you can't see it, does it exist? The *New Scientist* reported that young people can't remember how much more wildlife there used to be. "Walking in England's New Forest in 1892, butterfly collector S. G. Castle Russell encountered such numbers of the insects that they 'were so thick that I could hardly see ahead.' On another occasion, he 'captured a hundred purple hairstreaks' with two sweeps of his net. Patrick Barkham, who recounts these riots of nature in his 2010 book on butterflies, laments never seeing such a sight. However, new research suggests Barkham is

a rarity, because a lot of people are forgetting, or just don't appre
ciate, how much wildlife there was."[20]

How can you remember what you never knew? How could
we believe in viruses before we had microscopes? Some people
still don't believe in, or understand, how bacteria or viruses work.
Invisible gigantic forces are even harder to see than invisible
small forces. Absences are hard to quantify. Walking in the forests of Salt Lake City, I don't remember much wildlife although
once my sisters and I found a tarantula in our backyard. Salt
Lake Valley at one point had been filled to the brim with deer
and badgers, mountain lions and coyotes. But the Midwest the
Mormons sought to turn the valley into had shed its wildlife
by the time Paige and Valerie and I were born. Now, in winter,
my sisters and I count the particulates in the smog. We count
the number of days you can't have fires. We can't count the CO_2
molecules glazing thick glass. We can't count the mountain lions
because they are not there to count. We count the stuff we can
see as if sight is the only sense we know to use.

Perhaps if we really want to remember, we have to smell it.
Or touch it and listen to it. Taste it. What can I remember about
Michigan except for the time I tried to make pho? If I'd wanted to
make it feel like home, I could have made stroganoff. But I didn't
have time. We stayed only twenty months—not time enough to
mark it as home with Mom's old recipe. Western Michigan was as
gray as Portland but twice as cold. In January, the idea of summer
seemed impossible. It snowed so heavily, it was as if the clouds
had gathered up Lake Michigan and dumped it in frozen form on
top of our house. But I was sad to leave too—I would have liked
to have tried to grow tomatoes someplace new. I would have
liked to hunt mushrooms, too, but we left in April, right before
what was to be one of the best morel springs of the decade.

In Flagstaff, I would have to, for a while, rely exclusively on
grocery stores for tomatoes, and farmer's markets where the

vegetables are grown down the hill in well-irrigated and always warm Phoenix, Camp Verde, or Chino Valley. In my backyard garden, there are no tomatoes. I have no garden. Flagstaff is built on mostly volcanic rocks. If I had to live on food grown on my own, what could I grow? Now that I had left Salt Lake and my tomato garden and the newfound butcher a block away and dirt that was clay-y but not 90 percent rock, and all my hoarded packages of Knorr, I realized that if I had to live off the land here, I would most likely starve. In Flagstaff, unlike Portland, there are no blackberries or asparagus or watercress in the forest wilds to guide my planting season or my seed choices. The neighbors say the ground is so full of limestone that they have to import dirt to get anything, even penstemons, which are native wildflowers in some parts of the area but not, apparently, in our backyard, to grow. And, even though it's mountainous and monsoony, the air and dirt are still very dry. I would have to import water too from the reservoir, through the pipes, into my hose, just like I had to in Salt Lake. But unlike in Salt Lake where summer nights are mild, the temperature at night here, even in July, can drop below freezing. In Salt Lake, the wind doesn't reach hurricane levels worthy of blowing whole trees over, let alone tomato plants.

There's a reason Flagstaff wasn't settled by white people until 1882—the ability to transport earth and water had to come first. Before that, the Anasazi, Pueblo, Hopi, Yavapai, and Havasupai peoples who settled around the area were much more flexible about the plants they grew. They gravitated toward the patches of ground that held more soil than rock, to the springs where the water already was. Plus, the climate was different then. A little wetter, enough to make Walnut Canyon run perennially. Also, the Wupatki people were mobile in ways that I and my two-hundred-pound couch are not. They followed water. They did not force the water to follow them.

On my way to visit some of the ruins built in the 1200s at elevations below Flagstaff, where there's less limestone but more basalt and malapai, I shake my head the same way I shake my head at the city of Phoenix. It is dry as a bone here. Cactus grows. A few grasses. There is no obvious way to stockpile water. However, the building's infrastructure seems strong—thin, sandstone rocks mortared in layers became walls. The walls are built into the landscape upon a secure, gigantic red rock foundation. The Hohokam canal system laid the groundwork for what would, centuries later, become the Central Arizona Project. Between 700 and 1350 AD, the Hohokam built, in the end, over seven hundred miles of canals spread over one hundred thousand acres. The Hohokam left in 1450 (about the same time as the Wupatki and Sinagua in Northern Arizona), but when the Spanish arrived, they saw the Pima people still using the old Hohokam canals to gather water. Must have given them an idea.

How do you know when to trust your vision and when not to? If we could see the changing climate—we will be able to see more evidence as the crisis develops—will we do something? Or is the modern human too distrustful? Perhaps we have been trained not to believe our eyes. Perhaps this is the millennium of losing our last sense. Just as we look at people on respirators and still think we're immune to the raging pandemic, so too will we look to the shrinking rivers and say, but the tap on my faucet still turns.

The Wupatki ancient structures look like giant terra-cotta pots whose plants have outgrown their homes. I can see where the people had built their fires, where the draft came in as a bellows and where they vented smoke, where the food stores would have been kept but I can't see where the water would have been. The park literature describes an old spring that dried up long ago.

It's as if, after a long, dry fall and a cold, frozen winter, in the spring, the woman who carried the water from the little spring a hundred meters from the house went out to break off the thin ice and found there was no ice to break, just a layer of cold mud. She waited it out another couple of days or weeks, maybe, until tribal memory kicked in from the last time that this happened. The elders reminded her that once the spring is dry, it is dry and it is too far to climb those twenty miles toward the San Francisco Peaks to see if a creek is running. She packed up her husband and her papoose because that spring was done. Goodbye house that took sixty years to build. Goodbye little plot of land that, in this desert plain, held the one plot of hummus-y goodness thanks to the nearby stream, the dung of buffalo, and the compost of a few hundred pounds of composted corn husk and tomato vine. Goodbye beans and squash. Goodbye tomatoes and potatoes. See you in the old world.

If one learns how to move one's house to a more ideal kind of home—the kind where water is, where tomatoes grow, and where on the way one might find some mushrooms, the more likely one is to survive the droughts and privations. Sometimes, home means an ability to move and find what you need when you get there.

Mushrooms grow everywhere. They're not one of those, we'll-have-to-grow-them-so-we'll-survive kind of things but they do count as food and they are a sign of water. They keep it in their pores—boletes do it best in the sponge-like gill-tubes that make their caps thick and meaty. Unlike water, mushrooms don't need to accumulate to be usable. It's hard to extract one drop of rain from the edge of a leaf, but one mushroom shooting up from the sea of mycelium percolating under the ground holds ounces of water. The tiniest amount of rain can make that mycelium bloom like popcorn or, for those who don't like mushrooms, like the full rush of eczema.

Humans have always eaten mushrooms. The food timeline suggests that in the order of humans' ability to fend for themselves, first they gathered water, then salt, then they learned to fish.

Right after that, they collected mushrooms—not wild wheat, not wild tubers, but mushrooms. Mushrooms are ubiquitous. You can find them in high-altitude and lowland forests. You can find them in marshes and plains and meadows. You can find them on a rock, growing on dead trees, or in your carpet. They are meaty when there is no meat. People often think mushrooms have no food value but they are full of protein, amino acids, some B vitamins. They make soup worth its salt. They sauté nicely with fish.

Sometimes I wonder why I left Oregon. All that water. All those mushrooms. My boyfriend Andy and I spent every weekend combing the Cascade Mountains. It was November in Oregon; therefore, it was raining. There was no trail. The rain looked innocuous, but though the drops were tiny, they fell in the thousands per square inch. We parked the car on the side of the road and stepped into the woods. My coat was waterproof but my Levi's were not. Every time I walked into a fern, the water-collecting talents of the plant drained their collection on me. I love the idea of water, but not so much being wet. I am from Utah, where my skin was born dry. Where I did not need to wear Gor-Tex pants. Where tomato plants actually grew red tomatoes and didn't just wind and wind their way up in some great pyramid of green. Portland was too slippery to ever feel like home. I never found a neighborhood butcher in Portland, either, but maybe I just didn't look hard enough.

My mother-in-law, Ellie, comes to visit us in Flagstaff. Flagstaff's proximity to Salt Lake was the main thing that drew us here—but Flagstaff is not Salt Lake. There's just the one mountain, really, and though the peaks are nice, they don't suggest range or a place to escape if the hordes come marching through. Still, driving up to the San Francisco Peaks with El and Zoë, now three, toward the ski resort, we move into something familiar—ferns remind me of Hood River, Oregon, the aspens remind me of Alta, Utah. We see no rivers—the peaks had sloughed off their snow into the ground and the canyons months ago—but the dirt looks dark and loamy.

The Humphreys Peak trail begins under the chairlift, then takes a sharp left into already-dark woods. Even before we leave behind the sound of the machine whirring the lift up the mountain for tourists to try to squint out the Grand Canyon, we see evidence of fungal activity. Zoë, being close to the ground, spots the first mushrooms. We see shrimp mushrooms and puffballs and little brown jobbers. Ellie, who has never been mushroom hunting, brings me sample after sample—we have one bag to carry specimens and we reserve one bag to carry what we hope turn out to be edibles.

Unlike Oregon, where mushroom hunting is most reminiscent of swimming and the raindrops, though the drops are tiny, fall in the thousands per square inch, and soak every inch of the Levi's you mistakenly wore, here the sun shines in a sharp blue sky. The moss is emerald and the combination of sun and shiny green combines my two home places—Oregon and Utah. El offers Z a gummy bear to hike up just one more hill. She turns to the left and asks me to come over. She points to something crenulated and undulating. Chanterelles. In not Oregon. In the middle of what is mostly desert, we found the most moisture-loving of mushrooms. We offer Zoë another gummy bear. She climbs over basalt and malapai, underneath ferns as big as her head until we fill the bag with the most edible—mahogany-buffed king boletes that I'd never found in Oregon's coast range and umbrella'd chanterelles, that I used to find all autumn long—of mushrooms.

Perhaps the idea of home is, paradoxically, importable. With my mother-in-law and Zoë in the middle of the forest, I felt at home. In the shopping cart at Meijer's meat market with my mother, I knew what to call that place. It seems I want to live somewhere where water is plentiful but not in a place that wants to get me wet. Utah is home but I never found there the loam that grew lovely mushrooms. I miss the 8th Avenue market because it reminded me how to make my mother's stroganoff—which is where I lived, once a week, at seven p.m., for fifteen years. I've lost a lot in moving—a house, a nearby family, a place to grow tomatoes. I wonder if what I've gained has been worth it.

But if habit is home, maybe that's where we've gone wrong. Our habits are not necessarily our best characteristics. Habits are static. They wear grooves on our brains. They make it hard to change. Stroganoff is a habit. Not seeing animals is a habit. Fossil fuels are a habit. The most expensive cuts of meat are a habit. Meat itself is a habit. Knorr products are a habit. Perhaps learn to make béarnaise from scratch. Try to make a vegetarian stroganoff with mushrooms alone.

I found a new butcher in Flagstaff, just down the road. He doesn't have aisles of products. There are no pretzels or Ovaltine, Rice-A-Roni or Knorr products. Here, there really is just meat. The butcher, whose name I don't know yet, knows me. When I ask him about the difference between skirt steak and flank steak, he explains that "the skirt steak is the diaphragm muscle. It is a long, flat piece of meat, with a tendency toward toughness. But it has good flavor. The flank steak is the traditional cut used for London broil. It is long, thin, and full of tough connective tissue." He says to use the skirt steak for carne asada and fajitas. Instead of picking up a skirt steak though, he picks up a flank steak. "Here. I've cut it in half and tenderized it."

He doesn't tell me what to do with it. He trusts me. When I take it home, I dither. I plan to just make normal, barbecued flank steak with a Korean marinade. But I have fontina in the fridge and carrots and red bell peppers. I julienne the peppers and carrots. I grate some cheese and tuck the cheese and vegetables into the meat, roll it up, and grill it. I made something new. Which made me think of my mother too—who had made her stroganoff recipe and learned it by heart.

Now, I just need to find a place that sells Knorr products and learn to grow some tomatoes.

Although Flagstaff may be a little dry, a little windy, and a little bit too much in Arizona, it's not a bad place to call home for now. I'm trying to learn the lesson of the Wupatki people— take your home, in the form of recipes, mushrooms, and tomato plants, with you. Dig in, if you can. You never know what kind of disaster looms. Learn to compromise on the amount of water nearby but not on the proximity of a good butcher.

PORK
TECHNOLOGIES

A FLU PANDEMIC IS ONE of my favorite ways to freak out ala apocalyptic zombie movies. The threat of contagion. Holing up in your house with only Spam and cornflakes. Trying to find food for your dog. Trying not to eat your dog. What I worry about most is knowing that my child will die and I will just have to sit down and watch her waste away.

But then I remember, I am pregnant again. This time, easily, but it's no less frightening. I change my singular noun to plural: *children* not *child* will die. Watch *them* waste away not *her*, I correct.

Four months pregnant in July, I can't stop thinking about the H1N1 flu. Fearing the flu is almost as isolating as having it. People think you're an extremist. A germ freak. An overcautious nutter. Although possibly not as extreme as the Egyptian officials who slaughtered over three hundred thousand pigs to halt the virus or perhaps not as cautious as the people who wear masks on the bus or nervous enough to cancel travel plans to Mexico City where the epidemic started. But definitely extreme enough to think that the people who destroy pigs, wear masks, and cancel travel plans might be smarter than you. I ask my doctor if I should take my daughter out of school. She says no. I ask my doctor's doctor if I should take Zoë specifically, the daughter who had RSV, out of school. She also says no. I ask the preschool director what sort of safety precautions she's taking. She says she plans to ask the kids to wash their hands more often than she already does. I read an article the next day that suggests hand-washing does nothing to stop the spread. I read another article that says washing with soap is the only hope. I wash my hands. And then I smother them in Purell.

This is, of course, just a dry run for what will happen ten years from now. If one could hold on to one's panic, bottle it, store it up for every time you go to the store, maybe you'd remember to stock up on toilet paper. But apocalypse energy is hard to maintain. And usually, it's a lonely game.

During the H1N1 pandemic scare, I start stockpiling groceries. I buy twelve cans of Cento tomatoes, twenty boxes of spaghetti. It's not as if I think the grocery stores are going to close tomorrow. But I should start preparing—part as pure logic and part as an offering to the gods of swine flu. I buy two pork tenderloins, two pounds of bacon, and a saver-pak of pork chops. A little protein in the form of cheese won't save me but a lot of pig might. I'll fight fire with fire. I'll develop my own antibodies to the H1N1 out of bacon. I realize that it's not the pig that will kill me, but, lacking any other sort of game plan, I reason that pig is a prophylactic. I will eat him homeopathically.

The world is burning but there is some good news. Momentum builds to mitigate the climate crisis. Germany gave up coal. New solar technologies like solar fabric, solar asphalt, and solar skins should be ready for market in the next few years. Imagine a world, or, rather, an architecture, where windows and walls themselves absorbed and stored solar energy.

The very clothes we wear could be absorbing solar energy as we walk our fashion selves down the street. We could be our own plants. Right this minute, I am wearing a green shirt in solidarity with those plants. The technologies grow every year. But will they save us from our not-quite-plants-yet selves in time?

***

I am better at timing soufflés than timing my reproductivity. You'd think the stuff of the world—the tangible substances like albumen and membranes, shells and bones, proteins and sugars—would be manageable. That the effort put into getting air between the proteins would be similar to the stimulation of a zygote-ready endometrial lining. But the human body, unlike the tender egg, suffers under delusions of will. Not just desire. Not just choice. But layers and layers of mental proteins, laid upon the uterus expectantly. There was the time you were young and you wanted children. And the time, upon reading the Clearblue Easy stick, you most certainly didn't. There's the imagined possibility of you playing in the snow with your rosy-cheeked daughter and the possibility of you losing that child to the myriad of dangers like car crashes and cancers and drowning and cliffs and motorcycles and swine flus that makes you think having kids at all is a fool's errand. There was the panic when you got older that you couldn't conceive a child. Then there was a corrective to that panic: the moment when you sat back and watched your daughter spin across the room singing about a butterfly she thought she caught but telling you "I thought it was a butterfly but really, it was my hair." And you thought, "This is perfect. Don't mess it up being a nutter of a mother."

Then you thought about that daughter and how she had no sibling to pretend she was a butterfly to accidentally catch and to pull her hair. Or worse, something happening to that daughter and having no one left on earth with that same quality of hair, the same wild goose sounds coming out of her mouth. The uterus hears these things. I didn't believe it back when Erik's cousin Emily said that you could control your fertility with thought—but I was beginning to suspect she was right.

The human body is full of thoughts as sharp as glass. It lines up your arguments for and against. The shards cut off your chances and your choices. Or, sometimes, the shards shear a pathway through and you find yourself thirty-six years old, realizing that you're probably pregnant because you've pulled into the drive-thru of the Kentucky Fried Chicken, where you only go when you're pregnant. KFC is neither romantic nor as magical as soufflé but is still a carton of edible mashed potatoes and gravy of a sign. You wonder if, when you were trying to get pregnant, you could have set the uterine clock to zero, erased all that thought and trial and belief in choice and predictability just by going to the KFC. Who knew, four years later, that I was risking pregnancy by sneaking off to the KFC? What's in those potatoes anyway? An inseminating potato. A doubling gravy.

I dream of magical technologies—as magical as immaculate-conception-by-gravy. There are these tall, clocklike structures forcing themselves through the clouds, into the glassy CO_2. With whirring fans and complicated zappers, the machines press upon the CO_2 like a Norelco electric razor against a scruffy beard. The wheels spin and the carbons fall to the ground like baby whiskers. The oxygens stay in the sky and we humans, not plants this time, breathe them in, breathe them in.

We have restored the Holocene via the technologies of the Anthropocene.

And then I remember there is this thing called "tree" that already scrubs the atmosphere. I really would like to believe in magic.

Studies showed there were two kinds of people most at risk for dying from the swine flu—those with asthma and pregnant women. Actually, there were many others who were at risk but since Zoë had asthma and I was not just KFC-determined but Clearblue-Easy-determined pregnant, I didn't pay much attention to that list: parenthood makes us selfish. Save MY child, not yours, a mother with few inner resources thinks. I read about pulmonary edema and watched Zoë's chest to see if it expanded at an irregular rate. I remembered from her RSV days—anything over fifty-five breaths per minute. I counted to sixty and had no idea whether I was counting breaths or seconds. I received a message from my sister with a link to a *New York Times* article about a pregnant woman's ordeal with the swine flu and deleted the message without reading the piece.

I defrosted pork chops for dinner, brined them, and cooked them well-done although I hate chewy pork. The freezing and the brining probably would have already killed the nonexistent flu virus that was not at all lurking in my chops, but mind over matter! I was committed to pork homeopathy. The more pork I ate, the less the less the less the less chance the pig flu would get me.

The best amulet against the worst idea is always a small, bad idea.

It would be nice if worrying had its own positive effect. Shouldn't we, who risk looking like idiots by wearing the face masks, killing the pigs, calling the county every day to see if the vaccine had arrived yet, be the ones who miraculously avoided the flu? Worry as prophylactic.

Who doesn't believe trees have magic?

I woke up on Monday, October 19 at seven thirty to be the first to call the county to make a vaccination appointment for the following Saturday. By eight o'clock I had called five times. At first, I got a busy signal. Then voicemail. Then, nothing but dial tone even after I dialed the number. This is the way the world ends—the officials at the county health care center have been overrun by vaccine-needers, the building stormed by hordes of children and pregnant women and people with chronic diseases. Bad as zombies. Bricks hurled through windows. Consent forms flying. The nurses, armed only with syringes, try to fight them back but the vaccine-needers impale themselves upon the needles. They'll get the shot even if it means taking the needle home with them. Even if it means tackling a sixty-year-old nurse. By the time I used all three phones—my cell, Erik's, and our land line—and still found only a dial tone, I pulled my boots on. If kicking was required to get the vaccine, I had faith in my pointy-toed cowboy boots.

The vaccine will save me, I assured myself. It would save me from the virus but also from myself and this agitating self-concern. The antidote to fear, any fear, lies in the serum in the syringe. If I focused on the H1N1 virus I wouldn't have to think about this new baby being born with cerebral palsy, spinal muscular atrophy, cystic fibrosis, chronic lung disease. I wouldn't have to stay awake every night listening for this baby's breath. I had the shot! I won't worry about caesarean sections or pre-eclampsia or hemorrhage. The vaccine would save me from an early labor, a hard labor, a broken body, a NICU-imprisoned infant. The vaccine would prevent all the worry I wished I could have avoided the first time.

A vaccine for H1N1 became available quickly, largely because flu vaccines had been in development for years and the swine flu behaved similarly to our regular influenza. Regulations for the swine flu vaccine were adapted easily because the "egg- and cell-based platforms could be licensed under the rules used for a strain change."[21] Now the swine flu vaccine is included standard in the seasonal flu vaccine.

Vaccines for SARS, Ebola, MERS, and Zika don't follow the influenza pattern. Still, Dr. Nicole Lurie, in the *New England Journal of Medicine*, calls for platforms to be developed since new viruses are bound to surge. The trouble is, the will to make vaccines in advance of pandemic is short-lived. SARS disappeared before the vaccine was developed. Merck developed an Ebola vaccine, made it through testing stages, but since Ebola is deadly but not as contagious as SARS or even SARS CoV-2, the plans to make it commercially available are on hold.

But at the time, I didn't know how closely swine flu was related to regular flu. I certainly didn't know I was getting off easy this time.

I zipped up my coat and dialed the phone one more time. Miraculously, someone answered. "The lines have been down," the woman on the phone told me. "And my computer's down. I'll have to do this by hand."

Appointments taken by hand. Not since Y2K had I imagined the consequences of a lack of technology so whole-bodily.

She asked me to please hold. I imagined the appointments, along with the vaccine, disappearing by the second.

She came back on the phone. Her computer appeared to be back online. She scheduled Zoë and me for two of the first appointments—8:10 and 8:15 on next Saturday morning.

Instead of heading to the health department to kick some nurse butt, I took off my boots and cooked some bacon to celebrate.

That afternoon, Zoë came home with a runny nose. By Thursday morning, she had what I assumed was the swine flu. That night, I awakened at two in the morning and couldn't fall back asleep. I listened to her breathe. If I heard her wheeze, I would make the two a.m. drive to the hospital. If I heard nothing, I would presume her lungs had already collapsed into blocks of unmovable virus. I didn't go in and check on her because on the one hand I knew I was being ridiculous—a lung does not collapse in half an hour and on the other hand, I really could not imagine how I would survive finding Zoë in her bed not breathing.

The pathology of the H1N1 progressed like this at our house:

On Monday, Zoë's nose runs. It runs all the way through Tuesday and Wednesday. On Thursday, she is grumpy and feverish. On Friday, I call the doctor's office. The nurse says to watch for lethargy and for respiratory distress. I tell the nurse that the doctor promised to prescribe Tamiflu. The nurse says no. There is a nationwide shortage. And Tamiflu comes with side effects. If she turns blue, take her to the ER, she says.

I sniff and hang up. I have had a stuffy nose for days. To sleep, or rather, to not sleep, I have to turn onto one side, let my sinuses drain into one nostril, and then turn to drain the other side. I imagine white blood cells attacking, attacking and then succumbing, succumbing.

On Monday, I eat ham fried rice.

On Tuesday, I eat baked potatoes with bacon bits. Five slices of bacon, crumpled into bits.

On Wednesday, I don't sleep. I wake up in the middle of the night. I eat cold, leftover ham fried rice at two a.m. Full moon. I expect to see an owl out the window. At six I finally see some deer. Wednesday, Thursday, Friday—rebound! Zoë is up and around and not collapsing in my arms. We leave to get our 8:10 and 8:15 shots. The nurse says as long as she isn't wheezing or doesn't have a fever, Zoë can get her shot. She is not wheezing at exactly 8:00 or 8:30 although she is wheezing at 8:05 and 8:25. I hope wheezing or fevering at the exact moment the shot is given is what the nurses meant. I can feel the vaccine comingle with all the bacon I've eaten. I am inoculated.

That night, I relax my vigilance and make fondue. I eat no pork products at all.

In the morning, I make French toast and bacon. Just in case I missed something.

As the population grows, and as that same population eats more meat and becomes at risk for more zoonotic diseases, and as the climate crisis threatens to unleash microorganisms that haven't seen the sun in thousands of years, vaccine developers and regulators need to plan ahead. But even so, with the SARS

CoV-2, COVID-19 pandemic, no one was prepared. And then, even when other countries figured out how to be prepared, the United States doubled down on ill-preparedness.

Nicole Lurie's article in the *New England Journal of Medicine* subtly calls for more platforms to be made available to tackle pathogens. While diverse companies are working toward those new platforms that use both DNA and RNA to synthesize vaccines, requiring no fermentation or culturing process, no fully developed RNA vaccines had been approved by the time I was writing this. Thankfully, the Bill and Melinda Gates Foundation, and Nicole Lurie's et al.'s organization, the Coalition for Epidemic Preparedness Innovation (CEPI) devoted money and effort into making a vaccine as fast as possible. But COVID-19 is not the flu and the time I am writing this will never be the same time you're reading this. That is why one should always panic about the apocalypse. It's always coming even if it's already been here.

If Y2K was a case of extreme over-preparedness then climate change is a matter of extreme under-preparedness. Once the programmers saw that two placeholders for the year wouldn't suffice for our four-digit millennium, they could, even though difficult, wrench the computer code open to insert two more spaces.

Climate change is a case of extreme under-preparedness. Perhaps because, like a virus, we can't see it. Although carbon has been accumulating in our atmosphere since 1750, the sky today looks as it then did.

Eunice Foote, who is rarely credited with the find, discovered the effects of climate changes in 1856. Fully 150 years before we've even begun to stop arguing about its existence. "Foote arrived at her breakthrough idea through experimentation. With an air pump, two glass cylinders, and four thermometers, she tested the impact of 'carbonic acid gas' (the term for carbon dioxide in her day) against 'common air.' When placed in the sun, she found that the cylinder with carbon dioxide trapped more heat and stayed hot longer."[22]

If you imagine carbon dioxide as black as a gas as it is as a solid, we could see the thick layers. Like drilling an ice core sample to gauge the carbon, we could count layer-year by layer-year, from 1750 to 2020. Perhaps, were carbon as invisible as glass but as heavy, we could weigh the trouble. We could feel the heat more directly. But, like all gases, carbon gas is mainly weightless. The ceiling doesn't appear as heavy as Foote predicted it would be. And appearances, in terms of preparedness, are everything.

A cautionary tale about the thin ceilings: I lived with a pig once. Her name was Sophia. Although she made my boyfriend's apartment smell like overcooked turnips, she was a cuddler. If you were sitting on the couch, which you would be sitting on only for a moment while your boyfriend hurried to gather whatever clothes of his he could into a duffel bag to get them out of the apartment to take over to your non-pig-filled apartment before they too became stained with the long-flung scent of urine, Sophia would come up to you, like any golden retriever, and shove her muzzle under your hand and prod at your fingers until you consented to scratch her behind the ears. It wasn't her fault she smelled bad. The apartment was on the second floor and pigs are hard to get down the stairs for their evening walk. And anyway, she was living with guys who were too lazy to take the garbage down to the dumpster. What was the likelihood they'd bother to take the pig out for a walk?

What I remember most about Sophia the Pig was the lettuce. She loved to eat lettuce, and the garbage pile in the corner of the apartment was filled with lettuce. The pile started before Sophia came. Before the pile, there was Andy, my boyfriend who was quickly packing his duffel. And before Andy was Jonah and Robb. Jonah and Robb saved Andy from sleeping on the sofa of the student union. And after the pig came to live with him, Andy came to live with me. Still, we'd visit so Andy could pick up some books and clothes. He wasn't officially living with me, much like the pig who wasn't officially living at Jonah's and Robb's but doing what visiting roommates do best: reducing the piles of garbage. Unfortunately, the pile of garbage had been transformed to a pile of piss and shit in another corner. This apartment did not come with the factory farm's ingenious grate-underneath-the-cage invention.

Andy and I weren't at the apartment when the ceiling caved in. The pig pee had softened the floors. It had leaked through the floorboards and then the drywall. The pee turned the floor to mush and then, like any good mush, it let gravity have its way and moved the upstairs crap to the downstairs neighbors.

The ability of trees to transform CO_2 into oxygen as skillfully as Sophia transformed garbage into pee keeps me hopeful. But just today, a pool formed in the permafrost. The water still green, the last outpost for a cold-loving algae. Murky. Fizzing. Respiring more methane than a whole herd of livestock, more than cows and pigs combined. What had once been locked in, dying plants frozen mid-compost, a million years ago stunned into stasis, begins to ripple.

H1N1 has nothing on the viruses that threatened *Homo erectus* or earlier renditions of humans. How can we prepare a vaccine for a threat buried in what we thought was permanent hiatus? Take a break, virus.

Look in any freezer of an in vitro fertilization lab. Whole embryos can be stored for near eternity. Or at least as long as the would-be vitro will live. Viruses, masters of temperature fluctuation, patient opportunists, have been waiting for an immune system that can help them reproduce like any good baby doctor.

Even finding vaccines for zoonotic respiratory pathogens is new to us, and these viruses stem from the early Anthropocene. It's speculated that SARS-CoV-2 jumped from a bat to humans at a wet market in Wuhan, China, but the jumping back and forth between animals that humans eat and animals that humans live with and the habitats that are increasingly beset with humans means that whatever designs Nicole Lurie imagines now will need to level up exponentially, for the future.

I may have helped make a big baby by eating so many pork products and I may have staved off swine flu panic, but I hadn't helped out my blood pressure. Even medicated, it reached 150/98. Now, instead of 250 milligrams of Aldomet twice a day, my doctor wanted me to increase it to three times a day. She asked me how my boots fit. I told her that's why I wear cowboy boots. If I couldn't get them off, I would know that I had pre-eclampsia. I would need to get to the hospital fast before I or the baby died of HELLP syndrome. I looked at my boots and regretted the possibility that someone might have to cut them from my feet.

My doctor scheduled me for another ultrasound to measure the size of the baby. I couldn't tell if the doctor was worried or was reflecting my worry that labor would have to be induced to get my high blood pressure down. Two weeks until I'm thirty-two-and-a-half weeks pregnant—the week-gestation Zoë was born. I kept thinking I needed to get to that point but really, I needed to get so much farther. Eight weeks farther, in the human gestation plan. But I liked to give myself a window. Somewhere between five to nine weeks from now would be considered full term. I'm rooting for five. If this baby was anywhere near as big as Zoë was when she was eight weeks early, there's no way he'll be anything less than ten pounds at forty weeks.

But I felt contractions. At thirty-one weeks. I drank a glass of wine to mellow out the muscles and mitigate the bacon. I tried to go to bed and relax but I kept losing track of the contractions. More than six per hour and I was supposed to go in to the hospital. The hospital. A roach motel. Once you go in, you contract the swine flu or MRSA or *Clostridium difficile* and don't come out. I couldn't spend the rest of the semester on bed rest. I finally gave up counting and tried to breathe. Perhaps if what felt like a hundred-pound weight, the weight of a small pig, would get off my chest, I could breathe. If I could breathe, the contractions would stop. I turned to one side, then the other. I could hear Zoë cough in the other room. I thought *pneumonia* and got up to give her a breathing treatment. She fell back asleep. My contractions stopped but I felt cold. I lay there and thought of Zoë and this new baby, thirty years from now, standing on the edge of the Pacific Ocean whose shore edge is Sacramento. I thought about how there would be no fish left in the wine-dark sea. The sea would be the color of wine, all day. The oil drums piled up on the shore and the tar stuck to the beach sand sticks to their feet. They would have to laugh at the idea of polar bears. White bears? How can they camouflage against all this green? I wondered, what would there be for them to eat? For us? Perhaps in those big warehouses that line the beach, they still grow pigs like they used to at the turn of the twenty-first century. I hoped so. I still feel sorry for the pigs but the seaweed that my children are standing on isn't fit to eat.

Bacon on the Mormon Trail was necessary for survival. Flour, beans, and bacon. Would the pioneers have made it across five states without the energy bar that is the rasher of bacon? While packing for the trip, it might have seemed excessive and expensive. Heavy. Although think of all the things you can cook with the fat of bacon—beans, potatoes, dandelion greens. Bacon is doubly useful. Oil and meat. Salt and smoke. Calorie and flavor. Perhaps a love of bacon could be in the DNA of descendants of Mormon pioneers.

The Mormons brought pigs with them on their trek from Missouri to Salt Lake. There were no wild boars to tame in Utah.

They were more likely to find pigweed than pigs in the Salt Lake Valley. The Mormons turned a general lack of pigs into an overabundance of them, like at Circle Four Farms, where thousands of pigs stand snout to tail in cages, waiting for slaughter. Should my kids take precedence over these pigs? Maybe the virus is whispering something like "*no.*"

China made it to stage one trials for a vaccine for SARS CoV-2 by mid-March of 2020. That is very fast. Merely ten weeks after the virus's DNA had been sequenced. While the work toward developing a virus moves quickly, stage two trials require human volunteers. There are many vaccines—some might really want to be a guinea pig. Some people say they'll never permit anyone to inject them with a vaccine even in its later stages. If most people don't get the vaccine, herd immunity can't happen. Those who can't get the vaccine, like the immunocompromised or people recently recovering from chemotherapy, would still be at risk. The virus could mutate and the vaccine could have been all for naught.

My doctor says she and three other families have invested in a pig. It was going to be slaughtered that very day.

"Are you sad for the pig?"

"Not really. It had a great life. It ate good food. It was warm in the winter. We smartly didn't name it. A1 is what he's called. I wasn't going to get the bacon, because of that study about nitrates being nearly as bad as smoking. But then I read that as long as you eat some dark leafy greens, eating nitrates is not as bad as smoking a cigarette."

"So you got the bacon?"

"I haven't had bacon in so long. Any pork. The way they raise it. So many antibiotics. We have such a problem in the hospital with MRSA—some infections are just not responding to any antibiotics. There's a new kind of antibiotic-resistant infection going around in Georgia. Not even in the hospital. Right near a big industrial pig farm where they use so many antibiotics on the pigs."

"Poor pigs," I say.

"Poor us," my doctor says.

I am jealous of her antibiotic-free pork. That's the kind of pork that will keep viruses and zombies and the apocalypse away. At least that's what I'd like to believe.

A pork belly, not so jiggly when refrigerated, has a skin that must be peeled like a tongue. It has pink and white stripes like an exhausted candy cane. Usually butchered into squares, the belly has transformed from fat repulsion in the human to delectable challenge for the at-home charcuterie artists.

The recipe, if you can get pork belly, is simple: dry cure the pork belly with salt, brown sugar, and sodium nitrate. Unlike the pioneers, who cured without refrigeration, and whose intestines sometimes suffered for it, refrigerate your pork for one week. If you have a smoker, you can add applewood and cold-smoke it. To cold-smoke means to not let the smoke reach above 150 degrees. Building your own cold-smoker out of a metal garbage can should be easy. Take your regular smoker, heat it up as you normally would, and then connect a hose from that smoker to the garbage can. Install a grate for the belly to rest upon. Connecting the hose from the top of the Little Chief smoker to the bottom of the garbage can, now with grate, is the hard part. Don't be afraid to use tools to cut a hole in the tin of the can. My own bacon. Finally, I am free of the grocery store although now bound even more tightly to my pig-procuring and baby-delivering doctor.

The pig, naturally, does not want to go toward his own death just to make bacon for me. I did not, naturally, expect to get pregnant again. I did expect to go into labor early and dangerously. I did, naturally, feel sorry for the pig. I understand that the swine flu microbes just naturally want to percolate in my body, perpetuate and procreate themselves. I understand that the pig has no intention here. If he could, he'd roam the forest freely, looking for truffles. I understand that if I could, I would roam the forest looking for truffles. I understand that to the truffle we are the swine flu. Volition. The body wants to go forward. I feel badly for loving the pig at the very moment I'm eating bacon but it is a human's best skill—holding two opposing forces in the mind simultaneously. F. Scott Fitzgerald thought it a sign of good intelligence and it does seem like a good and a bad thing simultaneously to me—that human mind, it's so big and oxymoronic. It lies to itself but it also believes there is such a thing as verifiable reality.

At the second height of the COVID-19 pandemic, most people believed that the virus was a real thing, even if they couldn't see it. Other people believed that it was a conspiracy theory trying to take away their God-given right to drink at the bar. Other people just didn't know anyone who had gotten sick, so they thought themselves immune. The leap you have to take to believe in the science of the unseeable is a leap we take every day. Very few people eat raw pork, having heard of trichinosis. Dr. Nicole Lurie et al. would ask you to please heat your virus to at least 160 degrees Fahrenheit before inhaling.

It's a wild world that makes me yearn for technologies that help nature move along. IVF and carbon scrubbers. Vaccines and Pitocin. Albuterol and surfactant. Reproduction assistance. Respiration assistance.

And yet, I look to the trees and think: scrub this carbon like a better-built machine.

I look to the pigs and I say: come hither. Stay away.

I look to the permafrost and say: permafrost is an oxymoron.

I can never tell if I'm living in the best time or the worst time. It's that kind of indecision that lets you go ahead and reproduce, with assistance or without.

At thirty-nine weeks pregnant, close enough to the usual forty that there was no fear for the baby's well-being, the doctor decides my blood pressure has been too high long enough. That night I would go to the hospital to be induced. Instead of my talisman of bacon, I try to recreate the fancy cauliflower soup from the Tinderbox restaurant. I must not have sieved the cauliflower through a tamis enough because the soup is grainy. The blue cheese is harsh. I use the wrong kind of nuts. I think, I should have made bacon soup. My mom isn't in Flagstaff. Who will bring me Arby's as she did when Zoë was born?

I resist cooking up some bacon to garnish the top. Without the bacon, there's not enough salt, I worry.

We sit down to eat. I'm not at all excited to eat soup and then go to the hospital to be induced. I want to stay home. I want to have this baby naturally. Actually, I'd like this baby to stay inside me forever where he is safe from everything except for viruses and microorganisms and high blood pressure and worry.

My mother-in-law, who is staying with us to help with the new baby, passes the salt to me. "Did you ever think you'd have a baby in Flagstaff?"

"I was looking forward to avoiding doctors for a while." I pass the salt cellar back to El, who loves salt even more than I do. "You're lucky you have low blood pressure." I'm still missing the bacon.

"As soon as we moved to Flag, my blood pressure skyrocketed because of the elevation," I confess to my mother-in-law. Erik and his mom have low blood pressure. They can eat bacon without guilt—although his mom doesn't. She is a vegetarian.

"The doctor took me off the pill since birth control pills can make your blood pressure even higher."

Sometimes, two thoughts in your head at the same time is too much.

"I guess a high-elevation Flagstaff baby was the only second baby we were going to have," I say.

Having a baby at full gestation rather than prematurely like Zoë, at whatever elevation, is the way to go. As if you have a choice. As if nature didn't say, "Baby, be born naturally, unless. Except. Some other time. With Pitocin. With steroids. With forceps." Nature has a lot of opinions about what was natural. But this natural was particularly natural because I didn't have to be connected to the NICU. I could give birth in the same room I'd been induced in. I could watch TV. Erik put *Survivor Man* on his laptop and I watched episode after episode. I loved that he could make a snare using dental floss, a tent out of a canoe, an oar out of a branch and a found mudflap. He could take on zombies and viruses with a piece of bark and a clamshell.

Unlike Zoë's birth, which was full of head-spinning frenzy, Max's was full of body spinning. The baby moving down the vaginal canal felt like a snake eating a rabbit, like pushing toothpaste through a tube or frosting through a pastry bag, like a mouse collapsing his head to fit under a bedroom door. My body shook like it was trying to bounce him out of there. Eight and a half pounds. Almost twice as big as Zoë and about seventy times as painful. Bigger is better everywhere but in the vaginal canal. But God, how I loved the way he breathed right off the bat. On his own. Like breathing was more than luck but something you could actually rely on. Breath: a meaty substance.

ON ANGER

I LIKE TO IMAGINE AS I lie in bed, trying to sleep, listening out the ground floor window, that I can hear the almost-silent footsteps of a mountain lion. I like to think of his stealth. The way he's creeping by and not a single dog barks, no squirrels twitter. His heart beats so strong it signals to all the other animals to stay quiet. Only a thin piece of glass, some 1977 wood siding, and a sheet of drywall separate me from his massive muscles. He could, if he wanted, lunge at the window. He might, since there's a crack in the bottom right corner, break through. If he held a grudge, or had enough hunger, he could bust past the barrier. I think of his teeth in the back of my neck, of him pulling me through the window like I'm a broken gazelle. Why doesn't he do it? Isn't this his territory at stake?

The cougar's disappearing territory must have happened so quickly, the cougar barely noticed. Forests and plains replaced by human structures. First the train station. Then the general store. A few ranches. That's when the shots started coming. Then a couple thousand houses. That's when the food started going. One day, the cougar looked around. As far as he could see, he was the only cougar left.

Compared to the cougar, I have no right to be angry at anyone, ever. The humans won. This land is my land. And so is this land and so is that land. And yet here I am in the parking lot of my daughter's school at the daily drop-off. The daily drop-off.

How did I get here? Why is my daughter five years old already? Why does kindergarten start so early (both so young and so in the morning)? There is a line. There is always a line of Ford Tahoes and Chevy Suburbans, justified, I guess, because it snows here. In Utah, Suburbans signal big families, Mormons, mastery over the desert. Here, they mean the highest spot in Arizona. The anti-desert. The snow land. And yet, they drive Suburbans in Utah the same way they drive Suburbans in Arizona. They turn from the right lane as I wait in the left in front of my Honda. They stop the car, get out of the car to open the door for the kids, which backs up the line of idling cars all the way out of the parking lot, half a mile down the road to the car wash.

Although no one in Flagstaff seems to notice, there is a nationwide campaign to try to convince people to turn off their cars while they wait. Fifteen minutes of idling a gas-burning sedan produces 92 grams of carbon monoxide, 1.55 grams nitrogen dioxide, and 5 grams volatile organic compounds. Since grams seem small, this may not seem like a lot but if you consider SUVs' contribution to the climate crisis, they each deliver 121.8 grams of carbon monoxide, 1.85 grams nitrogen dioxide, and 7.68 grams volatile organic compounds. Just like the hordes of humans that crossed the plains and settled the West, it's the accumulation of these numbers that make the difference. Ten cars in the school line. Twenty cars. One hundred cars. Two hundred and twenty-three cars every morning and every afternoon.

Tempers are a bit like idling. They emit gasses and energy that seem like they're doing nothing—until the molecules accumulate. They say developing lungs suffer particularly from these respiratory pollutants. They say children who grow up in volatile environments breathe in that volatility.

***

I try to keep an even keel but Zoë's in the car with me and I'm not quite yelling at the cars in front of me. But the poor kid is buckled into her booster seat, trapped. Zoë will have to listen to me complain.

I finally pull forward and let Zoë off. I don't open the door for her. She's five. She can get out of the car by herself. I don't wait, though I want to, to see her make it into the school, because other people are waiting and I am a considerate human, except, like all humans, to the cougar. I signal to move back into traffic. The Suburban behind me ignores my signal, rushes past me, slides in front of me, and then stops. I slam on my brakes. I scream motherfucking asshole, which no one can hear through my layer of glass and their layer of glass. I see the Suburban's bumper sticker reads Obama equals hammer and sickle. I press on the gas. I am about to ram their bumper, mangle that sticker. Old, 1984 Suburban. Not even worth the wrecking. I wonder if they somehow think that the rich people they're voting for will buy them a new car. I wish I could go into politics, but I'm afraid I would punch people. Which is, I guess, not really governing. Although perhaps it's a kind of governing. I stop myself. Brake hard, again.

I wave my hands and scream, "Do you even know what socialism is? Is it the grave sin of letting someone merge in front of you?!"

Well, it comes out, "motherfucking fucking mother," but in my head, I make full sentences.

I should make my daughter take the bus, but she is five. I should weigh the anxiety I would have about her taking the bus alone against the anger that I have against the gas-guzzling monstrosities. I think she would prefer I stay home and try to maintain my blood pressure. But I like to go out into the wilderness of the drop-off line. I feel like I'm working on my anger management. For instance, I do not actually ram the Suburban with my own car.

It's not so far-fetched, imagining this cougar in the backyard. There has been a report of one in the Cherry Hill neighborhood, near downtown Flagstaff. The mountain lion was found one morning napping on a front porch. Napping seems too relaxed of a term. He must have been nervous. He knows our kind, right? The human, especially the western settler. The shotgun and the porch go together. That deep sleep is for those on the inside, behind the glass. Cougar. If you see glass, it had better be the zoo kind, because otherwise it means car or truck or house and that means the people will be scared, even angry, that you are in what they now call their backyard. You might try to make your case, that once this was your territory. But the fact of the gun will prove your argument wrong. This land is their land. Ours.

I am so tired of scrubbing this fake wood laminate countertop. I just wiped it down last night. I wiped it down today after breakfast. Now, I'm scrubbing it with Comet. For the moment, all I want in the universe is to not have to wipe it down again after lunch.

I think of the food in the fridge I could make for lunch. Quesadillas. Grilled cheese. Salad. Maintenance cooking is not the same as fancy cooking. Maintenance cooking is the same as vacuuming or matching socks or filling out a form. Put cheese (tab b) into white carb (slot a).

But Erik comes in from Sherwin-Williams where he bought more paint for the living room, carrying Max and the paint in one arm and nothing in the other.

"I thought you were getting lunch."

"I called. I didn't know what you wanted. I wasn't about to get McDonald's."

"So you brought home nothing? We don't have any food."

This is the bit of melodrama that probably sets off the little bombs in my head, which, unfortunately, make their way out of my mouth. I cannot stop them. "I cook every meal. Breakfast, lunch, dinner. Do you know how many times a week I scrub down this counter? And while you've been painting that god-damn room for two months, I've been cooking and cleaning and watching the kids with no help from you while you paint paint paint. And when you're done, you're done! I'm never done. I will still be cleaning this fucking countertop today and tomorrow and next week and the least you could do is once in awhile bring home lunch."

You would think a rant would be seen for what it is. A blowing off. An uncapped geyser that, once let loose, could go back to simmer.

But Erik is tired of painting and this rant isn't new.

"You go paint. You go paint and finish that room and I will cook and clean for the next year."

He didn't explode, but his voice was thin as a razor.

He went and got the brush. He handed it to me. "Go paint."

I didn't have any choice except to take the brush. I took it sobbing. Erik doesn't sob.

"You're going to do this, in front of the kids?" I asked him.

"Go paint," he said. His voice did not waver.

I tried to paint. He had left off cutting-in the stairs. My hands shook. With the first stroke, I touched the floor. I went into the kitchen to get a paper towel. Still sobbing, I saw he was making the kids tater tots. Perhaps there is a division of labor for a reason. Or, perhaps tater tots are delicious and not as bad as McDonald's.

Little bombs produce vapors. Paint produces volatile organic compounds. McDonald's produces methane emissions by cutting down the Amazonian rainforest to raise cattle for their burgers. The cattle produce CO_2 by kicking up the once rain-fed soil. Tater tots emit delicious smells and probably toxic chemicals. Toxic chemicals like Comet emit even more toxic chemicals. Sobs emit tears? What are the good things human industry emits? Clean counters? Well-painted walls? Grilled cheese?

Still, the argument with Erik was a political point. I did cook and clean more than he did. It didn't make it right just because I am a terrible painter. These battle lines seem so clear when the veins are pulsing. I made it halfway along a riser in the staircase before I gave up. The old brown paint, still lining the stairs, mocked my attempts at precision. Cooking forgives in a way painting does not.

Erik came in, gave me some advice. His voice calm and forgiving. "Just go slow." I wanted to throw the brush at him. I wanted to reach up on his newly scraped, newly drywalled, newly mudded, newly painted perfectly white ceiling and streak a fat, dripping line of "Netsuke"-colored paint across it. But I didn't. I redoubled my anger. Who was he to watch me fail? I handed him the brush and grabbed my car keys. I wanted Erik to think I was not coming back. I wanted him to think just how wrong he was to say "paint" in hate. I wanted him to yell, "I'm sorry, don't go," as I screeched out of the driveway, but he didn't try to stop me. That's where being so mad will get you: driving around alone, going to Target, wasting gas, wondering when you can come home, when your family will forget you've made a scene by storming out.

At least you have somewhere to go, you console yourself.

At least you have somewhere to go back.

A woman whom I have just met and am trying to befriend, Tutie, lives in Oak Creek Canyon. She has two boys and bought some property right by the river before the housing bubble burst and now instead of a would-be four-bedroom house built by her husband, she lives in a two-bedroom trailer where one of the bedrooms is dedicated to her husband's guitars.

She invites me and two other friends and their kids to play in her yard that is just out of sight of the creek that trickles through rocks made of limestone, sandstone, and basalt. Tutie serves the kids pizza and serves the adults the one luxury she allows herself—expensive cheese. This is an aged Gouda that I also love. We aren't friends yet. I just barely put her phone number in my phone. I still think one of her kids, Jack, is the other woman, Mary Ellen's, son. But we both like fancy cheese. This, I think, is a good start.

She tells us about this mountain lion that her parents saw on their porch. Probably not the same porch-loving mountain lion that was found porch-loving up in Cherry Hill. Two mountain lions! This makes me happy to imagine. It also makes me start talking about other good animal stories like the one about the polar bear who swam for nine days looking for an ice floe. At least that polar bear survived, unlike its cub, which drowned. "Fucking global warming," I say.

"The planet has always been warming up and cooling down," Tutie reminds me.

"Well, true, but not at this rate. Never have any ice-core samples shown such a rapid rise. It's definitely anthropogenic."

"It's not human-caused. It's a government setup to make you try and sell your car at a low rate. Do you know what's bad? It's the cloud-seeding. The government. They seed clouds with aluminum. Chem trails. Aluminum everywhere. That's why kids have autism. That's why I've got these headaches. And, do you know the FDA oversees our food more than the USDA? The USDA knows about chemicals and local farming. The FDA knows about drugs and how 'low-risk' means 'no risk.' The FDA doesn't even consider aluminum in our food a danger."

It takes everything I have not to let the little bombs in my head explode when she calls the global warming threat a government conspiracy. I try to channel restraint. I think of the cougar, walking by my window at night, every muscle tensed, but not pouncing.

I say, "Then that should be your job. To make sure the FDA and the USDA are separate entities always." Instead of walking out. Instead of freaking out. I try and stay in the conversation. Find an action plan she and I can agree on. I try to find some common ground, but inside my head, I'm exploding little right-wing bombs. I'm hoping that nodding and listening about the chem trails doesn't give me a stroke. I want to ask her more about the cougar. Had she seen it again? What would she do if she did see it? But I'm afraid her answer will be "shoot it." I don't think I could keep it together for that.

If I were a cougar, I'd be pissed. Mountain lion, puma, cougar, ghost lion. These are American cats and were in Flagstaff before the Anasazi. Once, in Provo, Utah, I went to argue for a law that would prohibit treeing cougars with dogs. Three of us were there to argue that Fish and Wildlife support the passage of the law. Everyone else, about a hundred men in baseball caps, swapped treed-cougar stories and offered discounts for ATV trips into the backwoods to look for the remaining cougars. They have their reasons: in the foothills, where the hills are the same color as cougar fur, mountain lions are spotted frequently. Sometimes the mountain lions attack. Not humans, but, you know, dogs. Not the dogs that would tree them, but small dogs.

When, and if, a mountain lion kills a dog or a cow grazing on public lands, the men climb with their guns and dogs onto the seats of their ATVs to save humanity from these monsters. The monsters look back at the humans and say, but there are so many of you and so few of us. Maybe they would say that. But maybe that's why they lose. They can't band together. They can't say to each other, what the fuck? We should get together and take those humans down. Anger, when it strikes randomly and individually, only scares and leads to your own demise. It changes nothing.

If fear of what you can see allows you to destroy a species, the cougar hunters make good progress. Eventually, the cougars will be as invisible as climate change, as a virus, as Black and Indigenous people's lives. If you can't see them, they aren't scary. I worry though. Zoë ran smack-dab into her grandma's extra-clean window. She didn't break anything but her nose hurt badly for a couple of days.

I try not to eat white-bread-type stuff but I have a lot of vegetarian friends. So I make pasta. Except all my pasta recipes have meat in them. So I make a vegetarian version and a meat version. For instance, cauliflower, pancetta, ricotta salata pasta becomes cauliflower pasta with ricotta salata. Broccoli rabe and sausage pasta becomes broccoli pasta. I add more salt. It's not quite the same thing.

Sometimes the life we're living and the life we think we are living are not the same thing. If I were truly an environmentalist, I would give up meat. But I'm obviously not. I'm a realist, maybe. A study just came out that said only three percent of the study participants were willing to try veganism. Ten percent were willing to try cannibalism.

Eating meat is so ingrained in so many families' lifestyles. Change what you eat and you might change how you fit in with your family—or if you fit in with them at all. My sisters and mom, sometimes we eat fish when we're together, sometimes pasta. But when my mom wants us to have a big night together, she sends one of us to Costco with a hundred-dollar bill to buy too-big steaks.

I try to exchange my meat-eating with other planet-conscious savings. I think of it as my own personal cap and trade program. I sometimes eat beef so I buy most of my clothes at thrift stores. I eat beef, so I drive less. I put solar panels on my house. I buy recycled plastic shampoo and conditioner. I don't buy plastic anything much at all. I do have whole days of vegetarianism. On those days, those hot nights, I let the air-conditioner run all night.

During times of crisis, we live at so many levels simultaneously: The crying level. The making quesadillas for the kids level. The staring off into space, trying to figure out what to do level. The paying the bills level. The worrying about paying the bills level. The dream level. The wondering if you should go to the hospital level. The what-could-be level. The level that has to turn off the TV because you can't see another video of a person being shot. The I don't think animals should die for my dinner level. The I really really want a steak right now level. Perhaps this is what is wrong with humans. Maybe the capacity to imagine too many things simultaneously forces us to give up fighting, give in to what comes easily.

Maybe I'm just a sensualist. Or I lack willpower. Or I think the typing is more effective than the chewing. Either way, I make penne all'arrabbiata, angry penne. The chiles make it spicy. The bacon makes it not even vegetarian, let alone vegan. My mother-in-law, the vegetarian, says she can pick the bacon out but it's just one more pan to dirty. I don't mind making two versions. Love is always two pans. Anger, only one.

I get a call from my boss on Friday afternoon. He asks if we could meet for lunch. He wants to talk about pressures. I say sure and hang up. And then I call him back to see if the kind of pressures he is talking about are the kind I'd been worried about.

"Well, the pressures. I've met with the dean who met with the provost. You'll still direct the program. But your course load will increase."

"Without a raise?"

"You know the Arizona budget. So yes, without a raise."

"What else will I have to do?"

"Just more of the same. Teach one more class and direct the program."

"I have a list of stuff I need to do. Maybe you can send it to the dean. Maybe he'll see that I already work a lot."

"It isn't the dean. It's the provost. The board of regents. The tuition increase we wanted to ask for isn't going to come back to the university. The regents will collect and distribute as they see fit. They say we can't use our reserves like we'd planned."

"But my list. There are twenty-seven items. Twenty-seven things to do today not including teaching, advising, and researching."

"You know you're important to us. You're appreciated. I care about you. I want to protect you. I just don't know if I can."

I felt exposed. Out in the wilderness without recourse. But I should shut up. At least I have a job, I tell myself. There are no other jobs like this—so good, I am so lucky, truly privileged to teach for a living—for me to quit in a firestorm of anger. Academia is a bloom-where-you're-planted kind of industry. But this bloom edict elides the fact that some growing zones aren't good for any kind of plants at all. They have me trapped. I can gnaw my leg off and leave, but then I'll just be jobless and footless and wandering the forest without even the pretense of protection. At least my boss provides a pretense.

We don't have a union. I can't fight this. The only fight is flight and there is nowhere to go.

I feel closer to protesters in Wisconsin who are pushing to keep their collective bargaining rights. If I had a collective. If I had something to bargain with. The Wisconsin governor claims he's not union-busting but without the option to bargain collectively, the teachers' and sanitation workers' unions become Kiwanis clubs. Public workers have protested for two weeks, sleeping in the capitol rotunda. On Facebook, friends were posting the phone number of Ian's Pizza so you could call in food to be delivered to the protesters.

It was late in the night on Tuesday when the Wisconsin Republican senators stripped the bill of the parts that required a quorum and then sped it through the house. The governor signed it before the Democrats booked their plane tickets to make their vote.

Ousted from the rotunda, the Democrats retreated. Maybe anger, combined, amassed, struck out, communicated, changes nothing either. I add to my work to-do list items twenty-eight through forty-two. Again I tell myself, at least I have a job.

But the occupiers bided their time. Their resilience is paying off. The recall effort against the governor swelled to six hundred thousand petitioners. Walker is confident he'll win a recall election, but six hundred thousand people is a lot of Wisconsinites. Accumulation can be a good thing, when it comes to people rising up, even if it's not such a good thing when it's CO_2 on the rise.

Numbers are how we measure but they don't make it easy to see. The number of humans protesting doesn't always make the news. The carbon dioxide bubbling up from the tailpipes as we idle our cars is invisible. The fights and the apologies, as long as they're even, cancel each other out. Who remembers who said what how many times?

In 2008, when Bill McKibben started his 350.org organization, he hoped to keep the carbon in the atmosphere to a safe 350 parts per million. Now, that number has reached 417 parts per million. The parts per million translate to a tiny two degrees Celsius, but that number may cause the death of millions of people. Already, over a billion animals have died by the Australian bushfires fueled by climate change.

Little numbers can be more disturbing than big ones. They counted down the number of eastern cougars left in the US until there was only one: the last known cougar was killed in Maine in 1938. Biologists performed extensive research over the past five years to document if there is any breeding population of cougar left anywhere east of the Mississippi River. They discovered none. Thirty years after the last cougar was killed, the species was declared extinct. Sometimes, it's harder to swallow zero than a billion.

I don't think Erik and I would fight if we didn't think about how long we might have to tolerate each other's annoying habits. If he was just visiting, I wouldn't be mad he didn't bring McDonald's. If I didn't live here, he wouldn't hold his painting skills against me.

My friend Beya said, if she had to plan a life where she'd have to hunker down in quarantine she would pick this place, Flagstaff. She'd pick her husband and her kids, she'd pick her friends and community. Would she pick the job she has? Probably not. But no one thinks their current job is the one they'll always have, which is how you survive the job. You imagine a different one. That same technique is contraindicated for marriage.

But the fights always end.

After a reasonable amount of time, Erik comes over to me.

He stands in front of me and crosses his arms and huffs, "Don't make me make you laugh."

Which is some version of "you're cute when you're mad," which I shouldn't accept as an apology but I do. Not that he necessarily needs to apologize. Not that I do.

"You shouldn't get so mad."

I have to say to him, "But I do. I really do. You're the only one who will fight with me."

It's not the fighting that's the problem. It's the fighting in my head, all alone. Without Erik, all the bombs in my head would have exploded by now, which is, I think, another phrase for aneurysm. I should thank him for saving my life.

"Come on. Let's put the kids to bed." A battle of its own, sometimes, but at least one we fight together. In the darkness of the kids' room, we sit on the bed, holding hands neither of us can see.

If I were an eastern cougar, I'd be pissed, but I'd also be extinct, so it wouldn't matter. They believe that the last eastern cougar may have been killed as long ago as 1933. No wonder they call it the ghost cat.

I imagine the cougar in my backyard heading back east through midwestern towns that have been abandoned for lack of work. Reports of cougar sightings have come from Wisconsin, Minnesota, Kansas. I imagine the cougar walking across what were once unmeasured seas of wild grass and are now acres of wheat. Perhaps the cougar hides his wheat-colored fur in the folds of a hill. Perhaps the cougar lurks in the white pines in Michigan. Between the ferns of the Adirondacks. On the banks of Hudson Bay.

Those occasional sightings easterners claim might not be ghosts. Western cougars are making their way east across the country in the opposite direction the humans migrated across the country. As small towns of the Midwest become emptied out of people and natural grasses, natural prey for the cougar returns. Perhaps their kind of restraint makes its own kind of progress. Not so much organized and not so much anger, but perhaps, with wandering steps and slow, a kind of calm and collected, bided time.

Somewhere in New Jersey, a cougar passes through a backyard at night. He can see inside through the windows. The kitchen emits its light. The dining room emits its light. The dishwasher runs, emitting a swooshing sound. A woman is making something that smells delicious, maybe even something the cougar would eat: elk or deer or even rabbit. But then, everything probably smells delicious to an always-on-the-move, down-to-eating-squirrels animal. The cougar watches the woman on the other side of the glass. She has stopped to listen—to what? Can she hear anything over the dishwasher? Whatever she hears, something makes her look through the window. She thinks she catches a glimpse of something outside.

She looks and, although she mostly only sees her own reflection, yellow eyes flare in the space in the window where her brown eyes would normally be.

A cougar was spotted in the suburbs of North Chicago. This sighting was confirmed because someone shot the cougar. But this one cougar couldn't take on the whole of Chicago—he probably didn't even want to. He's just as surprised to have wandered into the Midwest as the Chicagoans were to see him. His wandering wasn't just for territory, just for food. The cougar walked so far, as far back as the Mormons went ahead, looking for someone to join forces with, another cougar to confirm his own existence. If cougars could talk, they could organize. They wouldn't have to fight alone. Maybe we humans and they could even come to an agreement, settle on a deal, give them a territory of their own. Perhaps Wisconsin will become available.

But perhaps they are winning in their own way. Unlike the other big cats across the world, the cougars' numbers aren't shrinking. You can find them in every part of the Americas. Perhaps, even without strong rhetorical skills and legislative districts, they've found a way to not only survive, but thrive. They ignore us, for the most part, and therefore win their shared, invisible territory. Their dimension is the night, the vacation home, the emptied pueblos of the Sinagua Indians. They seem to have pushed the bounds of physics, claimed the only boundaries to exist are those formed by light. In the dark, they have found a silent way to say, we can all live here.

I don't know if that is true, but I'd like to think it's possible just like I like to imagine the cougar outside my window, occupying invisible ground, breathing invisible air. Erik lies next to me, breathing the same air. We're all breathing the same recycled air as the Sinagua Indians breathed. The cougars seem to be onto this, which gives them a calm, patient kind of power.

AN UNKINDNESS
OF RAVENS

"I'M GOING TO KILL HIM," Erik says. This seems like a normal response to finding out someone molested a little kid at the day care where your son goes every day.

"Don't kill anybody," I say, which also seems like a normal, if predictable, response to say to someone who claims he's going to kill anyone. But I envy Erik a little. He knows which side of good he's on. I am never all that sure.

I had just gotten off the phone with a woman named Andrea, the mother of a kid who goes to the same school as my son Max. I already knew what the phone call would be the second I opened the email that asked me to call her.

I knew what she would say as if I had always known it. In my bones. In the past. Wisdom is nostalgia for the dream that you can predict the future.

I let her tell me anyway. "This is so hard to tell you. Someone, a little girl, was molested by Melinda's son." It is my job to say it's okay, even when it's not. I don't say okay to mean it's natural. I say okay to mean, don't kill Melinda's son.

"Max is okay," I tell Erik.

I know Max is okay, I tell myself. He is okay. He's the same kid now as he was before day care—kind of stubborn, a little bit yelly. He's no more clingy, no more scared of strangers, no more likely to rub his penis against the couch. And, even if something happened, which it didn't, I'm almost sure, I don't know that it necessarily justifies the killing of someone. I don't think it's okay. I don't mean to minimize, but even if something happened, Max would be okay. Okay. Normal. Fine.

Except, I say to no one, why am I always the one balancing equations, seeking to find the median, the middle ground, the status quo? Can't I just let a bad thing be bad?

*

Ravens are scavengers. Incredibly smart scavengers that will gather keys and glass and marbles in their nests but scavengers nonetheless. They eat already-dead things. So what was this raven doing, attacking this live mourning dove in the middle of the road? Ravens aren't killers. I needed to intervene. This isn't how it works. I ran up to the raven, tried to scare him to fly off. He bounced a couple of feet away but didn't fly off. The dove hopped around in circles. Maybe he was sick and the raven knew it. A preemptory scavenge. The prediction of a short future. Darwin's natural selector.

But maybe he just sensed weakness. Doves aren't so smart. They collect nothing. Perhaps ravens do attack and kill. The idea that ravens only scavenge is only a dream I had about intelligent creatures and their unwillingness to hurt other living things. Perhaps I am wrong about everything.

*

The district attorney held a meeting. Social services, victims' advocates, Flagstaff PD, attorneys in the juvenile system, and attorneys for the rest of the system. Andrea wanted to know what went wrong. I bit my tongue. What went wrong? Don't you watch *Law & Order: Special Victims Unit*? This happens everywhere, every day. I understand the outrage, but not the surprise.

One of the kids' moms said, "I work at an elementary school. This would never happen in public school systems." I thought of public schools—closets, empty classrooms, bleachers, offices, bathrooms. Such great places for pulling down a girl's pants. Almost as easy as at your mom's bathroom, in her day care, while the other kids played innocently outside the closed door. Or, perhaps not so innocently. My thoughts are bad thoughts. I can think the worst of anyone. I wonder when the good kid shifts to bad. Or, rather, when the kid does the thing he wants regardless of its goodness or badness. When he does what he wants and want pervades like scavengers at roadkill. How pervasive do these things become? Did normal shift to the new normal? Will Max, when he's sixteen, think, this is what five-year-old girls are good for? Opportunities to talk to five-year-olds exist everywhere. Sixteen-year-old boys—natural opportunists?

I think about Clay, the sixteen-year-old boy who molested a girl at my son's day care. Possibly when my son was right there. In the other room. Even Erik, who does a much better job than I do drawing boundaries between right and wrong, wonders if something similar happened to Clay. What sixteen-year-old kid does think that it's okay to pull down a five-year-old's underpants? To put his fingers inside her? When was he insided out? You've spent so much time thinking it happens to little girls. Don't let yourself think about what might happen to little boys. What happened to Clay when he was five? Never-ending chain?

*

As soon as I leave the dove and walk back to the house, the raven returns. I only watch out of the corner of my eye. Is he pecking him to death? Is his beak strong enough to crack his throat? It must be. The dove's head looks limp, tilted upward, skyward, ravenward. The dove seems as confused as I am.

Box, my cat, who wasn't afraid of anything, was afraid of ravens. In Salt Lake, he took on raccoons and once a fox. In Grand Rapids, owls and skunks. But in Flagstaff, where the ravens are twice as big as my head, Box wouldn't go outside. He turned himself from an outdoor cat to an indoor one. When he was dying, he lay looking out the window. The sight of a raven startled him. The number of ravens flying into the yard doubled, then tripled. Before Box died, the backyard turned black with wings.

*

Inured. It's one letter removed from injured. What amount of suffering removes a *J*? My mother uses the word *diddled*. A word that, inured as I may be, still makes me cringe. What can you get used to? Incorporate first natural things into your nest: grass, feathers, sticks. Then, ribbons, hair pulled from a hairbrush, marbles, baubles. Pretty soon, your nest is as normal as the next, just heavier. Thick.

Ravens are a lot like people. Adaptable. You can hear the worst news. You can live through a famine, a pestilence, climate change. You can see videos of murders by police and a little boy handcuffed to a chair. You can see hundreds of children in cages in towns you've driven through and still go on. Ravens and humans. Nothing they can't get used to.

*

Ravens are scavengers. They'll eat anything. That doesn't mean if you invited them over for a dinner party, you wouldn't plan a meal. What would you cook for a company of raven? What do scavengers prefer? Not eggs, I imagine. Not chicken or turkey. Not that they wouldn't be cannibalistic, just that it wouldn't be the best. Stroganoff would be too rich and minestrone would be too messy. For the ravens, I think I would make spaghetti. Maybe with Bolognese. Brown the hamburger (small bits of meat tiny enough to fit in their beaks). Add onions (they're not dogs. They're not allergic). Add carrots and celery (we all like flavor). And tomatoes. Put up during the last days of summer. Are the ravens worth home-canned tomatoes? Are any of us?

*

I don't mean to empathize with my son's day care provider and mother of a child-molester, Melinda. I don't mean to think about what her neighbors are saying. I don't mean to imagine what horrific conversations happen at her dinner table. I don't mean to feel badly for her when I imagine the police coming to her door, arresting her for failure to report, for child endangerment. I don't mean to forgive her. She moved the day care out of her house, next door, to her dad's house. She claimed her father wasn't feeling well. Who was feeling well, in that family, at that time? She thought she was keeping the kids out of harm's way. Except one of the dads remembers Clay lounging on the couch one post-incident afternoon. The dad didn't know about the incident then. He just thought he was a normal boy, lying normally upon the couch, where normal boys normally lie and normal parents like to know where their children are, lying on the couch, normally.

But perhaps a normal person, a person who wasn't Melinda, might have made an excuse to close up the day care. "My father is ill. He needs my help," was the excuse she gave to move next door. Such an illness would have also worked to say, "I'm sorry, you'll have to find another place to take your child." But finding a day care for a one-year-old in Flagstaff was nearly impossible. Hers was one of the only places that would take babies. She felt for us. She was doing us a favor.

Late at night, when I can't sleep, the wind whispers what I already know: "You should have quit your job. You should have quit your job." Even though my job is the reason we live in Flagstaff where the university offers no day care. You are on your own. You did what you could to vet her. Half the people in town claimed she was "the best." State licenses all look alike, don't they?

***

After Melinda and Clay told their neighbor, a counselor, what happened and asked her advice for what to do, their neighbor said: "You must go to the police." "You must close your day care," she said. "You must get your son into counseling," she said. Clay went into counseling but the neighbor noticed that the kids continued to be dropped off every day. Eventually, after seeking counseling herself for her nightmares, and then her insomnia, that neighbor called one of the kids in the day care's parents. Otherwise, none of the parents would know. The day care would still be running. The police say "alleged." The police say "moved next door." The police say "she wasn't truly licensed," which makes it our fault, I guess. When you don't have much choice, you don't look too hard at the license. Everyone else was leaving their kids with her. It must be okay.

In the exact same spot where the raven attacked the dove, a squirrel has died the natural way. Or rather, the common way— being hit by a car. A raven does his normal work of cleaning up the streets. The same raven, maybe, that killed the dove stands over the flat mat that was once a rounded squirrel. Ravens are so black, from eyeball to talon, that it's hard to tell them apart. This one was huge and brave. I drove toward it as it pecked at the open wound of the dead squirrel. It didn't seem like he was going to move but as I nudged the car nearer, he hopped away. In my rearview mirror, I could see the raven hadn't returned. Maybe it wasn't the same raven at all. Maybe all ravens are not the same.

*

Some people, I think my mother is one of them, believe all men have the capacity to rape, that all boys have the proclivity to molest. Sometimes, I'm in that camp. In some ways, it's easier to believe that. You're never surprised when you hear about how an uncle molested his niece, a neighbor boy, his sister, a father his daughter, a grandfather, etc. But when you think of individual people. My husband. My daughter. It doesn't compute. I could never consider any male in my family like that. But then, some dark part of me chides that "never." Never say never, my mother does say.

This is where I go wrong: acknowledging that it's common, recognizing that it happens all the time, that everyone is capable, normalizes it. It's so normal, it's almost natural. Goethe said, "There is no crime of which I cannot conceive myself guilty." Me and anyone else. The aberration becomes the norm and I'm painting the whole world with one wide, black-feathered brushstroke.

When I told my friend Okim, whose daughter had been in the same day care as my son, she asked all the normal questions. What happened? How did you find out? What is going to happen now? She didn't ask the questions that I couldn't answer. She can't say it (not her daughter not her daughter not her daughter) aloud. I can't say no for certain so she doesn't ask. She's not stupid. Only in not asking can it have not have happened. I could ask her, however, if she wanted me to keep her updated on news from the DA. Will they file charges, etc. No, she says. She doesn't want to know. She can't drive past her house anymore, even though it's on the way to the Grand Canyon, even though driving past is the only road toward the mountain peaks. I nodded my head. That seemed about right. If you can't get to wisdom the regular way, take a detour. Head south, head east. Avert your eyes. No one really needs to go north.

This is another place I go wrong: by facing it, throwing my body full tilt into it, it becomes a part of me. I can think these thoughts. I can picture the young girl in the bathroom. It lodges normal inside of me.

***

I love winter. I love to ski—cross-country more than down-hill, but both. I love to run in the cold. I can run faster than I can in the heat, which feels heavy and weighs me down. I like to take Max and Zoë sledding in the forest behind our house. We trudge up the hill. I hold on to the slippery sled. Max clambers on first. Zoë holds tight around his waist with her thighs. She steers. They fly. The dogs chase them to the bottom.

When we first moved to Flagstaff, it snowed 115 inches one weekend. It hasn't snowed that much since. Not even across the whole winter. I talked to the guy in line with me to pick up Zoë's prescription at Walgreen's. When I said, "Sure is cold out there," he said, "This isn't cold. When I moved here in 1970, negative forty-one degrees that next January. That's cold. It used to actually be cold here." I checked my phone. The weather read thirty-nine degrees. That's normal, I thought, for Flagstaff in January. I know that weather isn't climate but that weather is a good example. I thought I knew cold. Maybe I know nothing about winter.

*

How to cook a raven? It could not be delicious, all wing and bone. But say it's all you had. Say it's the apocalypse. You've eaten through all of your canned food. You've wet your finger with your tongue and pressed your finger into every empty cupboard, coming up empty for crumbs. You've eaten grass, leaves. You've even drunk powdered milk. A raven in a tree, a slingshot, and an aim only hunger provides and now there's a dead raven at your foot.

It's amazing how, during the quarantine, we got used to seeing no one. We got used to not going to restaurants. We got used to not driving. Used to eating beans. You even laid in a store of wheat berries. What is your limit? When, once you thought you'd reached your limit, did your limit become normal?

For the raven, I recommend barbecue. The residual feathers will burn off. The hollowed-out rib cage makes for easy rotisserie. Let the meat, what there is of it, roast until it's done. Like any normal meat, the bird will let you know when it's ready to be flipped to the other side.

*

Zoë, who never went to Melinda's day care (and yet, so what? She has left my sight before. She does go outside. To school. To public school. To bathrooms. Who am I to be confident about anything? Confidence is for people from families not prone to molestation, which, as far as I can tell, is almost none of them), asks me why I like birds so much. Why I like hawks and eagles. Because they're rare, I say. You hardly ever see them. We're lucky to live in a place where you can see them, once in a while. A bald eagle sits atop a snag five houses down from ours. A blue heron stands on a rock in the pond, a quarter mile away from my front door. A red-tailed hawk, its belly feathers white for winter, circles overhead. I could reach out. I also have twenty-four ravens bouncing in my front yard. They like the rocks. Or maybe the scent of my dead cat's old fur. Perhaps we spill more food out here than I thought. Or, perhaps we're dropping more baubles for them—paper clips and marbles, plastic bracelets and bottle caps. Ravens must love messy children. When Zoë asks if I like ravens, I shrug. I guess I do. They're smart. In some ways as smart as humans. But maybe that's a reason not to love them. Plus, there's so many of them. It's hard to be surprised by the presence of a raven. I'll take a stupid, irregular owl any day.

Climate change threatens forests. As weather patterns change, droughts become more frequent. Drought stresses trees, inviting bark beetles and other tree-decimating insects. The drier forests are susceptible to high-temp forest fires that kill more than the brush underneath. The flames rise high into the canopy, catching needles on fire. The number of meat-eaters across the planet grows. Whole forests are cut down to provide space for meandering, delicious cows.

If the forests could just move a little—toward wetter and cooler lands—maybe they could outrun cows. The cows, as a whole, are pretty slow.

Ravens may provide some help. Ravens, like humans and trees, like it cooler and wetter. They're also very good at finding the best seeds and hiding them in wetter and cooler places. The ravens, smart beings that they are, still aren't perfect. They can't remember everything. If they tuck some pine seeds into the duff somewhere a little northerly, the forests can be on the move. Ravens are good at finding the best, most productive seeds.

I can't tell if it's a great story or the saddest story that ravens have to move whole forests to get out of the human's way.

*

I went to the meeting with the DA. The case is ongoing but I tell myself it's the last one I'll attend. I'm going to Okim it. Turn my head away. Stop driving by the scene of the crime. At the meeting, the other moms are so disgusted by the system, by the fact that Melinda won't do time for failure to report, that Clay won't have to register as a sex offender. How do we know he won't take one of the childcare classes taught with real live children at the high school Clay attends? they ask. How do we know Melinda isn't still running a day care? That Clay isn't taking those kids into the bathroom? How do we know this won't happen again?

The DA looks at these parents. How can he say anything? He is only a wise man. He can't predict the future. All he knows is that this will happen again somewhere, to some other children, by some perpetrator. Knowing this perpetrator's name is a pretend kind of solace. A clanging placeholder for knowledge where only wind whispers in the hollow. Still. I suppose my job, the best thing I can do for my son, is to make a sound. Hear me clamor.

All summer long, I've been seeing ravens dead in the road. I'm up to four and it's only July. I've never seen this before. Ravens are smart. When they're chewing on the ear of some sad road-killed squirrel, they wait until the last minute to jump away. They always make it. At least I thought so. But these four. They're making me wonder. The roadkill-eaters have become roadkill themselves. I feel bad for them. Their job is to eat decaying squirrels. Humans are the ones who paved the road. Humans are the ones who drove the cars on the asphalt, be damned squirrel or raven in their way. This training of nature, making it conform to such straight, yellow-lined paths—that's what's not normal. Maybe ravens would be happy eating lizards in the forest. Then again, without the roads and the cars and the poor squirrels just looking for a fast escape, maybe there wouldn't be any ravens here at all. But there's no real way to tell what ravens would do without dead squirrels and asphalt's future is a long one. Maybe Flagstaff isn't even their natural habitat. Ravens go where the cars go.

*

Erik came up the driveway with the mail in his hand. He stopped on the porch. I could see him through the window. He opened a letter, read one side, turned it over, read the other. When he came in the front door, he handed me the paper. District attorney. Victim's registration. If we wanted to be considered victims, we had to submit this form by this date.

I walked it over to the recycling. Erik asked what I was doing.

"What? I'm recycling this. I'm done. It's over. Nothing happened."

"But he was there, Nik. Our son. He could have been there when it happened. It happened just five steps away from where he played with the trains. This letter is for the trial against Melinda. For endangering our son. Child endangerment. It's a thing."

"She moved the day care."

"She moved the day care? That's it? That's all she had to do and you're okay with it? That one dad said he saw Clay over there. Do you have no idea how wrong that was?"

So I went to the next meeting with the DA. The DA told us about his daughter who, twenty-eight years ago, was in a day care. His daughter came home from day care one day, started touching her vagina in front of him and his wife. She was three. They knew immediately what happened.

"We got her counseling. We talked about it as a family. And now she's thirty-one, she's a lawyer with three kids of her own. She's okay."

And I wonder, is he being complicit? Am I being complicit? Is believing that our kids will turn out okay anything other than being complicit to a false hope? It's like loving the forest behind my house for the cool breeze and yellowing leaves but ignoring the one deer who limps through the forest, his leg broken by deep snow. The vulture stares patiently. The cougar watches from his invisible perch. I walk along the path. I see no cougars. No ravens. Nothing red. No tooth. No claw. My woods are a "nature-scape." I see a dog leash hanging from a tree. Some kind neighbor wanted to be sure it was returned to its owner. Humans are everywhere, taking the cruelty out of nature, replacing it with a park, a place where predators gawk at children, a different kind of cruelty. "The woods decay, the woods decay and fall," says Tennyson.

Optimism is a human characteristic, not one derived from nature. I am a landscaper, not a woman who lives in the wild. I smooth and trim. I adorn. It looks so natural by the time I'm done with it.

***

At the Arizona State University Biodesign Institute, they have discovered cyanobacteria (similar to algae) that, when propagated in water and let to photosynthesize in the Phoenix sun, converts sunlight into tiny lipids. If you stick your hand in the water to feel the bacteria, your fingers feel the slippery, soapy surface. These fatty lipids are industry-ready. You can slip the lipids from the surface of the water, slide them into tubes, pump them into regular old oil trucks. Ship them to a refinery and let the refiners do what they do—take oil and turn it to gasoline. Back into tubes, into trucks, and into your local gas station.

Humans are very good at screwing things up. They're also pretty good at fixing things. The only problem with these slippery by-products of human-helping microorganisms is one of scale. How much water do you need? How much sunlight? How many tubes?

*

In the poem "Thirteen Ways of Looking at a Blackbird," Wallace Stevens wasn't lecturing about sequence. He was doing the quantum math. Each number, its own universe. How many ways can you look? In section two, he writes,

> I was of three minds,
> Like a tree
> In which there are three blackbirds.

The blackbirds are always in trees. In section four:

> A man and a woman
> Are one.
> A man and a woman and a blackbird
> Are one.

They multiply, with man, with woman, with words. The blackbird is a link between the eye and the you, the I and the me. The blackbird is the object and the direct object.

The river is moving.
The blackbird must be flying.

There are so many blackbirds. Thirteen infinity. The blackbird is the linchpin. There are so many blackbirds. They are natural. They are nature itself.

I read the poem to Zoë last night. She asked, "What if each second was a year? Or each year was only a second? Would we live forever?" By imagining when we'll die. If we died in seventy-two seconds, would seconds seem longer? If we lived as long as a raven, would we live as long as a river?

As the river flows. That's how I managed time in the middle of COVID. During the pandemic, I only saw my two friends. Saw them once a week. Or once every three months? I had just finished teaching last week. Or was that last year? When you measure time by anomalies, time itself collapses. You will live forever if you stop counting.

"I want to live for a long time," she said.

"How fast does time go, Zoë?" I asked her.

"It goes very fast," she said.

It is hard on me to hear that she already knows the same thing about time that I know.

*

One of the problems with climate change is the time problem. We aren't very good at imagining the future. What we do now: it's hard to measure what effect that will have on our futures.

I mean, supposedly we are good at adapting for the future. Shaena Montanari writes for *National Geographic*, comparing ravens to humans. "For instance, a trademark of being human is the flexibility to plan for future events, such as saving for retirement or figuring out a meal for the next morning. Scientists previously believed these behaviors were unique to hominids—humans and great apes—because no other animals, including monkeys, were thought to have such abstract thinking skills."[23]

If you look at most people's retirement savings account or their plans for breakfast, I think you can lump humans in with the monkeys and let the ravens have the "forethought" category to themselves.

"In the final experiments, the ravens could choose between an inferior immediate food reward (a smaller, less-tasty piece of kibble) and a token for their favorite kibble they could trade later—a concept called delayed gratification.

"'Humans devalue things that take place in the future,' says Osvath, emphasizing people typically go for instant rewards. Ravens seem to be a little more patient, selecting the tool or token that would get them the better food in the near future over 70 percent of the time." [(Ibid)]

When Clay turns eighteen, no matter that he was indicted, arrested, prosecuted, and convicted, his record will be wiped clean. Time can move backwards, at least in this case, erasing all documented knowledge. At eighteen, he will go forth into the world, returned to innocence. Innocence isn't a sweet place though, necessarily. Innocence is the first natural state. Real nature—not the park-like kind, is innocent, unknowing, but still covered in squirrel guts, twisted dove necks, lame deer. You can't remake a nature but maybe you can make a park or a naturescape. Something flawed but natural. Human. Raven. Except the difference between humans and ravens, scavengers both, adapters both, internalizers both, is that the raven doesn't spend its days demarcating: this is normal/this is not. The bauble and the grass. Maybe that's wisdom—not insisting on a category called normal.

*

I also have to return to a kind of innocence/ignorance. I have a job. I have to take Max back to school—another school, this one at a church, this one closer to home, this one with many more adults and very few (zero) teenage males. Max cries when I leave him. The day care lady stands there, not holding him, just letting him cry. I'm half happy that she's not touching him. No one should touch my kid. And I'm half collapsed that she won't pick him up and make him feel better. Who is to say what does the most damage? There are finger marks where I pull his arms off me.

I turn and go. I almost run, try to outpace my imagination. Try to fend whatever shiny baubles in the form of wisdom are trying to stick with me. I cannot know and so I don't. I am guilty. The car goes forward on the asphalt. I do manage to avoid running over a squirrel that darts in front of me. A raven swerves to miss the car. Small, steering victories. Even in nature, on the road, not everything collides just because it can. I am able to leave Max behind because, whatever inherent order there is in nature, people will clean it up, and nature will mess it up, and people will mess it up and then nature will clean it up and who am I to say which is the order and which is the mess? They both look pretty normal to me. I drive. I turn. The raven turns. Grass and baubles everywhere.

PERSUASION

M AX, THREE AND A QUARTER years old, wakes up in the morning asking, rubbing the sleep out of his eyes, "Do I have to go to school tomorrow?"

"You have to go to school tomorrow and today."

"Today?" He is crushed. Tears. "But I want to stay with Mama." Who doesn't? I'm lots of fun, staring at my computer all day and complaining about the news.

I pick him up and cuddle him but then leave him to his own devices. I have to make his and Zoë's lunch. He comes out wearing shorts, a long-sleeved shirt, red cowboy boots, gloves, and a helmet. It is thirty-three degrees outside.

"Too cold for shorts, bubba."

"But I want shorts." If this kid wins any records, one of them will be ability to sustain the word *want* for forty-five seconds.

"Fine. Freeze." This is not a good thing to say to a three-year-old and yet, it's a good thing to say to Max because you will not win. You will not offer him candy to change. You will not threaten him with punishment. You will not carry him and forcibly change him. Even if you manage to physically restrain him, he'll run into his sister's room to put his shorts back on.

"Grandpa's wearing shorts."

"Grandpa is not even here."

And then he sees his dad, who is wearing flip-flops. Off go the boots.

I let him wear his flip-flops and tuck his Nikes and a pair of pants into his backpack. It seems cruel to make the preschool ladies fight the battle, but trying to convince Max to do something he doesn't want to do is like trying to convince a pig to understand the greatness of bacon.

Max's teachers probably won't take up the battle. He will be cold but he won't die of cold. It will warm up by noon, I tell myself. It's perfectly normal to wear shorts in February, I think. He's really quite warm-blooded, I say to myself.

I can go to great lengths to change my own mind.

Farm-to-table has become tail-to-snout kind of dining. This works best when you're talking about a fish. I love the whole trout. Hamachi cheek is my favorite food group. I can make good progress with a chicken. All the meat. The guts and bones for broth. I have eaten chicken feet before. The whole cow? Tongue. Sweetbreads, the thymus gland. Oxtail soup. I have made a lot of progress on the cow. The idea behind the eating of the offal is to let nothing go to waste. It stems from a kind of environmentalism—if you're going to do the evil of eating meat, you should at least have the sense to make use of all. It's tied to a respect for Indigenous cultures—Native Americans used the whole animal. It's tied to the DIY food movement—butchering, cooking, smoking, curing your own meat is a sign of self-sufficiency. It's a sign of respect. You have to believe that eating the whole animal is for the greater good. The greater good becomes a kind of religion. This religion, like all religions, comes through the stomach and convinces through intestinal satisfaction. You have done the good work. You have ingested the good thing. Transubstantiation. Voila, animal is God in the belly. Voila, you are at once person, cow, and God. To make it all the way to heaven, you have to be a stubborn convert, eat the ears of a cow in the form of the ears of a cow, not in the easy form of hot dog. Eating requires not religious conversion, though it can become the kind of religion you're born into.

***

I am in the process of writing postcards to encourage people to vote: Dear friend, please vote. I cannot take this anymore. I'm in the process of making business cards to hand out to people who idle their cars: each car idling contributes 30 million tons of CO_2 to the environment. Americans idle their cars for an average of sixteen minutes per day. A four-cylinder car would save thirty-two gallons of gas, 704 pounds of CO_2, and 116 dollars. An eight-cylinder car would save twice that much.[24] I am in the process of trying to convince my son to turn out the light in his bedroom. I'm in the process of asking Zoë to take five-minute showers. I'm in the process of buying locally grown kale, which can only be so local in Flagstaff in February. I'm trying to persuade my cat to come in the house. I'm trying to convince my students to register to vote even though they feel the whole political system is corrupt. I tell them, put your vote on the pile. It will add up. I add my postcard to the mail. I submit my order for the idle-accounting business cards. The CO_2 is adding up but the business cards add up too.

When I pick Zoë up from second grade on Wednesdays, I bring her a smoothie so she has some energy before gymnastics. I make one for Max too and pick him up after I finish my grading during Zoë's tumbling. One Wednesday, I had a late meeting. I couldn't get home to make smoothies. I picked up some Pirate's Booty and Strawberry Monster Odwallas at the grocery store.

This was good for Zoë. She loves Pirate's Booty. This was not good for Max.

"But I want my yellow cup."

"Look Max, this is better. It's got more sugar!"

"But it's not in my yellow cup."

"Pirate's Booty! Full of salt AND sugar." I try to convince him. "It's delicious."

"It tastes like Styrofoam."

Unlike Zoë, Max learned to talk very early. Too early. Lesson to take from this: Do not teach your kid to eat the edible packing peanuts shipped with Apple products. Do not teach your stubborn kid the word *Styrofoam*. Only stubborn kids will learn the word to use it against you. Do not indulge your kid with a yellow cup every Wednesday. Maybe just every other Wednesday. Kids love rituals but they should love sugar more.

At a farm-to-table restaurant called Estragon in Boston, whole pig head is served. Wait. The passive voice is wrong here. Estragon serves a whole pig head. A server brings the head to your table. The pig's head has been roasted. Or, rather, a chef stuck a pig's head in an oven. It looks like luau pig. The skin is crispy brown. The head is small. It's a baby pig. "Look at that." (Many syllables on the *that*). "Hello, baby," someone says. A table of four cannot be expected to eat an adult pig's head elegantly. A table of four cannot even be expected to eat a baby pig's head elegantly. Fingers will be involved, but not at first. At first, feign utensil skill. The cheeks come off easy enough. Slice them like chicken breasts off the bone, then slice them crosswise. Serve a slice to the diner to your right. The other cheek, let your friends on the other side of the table carve for fear too much reaching will soak your fancy sleeve with grease. What is it like? Carnitas. The most carnal carnitas you've ever had. Shredded pork shoulder has nothing on pork cheek. This cheek is not just on the bone but is braised in pig fat. There is a lot of pig fat. Do not bother to wipe your hands between head parts. There is nothing better than pig fat. There is more. You go on. Tongue first. Can't be worse than the tacos de lengua you order quietly when they order carne asada. The skin? You've heard of cracklins. You suspect this is what they taste like although admittedly, you've never had cracklins. The snout? Iconographic pig snout is the cutest part of the pig. You take a tiny bite for the collective cause. The brain? You know you're not supposed to eat cow brain, for fear of bovine spongiform encephalopathy. You pride yourself on knowing what's new in medical news as much as what's new in foodie news. There is no porcine encephalopathy that you have heard of. You take a bite. The fattiest pork fat. The closest thing to foie gras. But the eyeball. You just close your own eyes and put the pig's in your mouth, gnash it quickly. Most religions rely on a cross between knowing and not knowing which is sin and which is not and you don't want to know too much about the chewing and swallowing of eye. The sin is in the membrane popping.

*

In terms of carbon dioxide produced by pigs compared to cows, pork doesn't account for nearly as much: producing one hundred grams of beef produces 25 kg of carbon. Producing one hundred grams of pork produces only 6.5 kg of carbon. Pig meat contributes less carbon than coffee production. Part of that, though, is thanks to the cruelty of pig farming. Pigs housed in too-tight cages, spending their lives in cells too small to turn around.

When you try to convince the pig farmer to maybe give the pigs some open space, he looks at you like you're crazy. Would you give a coffee bean more space? A carrot? To him, the pig is a noisy cabbage—worth more because of its belly, ribboned with fat and flavor that a cabbage can only approximate. Bacon is its own persuasive force. And eaters are as good as farmers at thinking of bacon as a vegetable.

"I want to wear my cowboy boots."

"You are wearing your cowboy boots." Max is indeed wearing his red cowboy boots.

"I want my cowboy boots."

"Come here." Max walks over to me. I pick him up. Poor baby. He puts his head on my shoulder and pats me on the back. He's sorry his mama is so confused. So is she.

The boots fall off one by one. He points to them on the floor. "See. I am not wearing my cowboy boots."

Reality conforms to those who want it most. He wants it so much he makes it happen. I am proud of his rhetorical skills in an exhausted kind of way.

Do you have to talk yourself into eating pig's head? Do you have to talk others into joining you? What words do you use? When you ask the diners what they thought about the experience, they say, "It is a lot of work." If you ask them, "Would you do it again?" they say, "No. Lobster's a lot of work but I know where the cache of meat is. With the pig, it was too much work to get to the stores of meat. Same with crab. It's too much work."

You cannot eat a pig's head alone. The first rule of a religion is that it's not a religion if you do it alone—it's a psychosis. You are going to have to find a way to bring the pig to the people. If you can eat bacon, which is the fat then muscled layers of a pig's belly, then you can eat a snout! But we must make the word sound more beautiful than snout. To sell it to the less adventurous food-lovers, you're going to have to rely on some words that convey a happier reality. Try *liebe*. *Ich liebe die Schweine*. The Germans won't mind. Martin Buber, a major Austrian-born philosopher, promoted immanence. Austria is practically Germany. Love, love, love, liebe, liebe, liebe is everywhere.

If you can persuade a pig to come when you call it, does it make it smarter or less smart than a human? Humans put a lot of stock in being stubborn. Pigs can learn, and teach, a wide variety of things. In a study called "Thinking Pigs," researchers found that

some of the more interesting studies demonstrating emotional contagion in pigs involve responses to other pigs' anticipation of positive or negative events, revealing the importance of social factors in emotion. In one study, naïve test pigs were exposed to pen mates who had been trained to anticipate upcoming rewarding events (receiving straw and chocolate raisins) or aversive events (social isolation). When the naïve pigs were placed in the company of the trained pigs they adopted the same emotional anticipatory behaviors (e.g., ear and tail postures, increased cortisol release) as the trained pigs with the direct experience.[25]

Who is smarter, the animal that can anticipate the future or the one who pretends he can control the future? The one who eats bacon alone or figures out how to share his chocolate raisins?

It's hard to imagine how much alone-eating we would have to do in the future. Food can be eaten alone but meals not so much. If nothing else, an entire pig's head persuades us to eat together. In the future, we'll be eating bags of cracklins and pork rinds, sitting on the couch, watching *Chopped*, wondering when we can bother to roast anything ever again.

"Hey Max," I call from the other room. "Zoë wants to go to sushi. You want to go?"

"No. I do not want to go to sushi. I want to stay home."

"Why do you want to stay home? We've been home all day."

"Stay home. Stay home. Stay home."

"You can't stay home. You're only three. Let's go eat."

"I like my home."

He wins this one because for sure we don't want to go to our favorite sushi place and have him scream, "Home. Home. Home. I want to go home."

I turn on the oven. Put some potatoes in to bake. I quick-brine some chicken thighs. Seven minutes before we sit down to eat, Max looks at me and says, "I thought we were going to sushi."

I would like to stick my hands into his head and turn his brain around. I would like, at that moment, to massage some consistency into his head. But then, if consistent, he would not be Max. Or Max at three and a half years old.

*

How do you talk people into doing things? How do you convince three-year-olds? Is the process the same? Think of the poor vegetarian. He wants to convince you that eating animals is disgusting. It's bad for your health, for the planet, and for the animal. You'd think the best way for him to start was to serve you a pig's head, make you confront your demons, your evil, your sin. But something happens to the human mind. It resists conversion, at least when it comes to fat and meat. The stomach that a moment ago churned against the idea of popping an eyeball now somehow sends signals to the salivary glands to make them water. The vegetarian is aghast that you are chewing on an ear right in front of him. You offer him the other ear. He does not take a bite. You are at an impasse. No converts this night.

I spend half my life trying to convince Max to do what I want him to do. To put on shoes. To eat some broccoli. To go to sleep, my God, please go to sleep. But the point of having kids in the first place is to be converted unto them.

"Yesterday, there was a bird on my bed who told me I should be Spiderman and he gave me webs. I should take my webs outside and fight the bad guys."

"Who are the bad guys?"

"There are no bad guys, Mama. Come outside and see." And Max takes me outside to show me where he would shoot his webs if there were bad guys but now there are only hummingbirds.

"See? No bad guys. No webs. Hummingbirds."

"You like hummingbirds, Max?"

"I love hummingbirds."

And thus, the religion of Max.

***

If you name the pig snout "liebe," you have a naming strategy akin to religion's. Eucharist for cracker. Wine for blood. If you make eating pig head something you do every six weeks when Bob and Sue come to town, you have the routine of Sunday churchgoing, Easter, Christmas. If you repeat it in the right order. If you anoint the pig's head with olive oil, if you say grace in the form of, oh my God, I can't eat that, and then do, you will have your Christ. Your farm-to-table religion. You are leading by example. While everyone else eats bacon, you are sacrificing by crunching an eyeball between your teeth. Transubstantiation. The idea of transforming yourself is what religion is really good at. Conversion is as satisfying as eating pig fat. It's even better that you had once been so confirmed in your original morality: no eyeballs for me! And yet now, you wake up some nights craving the jelly-pop of eye.

Max convinces me every day, not by the power of persuasion but by the power of naming and ritual. Those are not cowboy boots. I want juice—not in a cup but in a cup. My face is not dirty. This is not even face. It is dirt. And dirt should be dirty.

"Mama, you should sleep by me."

"But this is not my bed."

He points to his bed. "It is your bed." He pats the pillow. "Sleep by me." I lie down. I can sleep in my bed tomorrow, I tell myself. Perhaps conversion is a daily thing.

I used to think I was a bad mother for Max. I had been, to my mind, a good, patient, not-argumentative mother with Zoë. But lately I've been thinking that Zoë converted me first to her own religion. She wanted to keep the tent up in the front room for six weeks on end. We let her. She made me and Erik lie down on the floor so she could cover our faces with washcloths and say "go to sleep." We did. She only ate food cut into the shape of squares. Max has a whole different list of jobs for me. How do I become the better mother for him?

It is hard to persuade anyone to change their mind or their behavior. The more educated you are, the more likely you are to search out facts that agree with your already-formed opinions. Hypocrisy may be our most human trait. It might also be the best and worst thing about us. As I said before, F. Scott Fitzgerald says the sign of true intelligence is to be able to hold two opposing thoughts in your mind at the same time. It's pretty amazing that we can love the pig while eating the pig. We see ourselves in the pig. We love that he eats chocolate raisins and doesn't idle his car. We love that he knows he will die one day. He's sad we love him more dead than alive, but we are also so sad for and so in love with all we have killed and all we have borne.

Max asks for hot juice.
"You mean cold juice."
"Hot. Juice."
"I do not think you would like hot juice."
"I want hot juice. Please."
The "please" convinces me. Maybe hot juice is the new thing. I get out the orange juice from the fridge. I take out a pan. I pour some juice. I turn the heat on low. To what temperature should one heat juice?

I drain the warmish juice into a sippy cup. He takes a sip. Hands me back the cup. "I don't like it."

Ha! I've won, I think. But then who is the person getting up, pouring out the hot juice, replacing it with cold, washing a pan that did not need to be washed five minutes ago. Converted again.

The pig, too, with its hot, juicy fat, wins the argument. Pig is persuasive.

***

I read something the other day about a woman getting her family's priorities in order. Love God first, then love husband, then love children, she wrote. If you take it to the next level, what you love keeps spiraling downward but I don't believe in hierarchies. Love husbands. Love children. Love eyeballs. Love pigs.

I love the hard work of finding crab meat even in the tiny tendrils of legs reminiscent of insects'. Maybe, though, work isn't the way to get to God. Maybe the easiness of tofu is.

Convert means to turn and look the other way. Max says, "Look here," so I look. It's easy. The doing is as easy as the saying. What do I see? I see the lilacs he calls birds and the squirrels he calls punch guys and the hummingbirds with spiderlike webs and I am born again. I call my pig cheek *pork*. That is easier too.

*

My friend Jesse called me the other day. Jesse's a former tow truck company owner, former bouncer, former meth head, my former student, present adventurer. No one really grins anymore, but Jesse grins.

"I found one."

"One what?"

"A pig's head."

"From where."

"My friend. He raises pigs down in Camp Verde. He'll give us a baby head." At Uptown, the bar where we hold most of our student poetry readings, I had mentioned just in passing to Jesse that I wanted to cook a pig's head but now I'm having second thoughts. Jesse knows everyone. Even pig farmers, apparently. I should have told someone who had no friends in Camp Verde who grew pigs. I should have told someone who had no friends.

But it was my idea. Now he'd found a head. Now there were two. We needed more. If we were going to do this thing, we had to convince others to join us. We couldn't eat one pig's head between the two of us. It would be wasteful. We wanted to start a movement. We needed to persuade some people this was a good idea. Not just flavor-wise. Not just adventure. But that it's a good thing to do. Head to tail. Hard to do. Confront what you're eating. Literally face-to-face. If we're going to do this thing, let's do it. Let's make the big bigger. Come on. Come with us. One of us isn't enough to achieve critical mass. But two is enough for missionary work.

When Erik brings Zoë home from school, he and she find Max and me in our cowboy boots with gloves on. We are drinking hot juice. This time, apple. Out of a yellow cup. We are eating packing peanuts from Microsoft—the kind that are made out of cornstarch. We offer some to Zoë. She tries one. Says it needs salt. Max and I nod and shake salt onto the Styrofoam. We sing Styrofoam, peanut, Styrofoam, peanut until we convince Erik to try one.

"Tastes like Pirate's Booty," he says. We'll see if we can convince Erik's mom to try some next. She's a vegetarian so I don't have hope she'll join the pig-head-eating sect but the Styrofoam-peanut sect—a good backup choice, if all other bacon-y persuasions fail.

TONGUE

Zoë, AGE SEVEN, ASKED ME the other day how words become words. I told her about cavemen who must have pointed at fire and grunted, "fo," and someone grunted back, "fo," and someone else grunted back, "fo," and the word "fo" became "fire" and was thusly agreed upon, although probably not in English, to be the word for fire for as long as that language should live. I didn't go into the meaning of the word *etymology* even though she had the etymology dictionary opened to the word *coast*. She wanted to know if she could make up her own words.

I said, "Like what?"

"Mourzy."

I asked her what that meant.

"Grass."

"Sure. If you can get someone to agree with you that it means some special kind of grass."

"Purple grass."

"Okay. I'm with you. Now if we get your dad and brother to go along. Then maybe convince your friends. It's not the usual way language is made. You'll have to persuade people. A mourzy campaign. But if you can agree and it sticks, bravo. It's not the normal way, but it's definitely a way. But there really are no natural words."

"Except *buzz* and other onomatopoeia," her dad chimed in.

"What's onomatopoeia?" Zoë asked.

"Words that sound like what they mean. Like *buzz* and *whisper*."

"How do you spell it?"

"Onomatopoeia? No one knows."

"No, how do you spell mourzy?"

Parents are slow on the uptake sometimes.

"What's mourzy?" I had already forgotten.

"Purple grass."

So far, our great linguistic experiment was falling apart. "I guess how it sounds."

"How about m-o-r-z-i-e."

"Purple grass. Morzie. Got it."

If the world were made of agreeable parents who said okay to everything, the world would be a kinder, more senseless place.

Even in Grand Rapids, Michigan, at the one good, authentic Mexican restaurant, they served tongue tacos. Lengua lingua langua. I cannot help but think of cunnilingus. It's not right what they do to cows. It's not right what they do to tongues. And this conflation between human tongue and cow tongue inside my head is deeply just not right.

"Deeply," says the double entendre. She sighs as she lies back on the pillows, legs open wide.

Oh bad brain. I have an overly graphic mind. Every word is an image. Oh my own bad tongue. I should not say aloud what I imagine or what I think in the privacy of my own head.

What I do imagine is that you are supposed to cut the taste buds from the tongue before you cook it. No one wants sandpaper crossing their own sandpaper-covered tongue. Maybe that's the difficulty here. Cannibalistic. When I eat a steak, I don't think thigh or butt. But tongue on tongue. Girl on girl action. Eating you out never sounded so good. Or so bad. I should stop talking before the puns get out of control.

I would not eat those Grand Rapidian tongue tacos. Not even on a dare. I didn't know then that tongue was normal. I did not know that everyone ate tongue. That I was a jerk for wasting so much meat when I was eating the rest of the cow, his flank, his chuck, his tender tender loin.

On the television program *Chopped*, four contestants, over three courses, use mystery-basket ingredients to make a winning dish. From one square basket, they pull a square piece of meat. A smoked cow's tongue is nearly square. When they cut it, it looks as organized as Spam. The squares of meat look like processed meat. It's the strongest muscle in the body, they say. I thought that was the heart.

There is nothing sexy about *Chopped*. Which makes it safe. I could watch fourteen episodes of *Chopped* a day. Once, when I was depressed, I tried to compare *Chopped* to writing. Writing was a contest and who was next on the chopping block. What happens to the non-winners? I think if they lose, they have to write scripts for *Chopped*, trying to make *Chopped*'s host, Ted Allen, sound like he's speaking off the cuff. I always guess what Ted Allen is going to say next.

I eat tongue all the time now but only in a taco. A taco is as safe as *Chopped*. Nestled inside, the tongue could be any meat, possibly not as tender, probably not as agile as puns. I have eaten tongue but I have not cooked it. I have not cut the taste buds off in a long, thin slice. I have not cubed the meat. I have not put my cooking hands on any cow's tongue when that tongue is still in tongue form. But if I did, I would leave the taste buds on.

In Cheryl Strayed's essay "The Love of My Life," in *The Sun* about her mother's death and Strayed's infidelity to her first husband (no one talks about their current husbands. That is outside the taco. Outside the parentheses), Strayed uses the phrase "going down on me" twice to describe what her husband does to her as he tries to comfort Cheryl, his then wife, as she grieves her mother's death.

The phrase "go down on" is the right one. The giver's head is so tucked, you can only see the pate. Paté. Duck liver is so smooth on your tongue. As smooth as lip against lip. Luce Irigaray taught me about going down on people. Women have so many lips. Let them all speak. Let them all speak in pun.

The word *cunnilingus*, though linguistically correct, is so full of tongue both in the word itself and on the tongue itself, it becomes its own sandpaper—scratchy, anti-tongue. It sounds so ridiculously syllabic. No one wants to be a walking sex-ed class. No one wants their own tongue to trip on the too many vowels, too many consonants. On the other hand, "eat me out" is too graphic. Who says that except teenagers looking to shock their mothers? It's the opposite of cunnilingus. So in-your-face. So not quite accurate. No one, unless they're not so good at it, really chews. No one swallows, at least not much, in the real-woman version of going down on.

Strayed's essay turns on its title—"The Love of My Life."[26] The love of Strayed's life is her mother. No matter how much her husband goes down on her, he cannot persuade her that he is that love. That she puts love, mother, and "go down on" in the same essay gives me permission to write an essay that has cow tongues, language, and daughters in it. Because isn't that what language is for? To give you permission to write what you cannot say, to imagine disaster so as to ward it off? If only such a magic trick worked.

It took Zoë a long time to learn to talk. Long enough that she worried the doctor. He ordered an MRI, which revealed no bad news. It was with relief and not mocking that we started calling her Nell when she made little bird sounds that in some world, mainly hers, were meant to be words. The movie *Nell* stars Jodie Foster, whose mother raises her daughter in an isolated cabin. The mother dies before Nell learns to talk so Nell teaches herself a language of her own.

Like Nell, Zoë says, "Moshe melises," as she comes in from the backyard, covered in Michigan dirt and Dreyer's ice cream. She may be saying she wants more ice cream because that's what everyone wants. Moshe melises. One more, may I please. Or she may be wanting to wash her hands. She doesn't like her hands messy. In day care, when we could send her, when she was not too sick or her immune system too weak, she wouldn't paint with her fingers. She gets the paint on her hands and runs around the room, wiping them off on her teacher's pants, on the walls, on the chairs. She will be well-prepared for the twenty-seconds or two-happy-birthday-songs washing of the forthcoming virus, which you did not manage to stave off by writing this book.

When you're stuck with something you don't like, you don't discriminate. You just want it off of you, just like you want your husband out from between your legs when you're grieving for your mother. You will flail against any surface, like Nell, wild, feral, fluttering around in a cage. She wants. She wants. Why does anyone need to learn how to speak? Isn't that all we're really ever saying? I want. I want. I want. Birds who flail only want one thing. To learn how to sing their want.

A bird can fly but a fly can never bird but flies make the best puns.

To like something is to want that something in your mouth. Your mouth leads to wanting. Your mouth waters for that thing that you want, even if what you want is cunnilingus. Sometimes, you'll just let that thing fall loosely on your lips, then tip it backwards onto your tongue, like butter, like saying the word *butter* over and over. You will think of the butter you have eaten. Cold butter on hot bread. Hot butter on cold crab. Emulsified butter in béarnaise. Buttered crepes and buttered corn. Butter is so safe. There is so little morality to the cow attached. A little dairy, but at least you only used her udder, not her tongue! Feel it on your tongue. Utter deliciousness. A little cholesterol. A little heart attack. A little death.

We all have to die of something.

As much as the next person, I like being gone down upon, even if the past tense locution of that sentence makes it almost sound like no one went anywhere at all. It's a raw spectacle from all angles. Thigh and pubic hair and folds of fishy labia. The slight smell of sweat and of piss. It's a full-frontal sensory assault on the going-downer—as if that person is sucking away every sense but the nerve-ending one. I understand why being gone down on doesn't help Cheryl Strayed so much after her mother dies. Smell, taste, and sight are all gone to grief. You lie upon your pillow with your eyes closed. Electric shocks, the good kind, but shocks nonetheless reverberate up your stomach, down your thighs, into the small of your back, which you arch half spontaneously and half to show your appreciation, put on a good show, and you can hear a little slurping but without those other three senses, your mind is allowed to wander. First you think that you might like the tongue to go more to the right. Then you think maybe more to the left and then you think about how the sound smacks like gum. The word *gum* makes you laugh. Gum gum gum gum. Almost onomatopoeia for the gum in your mouth but not at all for the rubbery, chewable substance made by Trident. Trident should have been called gum-smack. But that is a different Cheryl Strayed essay and too punny maybe even for this one.

You think about Cheryl Strayed and the idea of *Wild*. How far out you have gone. Once, in the wild, you saw a bear. Actually, you've seen two. You work the bear into almost every camping story you tell everyone who likes to camp (who likes to camp?

replace? What is the substance of grief? It is a tongue in foreign land, fat and bitten. Puns are where the familiar lies and grief is a foreign country now you can say eat me eat me eat me all day long and still neither cents nor sense or lies nor lies or butt nor but make any difference.

You're wasting away. Perhaps you should try to eat some chicken.

I love the word *lengua*. How I'm not eating cow. I'm eating Webster the dictionary. I'm eating all of Spain, Costa Rica, Chile, Mexico, and El Salvador. I am swallowing all those beautiful words like *chica* and *puta* and *mujer*. I am not your mother but I suppose only your tongue would know. I let them taste me but my grief rubs against them like sandpaper. Even men know when to step away from ill-shaped, ill-bred, motherless Nells.

Now, later, years after her tongue began to make good decisions about the spacing between English words, Zoë's learning Spanish. She recites, "Avion avion ah ah ah. Bonita bonita ba ba ba. Cepillo cepillo se se se."

I ask her, in the middle of second grade, after she's been in the immersion program for two years, "Do you want to learn Spanish?"

She looks at me, incredulous. She has a choice?

"You understand, right, when you watch movies in Spanish, what *Shrek*'s about, what he says? I mean, you've seen those movies a million times."

She pauses. Looks at me like I'm Shrek. "I have no idea what is going on in this movie."

I wonder who or what to blame that she can't speak the language. Her dedication to Spanish? Her lessons? Shrek himself for his many inside jokes? All those puns? Does Shrek even make sense to her in English? Without puns, how do kids find ways to laugh at all? Later I find out from her teacher that it's me.

I'm the problem. She speaks Spanish fine. I just needed to ask Zoë if she likes Spanish en español.

In Strayed's grief, she argues she did not go through the five steps of grieving.

I did not deny. I did not get angry. I didn't bargain, become depressed, or accept. I fucked. I sucked. Not my husband, but people I hardly knew, and in that I found a glimmer of relief. The people I messed around with did not have names; they had titles: the Prematurely Graying Wilderness Guide, the Technically Still a Virgin Mexican Teenager, the Formerly Gay Organic Farmer, the Quietly Perverse Poet, the Failing but Still Trying Massage Therapist, the Terribly Large Texas Bull Rider, the Recently Unemployed Graduate of Juilliard, the Actually Pretty Famous Drummer Guy.

Who needs grief-steps when your mouth is full of wonder? I wonder, at the sucking, at the being sucked upon, how much this fills her with her mother. We know our mother's breast first, sure. But what about later? Zoë's always licking my arm. Sometimes, she licks my cheek. I wiggle my finger in her armpit to tickle her. She puts her thumb in my mouth and asks me to suck it. At some point, the kid grows up. She stops salivating upon you. The kid does not touch you. You don't touch the kid. Platonic hugs and kisses replace full-body touch. But later, after that spate, that absence, when the child goes on to find other bodies, go ahead, make yourself say it, to fuck and to suck others, maybe this whole sex thing is just a way to crawl back into the womb. Kiss me first. Open up. Take me home. Nestle me between your lips.

So let's take the tongue out of the taco. Time to face facts. Put your money where your mouth is. Call it what it is. Put it on the plate, front and center. Stop hiding behind niceties. Even if you can't say *cunnilingus* you can say *lengua*. Say it with me. *Lengua*. Another word for want. Do this, says the recipe. Act as if the recipe is your mother. Obey.

How to Cook Tongue

Rinse tongue well with cold water and place in a deep 6- to 8-quart pot. Add cold water to cover by three inches, then add remaining tongue ingredients. Cover pot and bring to a boil. Simmer, partially covered, until tongue is fork-tender, 2 1/2 to 3 hours.

Transfer tongue to a cutting board (reserve 1 1/2 cups cooking liquid) and, when cool enough to handle, peel off skin and trim any fat or gristle. Skim off fat from cooking liquid and pour liquid through a paper-towel-lined sieve into a large bowl, discarding solids. Keep tongue warm, covered.

How to Make Tongue Sauce:

Cook shallot in butter in a 2-quart heavy saucepan over moderate heat, stirring frequently, until softened. Whisk in flour and cook, whisking, 1 minute. Gradually whisk in reserved cooking liquid and cream, then bring to a boil, whisking.

Simmer sauce, whisking, until slightly thickened, 2 to 3 minutes. Whisk in mustard, horseradish, herbs, lemon juice, and salt and pepper to taste.

Slice tongue and serve with sauce.

Tell me what to do, recipe, how to make it, if not how to say it. The best thing about sex and cooking? In both, you have permission to use the imperative form. "Beat me, bite me, whip me, fuck me, come in my mouth," said a T-shirt I wish I'd bought when I was in the seventh grade, back when Cosmic Aeroplane bookstore still existed. Back when I could give commands and rebel against my mother, who would not have washed my mouth out with soap but may have suggested that I better know what I'm saying before I say it.

Zoë is obsessed with her tongue—what it can do, what it can't. Twist it sideways, scroll it inwards, bend it back. Her cousin can form hers into a W—Zoë's first real envy. Her brother Max can ululate with his uvula. He sounds just like a raven. Zoë's standing on the dirt, under the pine trees, twisting her tongue and turning it around and you say, this is where language came from. Not to ask. Not to name. But because otherwise, the tongue is just for eating. Physicality has its advantages but abstract acrobatics is where the fun is. Twist that word inside out. Make a pun. Eat me out is just figurative language unless you're a cow.

Still, I find myself repeating to Zoë what my mom always said to me: Keep your tongue in your mouth. It is not polite to walk around with your tongue hanging out.

I need to ask permission for this essay. I should send it to Cheryl Strayed. I should let my husband give the okay for both him and as Zoë's parent. I should probably ask my mother too. I would like to think I can write whatever I want but I can't. I am shaped round thanks to the sandpaper of my rearing. My rearing. My rear raised up high in the air. For fear of hurting this person or that animal, or for fear of getting it wrong or not making sense, I will carve these sentences into respectable shape. For karma or for old debts I will share a little too much but not so much that no one can stand me. I will limit and condense and round out for the sake of the husband who goes down on me, who would rather I not mention that on the page, but I still will say it because, like eating tongue tacos without the safety sheath tortilla, I feel I should be as honest with my tongue as I am to the cow's. It must be good for me, like confessing, like learning Spanish, because then you know with enough persuasion and repetition, enough puns and enough titillation, you will make some sense at the end. Sense is a whisper that barely requires the tongue at all. The cow is eaten because he could not talk his tongue into any sense. No wonder I worried for my daughter, that Nell.

A tongue can scrape, twill, twitter, buzz, cluck, drink, thrust. (Thrust.) But it's the lick that takes the edge off. When you are licking, you have nothing to say but something to do. The lick makes us beastly busy. We are not stuck up in our heads thinking about the way the word *lengua* ever devolved into the word for tongue. Who wants to be licked by a tongue? Let me lick you with a lengua.

We are licking. We are licking like the cow who licks the caul off her calf. We're licking all the *c*'s off. We are licking the wound better and we are licking our lips and we're licking the tongue taco without feeling guilty about anybody else's tongue.

When mothers talk, it's like the licking of the caul from the calf, training her from on-the-ground to standing up. The kind where language is an ecology of push and pull. If I give you some scolding here: stop licking me, I'll give you a bit of praise: wow, good use of the word *synonym*. Great job with your Spanish today. Great job practicing piano. Thanks for putting the dishes away. Don't forget to write a thank-you note to your grandma. The sculpting of a whole human being through tongue. That's why mothers talk so much. They're licking us into a person-shape—one with guideposts, with pauses between words, in a society, with etiquette, with balance, with an understanding of the problem with and the joy of puns, with a healthy love of synonyms, one with a tongue who can eat a tongue and say tongue and say love and lick back.

When our mother dies, no one cares anymore what we're doing with our tongues or how to make the word *morzie*. We don't have to ask permission anymore. It's just us, and Nell, and the ever-silent cows.

Still, you ask.

Still, the mothers say, "Take at least one bite. It's good. I promise you, it will taste good."

IMPURITIES

MARCH 12

THE WRITERS KRISTEN Arnett and Jami Attenberg read from their recently released books at Bright Side Bookshop. We didn't know it would be the last reading. The number of people in the audience was small because Chelsey, my colleague at NAU, and I, didn't know how hard to promote the event. Should we encourage people to get together or not? I'd just returned from a writer's conference in San Antonio. Chelsey had decided not to go because travel advisories had started for some places because of the novel coronavirus. I had gone because my ticket from Flagstaff to San Antonio cost $515.95. In those days, you couldn't cancel flights without huge penalties. But the conference had been over for a week and things were getting less clear. We talked about canceling the other readings with Arthur Sze and Manuel Muñoz. The Earth Day event I was speaking at was canceled. For a minute, the cancelations felt good. Who books a March like this? An April? If I had made it to the Earth Day event, how would I chair the seven theses defenses I had scheduled that week?

March 13

I visit my student in the ICU. He has been here since about the time we've returned from the conference. I sneak a beer and a hard cider into his room for my colleague who has been here all day.

"Have you eaten?" I ask as he slugs the beer.

I feel like my mother. Bring Arby's to the infirm or to those waiting for the infirm to firm up. Food courier is a good job for we who find both conversations around people who are lying down, bodies half exposed, and the panopticon of the hospital awkward. The hard cider helps but not much.

My student lies on his stomach. The nurses have turned his head to the left to accommodate the tube down his throat. Urine in his catheter bag looks brown. I shouldn't be looking at the color of my student's urine but I worry.

"Is he getting dehydrated?" I ask the nurse.

I touch his calf. If I press down and his skin doesn't return quickly, I'll complain that he's dehydrated, but it comes back okay.

I remember touching Zoë's fontanel to discover how dehydrated she was. That once we gave her that extra breastmilk she bounded back.

Liquids are magic but they've already drained fluid from his lungs as much as they can. Who am I to say what is the proper balance between touch and bounce, between input and output?

They have tested him for COVID-19 but the test came back negative. But he's twenty-four years old and intubated. What else can it be?

We let ourselves believe that it is COVID-19, so we can believe that we've contracted, sustained, and overcome the disease, and continue to believe that it's not, so we don't feel foolish for attending that conference the week before. So we don't feel foolish for sitting by his bedside, drinking a beer, eating breakfast burritos that are not Arby's but are just as distracting.

March 26

My friend Beya is going to come over to my house to sit on my porch. I so badly want to see her but I don't want to get in trouble. Erik is stressing very hard about the virus. He worries about Zoë's lungs. He worries about his boss who has a heart condition. He worries about his parents who are over sixty. I worry less. I don't know why. I'm calloused. I have spent time in the COVID-ridden hospital. I am generally optimistic, which is why I'm usually disappointed.

I think of Zoë's hard breathing in the PICU in Salt Lake City thirteen years before. The doctors taught me to count her ribs. If she retracted, to see one rib was better than if she retracted two. If I could see three ribs when she took a breath, push the button for the nurse. No, not that one. That one. They say COVID doesn't affect children. And then Beya, who sits on my porch eight feet away, tells me a twelve-year-old died from the virus in Florida. They think he had an underlying condition. Having a body seems to be an underlying condition. Having a body of color seems to make that underlying condition that much worse.

March 27
Beya texts, "I shouldn't have come."
I text, "I don't think I'm going to make it much longer."

April 4
Images of growing plants from vegetable scraps swarm my newsfeed. A garlic clove sprouts a green stem. I shove it in a pot of water. From romaine butts you can regrow lettuce leaves. The ends of onions will reshoot onion sprouts.

I'm a writer. I'm a big fan of revising. Retelling. Reinventing. Regrowing edible food from the stuff you were about to throw away.

I am the cook. So I cook.

March 14-June 8
3/14/20   Cauliflower and bacon pasta
3/15/20   Roasted chicken
3/16/20   Tomato soup and grilled cheese

3/17/20	Tacos
3/18/20	Grain bowls
3/19/20	Bolognese
3/20/20	Erik made chicken noodle soup for lunch
3/21/20	Pizza homemade (Flagstaff calzone)
3/22/20	Tacos
3/23/20	Korean ribs
3/24/20	Tacos
3/25/20	Baked chicken thighs
3/26/20	Lentils and soufflé
3/27/20	Karma
3/28/20	Pork chops
3/29/20	Chicken & dumpling soup
3/30/20	Pizza from Grimaldi's
3/31/20	Tacos
4/1/20	Filets, wedge salad, baked potatoes
4/2/20	Fried rice and chicken stir fry
4/3/20	Crab sandwiches
4/4/20	Pizza
4/5/20	Broccoli and veggie sausage pasta
4/6/20	Grilled chicken thighs
4/7/20	Hamburgers
4/8/20	Shift Restaurant Take Out
4/9/20	Cobb salad
4/10/20	Broccoli and sausage pasta
4/11/20	A stick of butter?
4/12/20	Ribs
4/13/20	Grain bowls
4/14/20	Strangely, not tacos
4/15/20	Pizza from Fratelli's
4/16/20	Filets, wedge salad, baked potatoes
4/17/20	Shift cocktails, Brussel sprouts, and chicken tenders after wine in the forest with Shamah and Lindsey

4/18/20	Flatbreads with kale, sausage, onions, tomatoes, pesto or alfredo
4/19/20	Kofta, spanakopita, Greek salad
4/20/20	White bean soup and sourdough bread
4/21/20	Tacos
4/22/20	Broccoli and sausage pasta
4/23/20	Grain bowls
4/24/20	Asado negro
4/25/20	Lasagna and salad from Coppa Café
4/26/20	Curry
4/27/20	Clam linguini
4/28/20	Tacos
4/29/20	Flat iron steak with béarnaise
4/30/20	Broccoli and sausage pasta
5/1/20	Tomato soup and grilled cheese
5/2/20	Lemon and rosemary chicken
5/3/20	Arctic char and roasted potatoes and artichokes
5/4/20	Chicken tacos
5/5/20	Brussel sprouts
5/6/20	Boiled potatoes
5/7/20	A lot of pizza
5/8/20	Ancient grain bowls (Lindsey's birthday eve)
5/9/20	Teriyaki chicken
5/10/20	Sausage and broccoli pasta
5/11/20	Turkey and mashed potatoes, sweet potatoes, and cauliflower
5/12/20	Beets and chèvre salad
5/13/20	White beans and tomato bake
5/14/20	Chicken thighs from Whole Foods
5/15/20	Proper Meats—chicken and sandwiches
5/16/20	Clam linguini
5/17/20	Chicken tacos
5/18/20	Tomato soup and grilled cheese
5/19/20	Ancient grain bowls

5/20/20	Homemade pizza
5/21/20	Tacos
5/22/20	Tacos again?
5/23/20	Sourdough starter bread and lentils and soufflé
5/24/20	Burgers with Beya—Veggie and regular
5/25/20	Popcorn
5/26/20	Broccoli and veggie and turkey sausage pasta
5/27/20	Barbecue chicken drumsticks and Swiss chard
5/28/20	Tacos—turkey and mushroom/pablano/oaxaca cheese
5/29/20	Crab sandwiches
5/30/20	Beyond Burgers at El's
5/31/20	Noodles and red sauce
6/1/20	Backpacking tasty bites
6/2/20	Steaks at El's
6/3/20	Backpacking stew
6/4/20	Spaghetti with Swiss chard and chickpeas
6/5/20	Fratelli's pizza
6/6/20	Barbecue chicken
6/7/20	Mac and cheese and pork belly and Swiss chard
6/8/20	Chicken and dumpling soup

Max asks, what are we having tonight for dinner?
He answers his own question. Chicken.
We do eat a lot of chicken. And a lot of tacos.

April 17
The garlic sprouts into spaghetti-length sprouts. Sturdy as raw pasta, as green as promise.

April 28
The garlic stalk is cooked spaghetti, bent and white. The bowl of root-ends smells like rotting onions. The romaine does sprout a leaf. We are having tacos and we're out of lettuce. Should I take this one leaf?

Memorial Day Weekend, 2020

The governor of Arizona has lifted all edicts to stay at home. He hopes that businesses and individuals will make the right decision. My friend who owns a clothing store downtown got cussed out for asking him to wear a mask in her store. Beya and I agree we've been so good for so long. We can still be good and see each other again.

I invite her and both her sons over for dinner on Sunday. We'll stay outside. They'll pee in the backyard. I'm just going to make burgers.

Burgers of the Pandemic

I have two recipes for burgers. One is for the very best hamburgers, from the *Washingtonian*. The other is for the very best veggie burgers, from *Cooking Magazine/NYT*.

The best beef burger recipe asks for 80/20 ground beef, a tablespoon of Duke's mayo per pound and one and a half tablespoons of fish sauce. If you don't have Duke's, add an egg to the mayo to enrich the already rich mayonnaise. Add the fish sauce because salt wicks away moisture but fish sauce wicks in flavor. Pat your patties. Divot them with your finger. Serve with potato buns and iceberg lettuce and fry sauce. They don't call it fry sauce because the *Washingtonian* isn't based in Utah, which is where fry sauce is based.

Utahns have been whipping together mayonnaise and ketchup since the beginning of time, or, since Hires drive-in opened on 7th East and 4th South. Crown Burger makes their own version with bits of pickles swirled in, which may make you think what I'm talking about here is Thousand Island dressing but I've tried that as a substitute and it's just not. The Training Table made their own version with hickory barbecue sauce, which went particularly well with cheese fries. Our first stop when my sisters and I got together, each of us coming to Salt Lake from out of town, was always the Training Table, where, from our booth, we lifted a telephone receiver to call in our order: one blue bacon burger, one grilled cheese, one club sandwich, an order of cheese fries, and three fry sauces. Black-and-white images of sports people explained the "training" part of the table. I'm not sure how the phone-in-your-order matched with the idea we were in training but we were definitely in training for how much fry sauce we could order. I ordered two—one for my fries. One for my burger.

However, it wasn't until I read it in the *Washingtonian* that I realized the secret to fry sauce is pickle juice. Now that it's pandemic times, I don't have to suffer that particular lack. Although fries themselves are hard to come by.

When Beya comes over, I make the hamburgers and I make the veggie burgers, which have more ingredients than fry sauce has story. Beets, red kidney beans, mushrooms, cotija cheese, tempeh, cashews or tamari almonds, egg, mayo, and brown rice. I use leftover farro from our ancient grain bowls because I refuse to throw anything away. That is, until it smells funny and infects my refrigerator with its own kind of moldy virus and then I throw everything away and feel guilty but also redeemed for cleaning the fridge, which I do less often than I should but more than anyone else who lives here.

The veggie burgers are red and textured. They look a bit like raw meat before they're cooked. They look a bit like raw meat after they're cooked.

I made oven fries but the oven kept turning itself off. The fries shrank and collapsed on themselves.

"I'm sorry, B. What kind of first-time-I've-seen-you-in-two-months celebration is burgers and fries?"

"I love your veggie burgers."

I, who had a regular burger and half a veggie burger, said about the veggie, "I just don't get it. All those ingredients and they still really taste like the bun."

"It's because you eat it plain. You need the bun. The cheese. The lettuce. Onion. Tomato."

I nod to agree but my meat burger tastes delicious on its own. My dream of becoming a pure vegetarian fails, just like any of my dreams of being purely pure.

THE BODY

S OME DAYS, IT'S ALMOST TOO much to cart your own body about. Monday mornings after a long weekend and a transition back to running after so much standing around, staring at your tomato plants, trying to get them to grow, even walking up the stairs burns. So what makes it sound like fun to hoist not only your own ever-increasing body mass but also your survival needs—food, tent, sleeping bag—onto your own back and climb into a canyon that probably would prefer you stay out of it anyway?

It has been a long pandemic. I hadn't sat indoors with anyone besides Erik, Zoë, and Max for ten weeks. To go backpacking with Erik's parents and his stepdad's brother, sister, and cousin seemed like a loophole—a way to get around the rules without breaking the rules. We could be together but we'd be outside. We could hang out day and night because we'd be doing this hard thing, with redemption automatically awarded to they who suffer backpacking.

It would be a good lesson for Max and Z. Get them out of the house and off their phones. Teach them to appreciate electricity and running water and soft, above-ground beds. Erik and I could talk to just each other because other people could listen to the kids. We'd figure out why we'd been bickering lately. We'd restart this whole summer. Nay, we'd restart this whole life.

***

The problem was, backpacking and this whole pandemic life aren't opposites, they're epitomes of each other. To organize for the trip, we leave for Torrey, Utah. Erik's parents, who live there full time now, shop at the grocery store in Loa where I fled to shore up Y2K apocalypse supplies. But this time, the grocery store really is out of ordinary supplies—not only toilet paper, like every store in the country, but milk and eggs and spinach.

"Someone came in with a horse trailer and bought everything out," my mother in law told me. "Now, you can only buy one gallon of milk, one pound of butter, one loaf of bread."

I'm reminded of the kid on the *Sesame Street* skit who has to remember four things to pick up for his mama from the store. The fourth thing, whatever it was, you can't remember, and to remind yourself, you have to see it in the store, where it isn't during the pandemic, so you can't remember and now you don't have any whatever it was anyway.

Not that we were faring much better in Flagstaff. When I stopped to pick up some backpacking dinners, the owner of Peace Outdoor Supplies opened the door a crack and asked through his mask, "What can I get you?"

"Mountain House. A couple of those freeze-dried backpacking dinners?"

"Don't have any. The government came in and bought out my whole supply."

"The whole supply?"

He nodded and shut the door.

Stumped but not defeated, Zoë and I mask-up and venture into Whole Foods. I look for dehydrated mushrooms. I can make my own stew. No mushrooms found, I buy some fancy beef jerky: bison and bacon bits, and some expensive bouillon. Backpacking without stew is as pointless as backpacking during a pandemic.

At home, I cook frozen peas, shitakes, onions, and carrots on a cookie sheet. I cook them until they shrink and cook. They're still moist, but I live in arid Arizona—the third driest state, after Nevada and Utah, in the country. I stow the sheet pan on the top of the cabinet in the living room. By the time we leave, they'll be as dried as freeze and individually reconstitutable to boot. Into a Ziploc, two bouillon cubes and the vegetables went. I packed a tube of tomato paste and the bags of jerky separately. I do not feel too righteous about my self-sufficiency. Backpacking may not require much fossil fuel, but the levels of plastic layered in my pack could a large raft make.

A body knows itself best at five a.m. It likes itself least at that moment and thus, recognizes it by every complaint. Reviewing where the body hurts is like sending out radar signals—are you here? Yes, I am here. Exhaustion is a capillary level event. You are 100 percent convinced of your existence even if not 100 percent awake. We had to get up early to start the hike where temperatures may reach ninety degrees by ten a.m. at the top of the gulch and one hundred degrees by noon at the bottom. It was a two and half hour drive just to get to the ninety degrees which, we were hoping, would only be eighty degrees at eight o'clock.

Hunger does a good job sketching the body, making the curve of the waist seem narrower than it is, making the cave of the stomach seem deeper. A perfect cave filling food is an English muffin with butter and also peanut butter on it. It also well-serves to flatten or even make convex the waist's would-be concave curve.

Although Eleanor and Rick's kitchen has been remodeled since I made chalky salmon to stave off Y2K, my body has not. I am still short and still am trying to lose ten pounds. They are probably different ten pounds—more peanut butter, more wine, less prime rib, fewer oysters, less beer.

We weighed our backpacks. I thought mine would come in ten pounds heavier than my hundred-pound daughter's but it was only a couple of pounds more. We each carried an extra gallon of water, which I repeatedly told everyone in the group weighed eight pounds. It had been the mantra on my last backpacking trip in the Grand Canyon. "I can't believe we have to carry eight extra pounds." "Wow, water weighs a lot." "Funny how we have to carry eight pounds of water when we're hiking down to the largest river in the West."

But in the Grand Gulch, the ranger told us the spring that normally provides water to hikers was dry. There was no Colorado River waiting for us at the bottom of this hill. Still, we imagined that some water might seep from the thousand springs that drew the Anasazi from Chaco Canyon and Mesa Verde. Thousands of relics and petroglyphs mark the hundreds, maybe even thousands of years people lived in the ledges of these cliffs. They made it through hundred-degree summers. Why can't we?

We walk down the sandy trail, pass through a gate made of old logs, and trip past the lives of people we can only imagine. I can imagine. I see shelf after shelf of possible living space. Squares of rocks that just behind might hide corncobs or squirrel pelts or even blue macaw feathers. Anasazi people with the Aztecs. The people in the town closest by, the White people, have pulled such evidence out of the canyon to display it at their museums and private show-off venues. The Hopi and Navajo, the likely descendants of these earlier people, call this place and the Bears Ears area that looms orange above like a sunset, sacred. But bodies carrying packs that weigh a third or, in Zoë's case, almost half, of their own bodyweight, don't feel the sacred. At ninety-five degrees in the sun, the sweat pulls the sacred out of your pores and leaves it in the weep of your bandana and the soak of your hat.

We found the alcove that we were looking for. Six tents would fit nicely. The looming red cliffs would shade us for most of the day. But we couldn't stay. There were no seeps. No springs. No extra water except the gallons in Erik's, Zoë's, and my packs. Not enough for nine people for two days at ninety degrees.

So for the one day, we watched the sun move as the Anasazi must have watched the sun move. We sat under an alcove. We scooted closer to the wall as the sun rose overhead. We moved down into the gulch to wait out the rest of the sun under a cottonwood tree.

It is no wonder people believed the earth circled the sun. The sun is far enough away that you can learn how to avoid it. It reduces its power, this hiding out under a cottonwood tree. Humans let that hiding-from-the-sun skill go straight to their heads. We should know, as the Anasazi must have, that the earth readies to flip you out of its hands and into the sun's at any given water-around-the-corner-believing mistake. We sat still, sweating in the shade, pulsing the earth right out of us.

The next morning, packed and out of there by five a.m. again, we hiked back up to the top, debating whether we should try another, more water-filled hike. As I looked off across the mesa studded with sagebrush, I noticed the water tanks making their own kind of shade. The pumps, powered by solar, filled tanks for the cows that came to check us out as we drank a nine thirty a.m. beer back at the car. The springs. Maybe they would have seeped if the water hadn't been drawn up here to keep the livestock from dying of thirst. The Anasazi survived in this canyon for a thousand years. We couldn't even make it one night. We have only ourselves to blame—whether it's the climate crisis or the cattle crisis or the way we misunderstand how deeply the sun revolves around our sweat, the desert will do anything for your water. We made our desiccated escape.

***

Your body may resist like it resists climbing up hills. It might resist like it resists falling asleep. Like it resists listening to you tell it to stop gulping wine. Like it resists veggie burgers. But listen. You can tell your body what to do. When we returned to the cabin, which is no longer really a cabin, in Torrey, Ellie made four veggie burgers and six regular burgers. Erik's uncle came over. He was in Vietnam. He's not eating a veggie burger. So I volunteered. It was a Beyond Burger, cooked in butter, topped with cheese.

Reader: it was delicious.

That night, Erik's family decides we should try again to backpack, this time at Blind Lake. It's only a one-and-a-half-mile hike. Straight up, but there would be water at the top. No one had to carry in extra gallons. We would have had the full range of the southern Utah experience. Desert and mountain.

In marriage, like hiking, there are vicissitudes. Although we didn't have to wake up at five, we had to pack the packs again. I packed the stew I'd dehydrated carrot by carrot, with the artisanal bison and pork belly beef jerky. And instant mashed potatoes. I'd hike anywhere for those.

Erik and I had to reorganize our packs when we got to the trailhead with water bottles and the food. Everyone else was already packed. They took off up the hill without us. I didn't know it then, but Rick raced off in case someone lagged behind. Rick could leave his pack at the top and come back down. In the rush, I forgot my wine. Box wine, like instant mashed potatoes, tastes extra delicious when camping, like Joël Robuchon's butter-pound for potato-pound homemade potatoes.

Thirty steps in, I stop. "Hey Erik, I can't get this front strap to latch."

"It's your pack. You need to figure it out." Back to the old operator error of 1999. I would have fixed it if I wasn't going to be left behind. Everyone else, including the kids, had marched off ten minutes ago.

Halfway up the hill, Erik swatted at my legs. "Your legs are black with mosquitos."

But no one knew where the bug spray was. We just hiked faster, catching up with Rick, taking a break then to tear through our packs for the bug spray like we had torn through them just a day ago, looking for the extra water.

But then, up over the ridge is a lake. I dump my pack and float along the trail. So much water. The air is cool. Erik rubs mosquito repellant into my legs. The mosquitoes don't take much notice, but some. It's chilly. Erik gets the tent up so Zoë and Max can crawl in and get warm. He finds my yellow long-sleeve shirt and tosses it to me like he remembered to bring some of the Grand Gulch heat up to me.

We walk, pack free, to explore around the lake. Max and Zoë stay in their tent because it looks like rain. We didn't bring much rain gear. But then the clouds part and the trail is flat and although I run, against my will, three times a week, at this moment, next to this water, at this high and cold elevation, I run, no will required.

The body can tell the brain what to do too. It can fall asleep in the middle of typing a sentence. It can throw up if you gulp that wine. It can fall down from exhaustion. It can sob in the bottom of a canyon. It can increase your blood pressure with every thousand-foot increase in elevation. It can increase your blood pressure because your dad had high blood pressure. It can increase your blood pressure because you took too long to embrace the Beyond Burger burger. It can lose teeth and layer fat. It can palpitate your heart when you hear about your friend's dad's death and then you hear about your other friend's high school buddy and his cousin's husband.

On your way to Torrey, Utah, you can drive through the Navajo Nation and read on your cell phone about the number of people here, dying in disproportionate numbers. You can look out the window across the landscape and not see a single person standing against the red-and-orange-lined hills.

Some bodies can resist the coronavirus. Most of the time, the body treats COVID-19 like a regular cold. You get a fever or lose your sense of taste or smell. You get a dry cough. You recover. But sometimes, your body overreacts, a lot like you did in that canyon that night. Your lungs create a lot of fluid to combat the disease.

Viruses hijack your cells and replicate the virus within them. Your immune system becomes activated. The white blood cells, and special cells called natural killers, destroy these hijacked cells. You still feel crappy but your body is actively ridding itself of the virus. But if things go badly, your immune cells will be overwhelmed.

A misfiring. Instead of seeing the virus as mainly harmless, your body sees the virus as hulking invaders, and instead of launching precision strikes against the offensive cells, the immune cells start blasting everything in sight. In the midst of this indiscriminate shelling, many of your good cells die and accumulate in your lungs, creating pools of fluid that cause severe irritation.

Some bodies have a harder time resisting than others, because they come in contact with the virus over and over again. Some say the virus spiked on the Navajo Nation because there was a big Christian gathering where members from across both Arizona and New Mexico came. Some say it's because not all houses have running water, partly because the Nation is so big and partly because the country has turned its back for so long on Indigenous Americans that no one paid any attention. Some say it's because white settlers wanted their water. Regardless of the scarcity of running water in some houses, after the Navajo Nation committed to a highly restrictive lockdown, they flattened the curve. The increase in number of cases in the rest of Arizona is higher than anywhere in the country—and we have all the water that can be pumped from the north, through the Navajo Nation, right into our pipes.

The brain must then process the body's reactions. At the edge of Blind Lake, I'm trying to attach the correct tube to the correct nodule. Erik had said if you get the tubes wrong, all the contaminants that you're trying to filter will infect the pump and the filtering will have been pointless. After half an hour of not being able to make the connection fit, I have Max go up to get Erik. He takes it from my hand, puts the "wrong" tube on the right nodule. I had it wrong the whole time.

The hike and the run and the walk and the remaking of the soup and the cold and the bug bites and the lack of rain gear and the five a.m. fill my body and Erik's comment of how I'm doing it wrong I can no longer resist. I cry into the water filter, probably contaminating it. Just like the sun pulled all the sweat out of me, into the air, the lake pulled all the water out of me, into it. Am I resisting the abyss or overreacting?

When we returned to Flagstaff, I purchased Impossible Burger non-meat from the meat section of the grocery. I made Erik and Max regular burgers with the mayo and the egg and the fish sauce. I incorporated the same into the Impossible Burger. I think the simulacrum is getting close here. Erik won't eat an Impossible Burger because he says the processed ingredients make his stomach hurt. I disliked the beet burger because it was too mushy although I liked each ingredient individually. Erik likes individual ingredients. It's hard to know exactly what's in an Impossible Burger since it's like some patented secret. As if the cow transforming its grass and sagebrush into meat isn't its own kind of processing and we will process by chewing on the beef.

The virus isn't over. My friend's dad just died. He was a truck driver, considered an essential worker, so he kept going to work driving his semi back and forth across the country. He finally got sick in Pennsylvania. He was in the hospital for eight days, then thirteen, then twenty-two. He was intubated, sedated into a coma, like my student. The nurses turned him prone. They put a phone up to his ear so his family could send words of encouragement. He was getting better, the nurses told my friend, until he didn't. He died so far away from home.

The virus isn't over. We wait in line for our tests. Duct taped x's mark the floor where we stand six feet apart. I wear the green mask my friend Mary Anne made for me. She sent six. I gave one to Zoë. One to Max. The other three, I sent home with my friend Bryson to his family on the Navajo Nation.

The nurse hands me a swab. I need to perform the test myself: to protect the nurse. To speed up the process, which feels very much like a process. Cows wait in lines like this, I think. People going to prison wait like this. To internment camps. I am lucky. I am just waiting for a test. She watches me as I push the long Q-Tip up my nose until my eyes water. I spin the tip, collect as much of a sample as I can. I look at the swab. It's a little moist? Is that Covid on there? I can't tell. I won't know for three days.

The virus isn't over. The marriage isn't over. The hiking isn't over. We decide to go camping with my sisters in Utah. This time it is car camping. We will have gallons of water at our disposal. We will have gallons of wine. Paige and Valerie and I, when we get together, host an *Iron Chef*-like battle. We've done Battle Citrus where Valerie made lemon capellini with caviar and Paige made grapefruit martinis. We've had Battle White. I made hamachi with ponzu sauce and Valerie made scallops in cream.

For the camping trip with my family, we try Battle Pink. I bring pork tenderloin with a plum chutney. Val brings salmon with cherry butter sauce. My mother-in-law, still the veg, will eat Val's salmon and my chutney. She brings beet pasta. Paige makes shrimp cocktail.

To the campsite, I will bring a Mormon dessert to the desert. White cake, forked with holes, covered with strawberry Jell-O, topped with Cool Whip. It is pink and full of preservatives. It is, mainly, except for the horse hooves in the gelatin, vegetarian. I'm not sure what Cool Whip is made of. It wouldn't sustain us forever through the apocalypse, but it did make the day feel like sustenance.

WORKS CITED
(ENDNOTES)

1   Dupont, Sam & Hall, Emilie & Calosi, Piero & Lundve, Bengt, "First Evidence of Altered Sensory Quality in a Shellfish Exposed to Decreased pH Relevant to Ocean Acidification," *Journal of Shellfish Research*. 33. 857-861. 10.2983/035.033.0320. (2014).

2   Brown, Claire, H., Climate Change Will Make Seafood Scarcer and More Dangerous. It Will Also Change the Flavor, *The Counter* (Sept. 26, 2019): https://newfoodeconomy.org/climate-change-seafood-taste-ocean-acidification-united-nations-ipcc-report/

3   Stokstad, Erik, "Our Growing Taste for Shrimp Is Bad News for Climate Change," *Science* (April 2, 2018): https://www.sciencemag.org/news/2018/04/our-growing-taste-shrimp-bad-news-climate-change

4   Abraham, John, "These Tiny Shrimp Could Influence Global Climate Change," *The Guardian* (June 7, 2018): https://www.theguardian.com/environment/climate-consensus-97-per-cent/2018/jun/07/tiny-shrimp-could-influence-global-climate-changes

5   Reilly, Laura, "The Impossible Burger: Here's What's Really In It," *The Washington Post* (October 23, 2019): https://www.washingtonpost.com/business/2019/10/23/an-impossible-burger-dissected/

6   Ritchie, Hannah, "You Want to Reduce the Carbon Footprint of Your Food? Focus on What You Eat, Not Whether

Your Food Is Local," *Our World in Data* (January 24, 2020): https://ourworldindata.org/food choice-vs-eating-local?fb-clid=IwAR2-D6nQnXXY5hlwI7EDUYApEWsTs7s136KDzSu-Zui-IGcgL0CDe22eM5OY

7   Ahmed Chinade Abdullahi, Chamhuri Siwar, Mohamad Isma'il Shaharudin and Isahak Anizan Carbon Sequestration in Soils: The Opportunities and Challenges, Carbon Capture, Utilization and Sequestration, Ramesh K. Agarwal, IntechOpen, DOI: 10.5772/intechopen.79347. (September 12th 2018): https://www.intechopen.com/books/carbon-capture-utilization-and-sequestration/carbon-sequestration-in-soils-the-opportunities-and-challengesAbdullahi, Ahmed Chinade et al., "Carbon Sequestration in Soils: The Advantages and Challenges,"

8   Lee, Hilde Gabriel, *Taste of the States: A Food History of America*, Howell Press: Charlottesville VA. (1992) p. 241-2.

9   Achatz, Grant, *Alinea*, Ten Speed Press. Berkeley/Toronto (2008).

10   Keller, Thomas, *French Laundry*, Artisan Press, (1999): 7 http://www.foodandwine.com/articles/become-an-intui-tive-cook-thomas-kellers-cooking-lessons#5steps

11   Kamal, Rabah, Julie Hudman, and Daniel McDermott, "What Do We Know About Infant Mortality in the U.S. and Comparable Countries?" *Peterson KFF Health System Tracker* (October 18, 2019): https://www.healthsystemtracker.org/chart-collection/infant-mortality-u-s-compare-countries/#item-

12   Howard, Brian Clark, "As the World Warms, Part of the American Southeast Cools," *National Geographic.* (May 10, 2014): https://www.nationalgeographic.com/news/2014/5/140509-global-warming-hole-southeast-climate-change-science/

13   Learn, Joshua Rapp, "Birds Talk To Their Eggs and This Song Migh Help Their Babies Survive Climate Change, *Smithsonian Magazine.* (August 18, 2016): https://www.smithsonianmag.com/science-nature/birds-talk-their-eggsand-song-might-help-

their-babies-deal-climate-change-180960168/?fbclid=IwAR1R-
wcEJwTRhBd6CeEvJzPg3bLR_9AtqYK79Yv_6T_--gmqfYSE-
UIkIt2aY#XwzdmejsMzRu8Qxr.01

14   Roethlisberger, Caronline, "Bags To Mats Program
Turns Trash into Treasure,"*Oxford Observer*. (January 11, 2019):
http://www.oxfordobserver.org/article/bags-to-mats-program-
turns-trash-into-treasure

15   Stefen, Luana, "Planting Trees in Square Holes Helps
Them Grow Stronger and Faster," *Intelligent Living*. (December
21, 2019): https://www.intelligentliving.co/planting-trees-in-
square-holes/

16   Rupa Basu, Brian Malig, Bart Ostro, High Ambient
Temperature and the Risk of Preterm Delivery, *American Jour-
nal of Epidemiology*, Volume 172, Issue 10, 15. (November 2010):
Pages 1108–1117, https://doi.org/10.1093/aje/kwq170

17   Preston, Richard, Folger, Tim (Eds) "Diet Is Not Destiny," Watters, Ethan, *Best American Science and Nature*. Mariner
Books, (2007).

18   Learn, Joshua Rapp, "Birds Talk To Their Eggs and This
Song Migh Help Their Babies Survive Climate Change, *Smithsonian Magazine*. (August 18, 2016): https://www.smithsonianmag.
com/science-nature/birds-talk-their-eggsand-song-might-help-
their-babies-deal-climate-change-180960168/?fbclid=IwAR1R-
wcEJwTRhBd6CeEvJzPg3bLR_9AtqYK79Yv_6T_--gmqfYSE-
UIkIt2aY#XwzdmejsMzRu8Qxr.01

19   Webb, Jonathan, "Zebra Finch 'Heat Song' Changes
Hatchling Development, *BBC News*. (August 19, 2016): https://
www.bbc.com/news/science-environment-37116728

20   Vaughn, Adam, "Young People Can't Remember How
Much More Wildlife There Used To Be," *New Scientist*. (December 11, 2019): https://www.newscientist.com/article/2226898-
young-people-cant-remember-how-much-more-wildlife-there-
used-to-be/#ixzz6AHVCSWKy

21   Lurie, Nicole M.D., M.S.P.H., Melanie Saville, M.D.,

Richard Hatchett, M.D., and Jane Halton, A.O., P.S.M. "Developing Covid-19 Vaccines at Pandemic Speed," *New England Journal of Medicine.* (March 30, 2020): https://www.nejm.org/doi/full/10.1056/NEJMp2005630

22 Wilkinson, Katharine, "The Woman Who Discovered Climate Change Was Long Overlooked," *Time.* (July 17, 2019). https://time.com/5626806/eunice-foote-women-climate-science/

23 Montanari, Shaena, "We Knew Ravens Were Smart. Just Not This Smart," *National Geographic.* (July 13, 2017): https://www.nationalgeographic.com/news/2017/07/ravens-problem-solving-smart-birds/

24 Spector, Kay, "Stop Idling Your Car and Cut Carbon Dioxide Emissions," *Ecowatch.* (December 12, 2013): https://www.ecowatch.com/stop-idling-your-car-and-cut-carbon-dioxide-emissions-1881837763.html

25 Bekoff, Mark, "Pigs Are Intelligent, Emotional, and Cognitively Complex," *Psychology Today.* (June 12, 2015): https://www.psychologytoday.com/us/blog/animal-emotions/201506/pigs-are-intelligent-emotional-and-cognitively-complex

26 Strayed, Cheryl, "The Love of My Life," *The Sun,* Issue 321 (September 2002).

27 Cousneau, Ruth, "Tongue Tacos," *Gourmet.* (June 2009): http://www.gourmet.com.s3-website-us-east-1.amazonaws.com/recipes/2000s/2009/07/tongue-tacos.html

ABOUT THE AUTHOR

NICOLE WALKER is the author of *The After-Normal: Brief, Alphabetical Essays on a Changing Planet*; *Sustainability: A Love Story*; *A Survival Guide for Life in the Ruins*; and other books. Her work has been published in *Orion*, *Boston Review*, *Creative Nonfiction*, *Brevity*, *The Normal School*, and elsewhere. Recipient of a fellowship from the National Endowment for the Arts and noted in multiple editions of *The Best American Essays*, Walker is nonfiction editor at *Diagram* and professor at Northern Arizona University in Flagstaff, Arizona.

TORREY HOUSE PRESS

Voices for the Land

The economy is a wholly owned subsidiary of the environment, not the other way around.
— Senator Gaylord Nelson, founder of Earth Day

Torrey House Press publishes books at the intersection of the literary arts and environmental advocacy. THP authors explore the diversity of human experiences with the environment and engage community in conversations about landscape, literature, and the future of our ever-changing planet, inspiring action toward a more just world. We believe that lively, contemporary literature is at the cutting edge of social change. We seek to inform, expand, and reshape the dialogue on environmental justice and stewardship for the human and more-than-human world by elevating literary excellence from diverse voices.

Visit www.torreyhouse.org for reading group discussion guides, author interviews, and more.

As a 501(c)(3) nonprofit publisher, our work is made possible by the generous donations from readers like you.

Torrey House Press is supported by Back of Beyond Books, the King's English Bookshop, Jeff Adams and Heather Adams, the Jeffrey S. and Helen H. Cardon Foundation, the Ruth H. Brown Foundation, the Sam and Diane Stewart Family Foundation, the Barker Foundation, Diana Allison, Jerome Cooney and Laura Storjohann, Robert Aagard and Camille Bailey Aagard, Heidi Dexter and David Gens, Kirtly Parker Jones, Elaine Deschamps, Patrick de Freitas, Lindsey Leavell, Laurie Hilyer, Susan Cushman and Charlie Quimby, Shelby Tisdale, Stephen Strom, Link Cornell and Lois Cornell, Rose Chilcoat and Mark Franklin, Betsy Folland and David Folland, the Utah Division of Arts & Museums, Utah Humanities, the National Endowment for the Humanities, the National Endowment for the Arts, and Salt Lake County Zoo, Arts & Parks. Our thanks to individual donors, subscribers, and the Torrey House Press board of directors for their valued support.

Join the Torrey House Press family and give today at
www.torreyhouse.org/give.